Shi'i Islam

A Beginner's Guide

ONEWORLD BEGINNER'S GUIDES combine an original, inventive, and engaging approach with expert analysis on subjects ranging from art and history to religion and politics, and everything in-between. Innovative and affordable, books in the series are perfect for anyone curious about the way the world works and the big ideas of our time.

Beginners
GUIDES

Shi'i Islam
A Beginner's Guide

Moojan Momen

ONEWORLD

Copyright © Moojan Momen 2016

The right of Moojan Momen to be identified as the Author
of this work has been asserted by him in accordance with
the Copyright, Designs and Patents Act 1988

ISBN 978–1–78074–787–3
eISBN 978–1–78074–788–0

Typeset by Jayvee, Trivandrum, India
Printed and bound in Great Britain by Clays Ltd, St Ives plc

Oneworld Publications
10 Bloomsbury Street
London, WC1B 3SR
England

Contents

MAP OF THE SHI'I WORLD

Map showing countries, regions and places mentioned in this book. Some of the boundaries shown are not agreed by all sides.

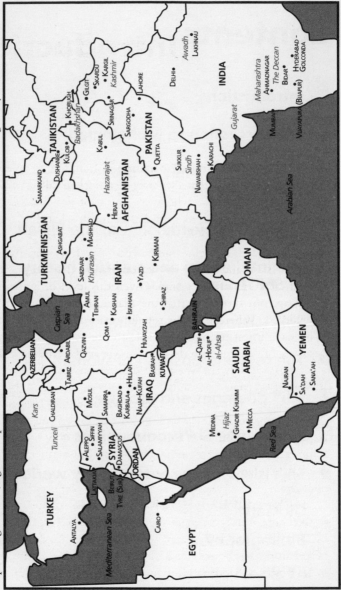

Introduction

Prior to the 1979 Islamic Revolution in Iran, few people in the West were conscious that a separate sect of Islam called Shi'i Islam existed and even those who were aware of this were not very clear who the Shi'is were, where they lived, what they believed or what made them different to the majority Sunni community. Even in academic circles, there were very few who had studied Shi'i Islam and there was little literature that dealt with the central concerns of this group. Given this level of ignorance, it is perhaps not surprising that the Islamic Revolution left many bewildered. Where had this revolutionary fervour come from? Why had almost no one been able to predict it? What was the best way of dealing with the new power in the Middle East?

It was not only the West that the Iranian Revolution caught by surprise. Many Muslims were just as mystified by what had occurred. For centuries, Sunni Muslims had been used to discounting the Shi'is, considering them an irrelevance to the politics and economics of the Middle East. In only one country, Iran, did Shi'i Islam seem to be of any importance and even there, the religion appeared to be taking a back seat to political concerns.

The Revolution was enough to put Shi'i Islam on the map but further upheavals arose from the newly-discovered phenomenon of Shi'i Islam. Suddenly people discovered that the destabilization of Lebanon was being caused by a militant Shi'i group; unrest in Iraq against Saddam Hussein was due to a Shi'i movement;

turmoil in Syria was found to be due to Sunni opposition to a minority Shi'i government; political unrest in the oil-rich province of Saudi Arabia was also noticed to be coming from Shi'is; and civil strife and violence in Pakistan and India were now being described as due to Sunni-Shi'i animosity. All this unrest had existed before 1979 but had been attributed to political and economic factors. Now everyone was seeing a religious dimension to these conflicts.

After the 1979 Islamic Revolution in Iran, a slew of experts promptly appeared and opinions were given about how Shi'i Islam was inherently revolutionary and destabilizing and how oppressed Shi'i masses were now demanding a voice and power in proportion to their numbers. These explanations were not incorrect but were often superficial and failed to provide an understanding of what was actually going on and the variations in Shi'i Islam among countries, regions and groups. To make matters worse, political decisions were then based on these explanations, leading to errors by Western statesmen and a widening of the gulf of misunderstanding between the West and the Shi'i world.

Relations between Shi'i Islam and the West since 1979 have been marked by a continuing series of surprise moves on the Shi'i side and paralysis and errors of judgement by the West. Every time people think the situation in Iran and in the Shi'i world is starting to settle and become more understandable, and therefore more predictable in terms of the sort of theories and mechanisms by which the West usually explains social and political affairs, the Iranian government or some other Shi'i group comes up with a surprise that requires fresh explanations and new models. The 1979 Iranian Revolution left many governments floundering in ignorance, not knowing how to approach the new government in Iran; but just as people were getting used to the idea of the Islamic Revolution and contemplating negotiating with the new government, in a break with the norms of international affairs, students seized the American embassy in Tehran and took 65

Americans hostage. A year later, the Iran–Iraq war began and again the West was badly informed and took the side of Saddam Hussein in the conflict, despite evidence of his war crimes (his use of chemical weapons). When America's intervention in the Lebanese Civil War culminated in the first major episode of suicide bombing against the United States (when the Beirut embassy and the American barracks were bombed in 1983), the attacks took everyone in the West by surprise and induced such a state of panic that within four months all American troops had been withdrawn from Lebanon. The unexpected twists have continued with the strong Green Movement that rose in protest against the 2009 election victory of President Ahmadinejad and the rise of the Houthi rebels in Yemen.

Iran is, in fact, a country full of paradoxes and these extend to other Shi'i communities as well. For example, people think they know that women are oppressed by the Islamic regime in Iran and while that is true, women in Iran have the vote, have levels of literacy comparable with women in the Western world, and make up 65% of university students (70% of science and engineering students) and 40% of the country's salaried workers.

There is thus a great deal of room for improvement in the West's knowledge of Shi'i Islam and this improvement is vital if Western policy decisions and initiatives in the area are to be more coherent and constructive. Although this book cannot claim to remedy this situation completely, it is hoped that it will at least shed some light on the complexities of Shi'i Islam and its role in the world.

This book is intended to be a brief introduction to the Shi'i branch of Islam for the general reader. In a short book such as this, it is not possible to give a detailed account of all the Shi'i sects and sub-groups. I have, therefore concentrated on the main grouping of Shi'is, the Usuli School of the Ithna-'Ashari (Twelver) sect of Shi'i Islam, which represents some 80% of the world's Shi'is. When reference is made to Shi'is or to Twelvers in this book, therefore, it is this group that is intended unless specifically designated otherwise. The early history of the other Shi'i groupings is included in Chapter 2 and a brief account given in Chapter 8. Also, when writing about doctrines and practices, I have concentrated on those areas where Shi'i Islam differs most from Sunnism, rather than attempting a comprehensive coverage.

In writing this book, there has been some question over what terminology to use. One problem has how to describe the main grouping of Shi'is in the world today. Some authors have called this group the Imamiyyah, but that is only used of them in the early histories and can be regarded as also being an accurate designation of another grouping of the Shi'is, the Isma'ilis. They are also sometimes, and in some areas, called Ja'fari Shi'is and Matawilah. Most call themselves the Ithna-'Ashariyyah to signify that they hold to a succession of Twelve Imams and so in this book I have followed this designation and translated this directly as the 'Twelvers'. The next problem relates to the adjective to use in relation to Shi'ism. In Arabic, the word Shi'ah is a collective noun and should be used only for a group of the followers of the religion. However, in Persian, Shi'ah is pronounced Shi'eh and is frequently also used as an adjective (and therefore also as a noun for a person of this group). This usage is also common among Shi'is of the Indian subcontinent because of the historic predominance of Persianate culture there. Since this usage is foreign to Arab Shi'is, however, I have used the word 'Shi'i' as the adjective from Shi'ism and only use Shi'ah as a collective noun.

Another problem relates to the designation to give to those Shi'i groupings that broke off from the mainstream of Twelvers and Isma'ili Shi'is, and are usually designated as the *Ghulat* (extremists, singular *ghali*) and their movements collectively as *Ghuluww* (extremism). But this is, of course, a designation given to them by their opponents, much as the Shi'ah were, and still often are, called the *Rafidah*, the Rejectors, by their Sunni opponents. No religious group regards itself as extremist. On the other hand, there is no agreed term by which all these '*Ghulat*' groups can collectively be called. It is possible to use the designation 'Mystical Sh'ism' since most of these groups have practices such as repetitive chanting that are typical of mystical groups, but this would be confusing since there are also Twelver Shi'i Sufi orders that could be thus designated. Anxious to avoid using the word 'extremist', and for want of a better term, I have called these movements 'Gnostic Shi'i Islam' since most of them have an element of gnostic teaching (in the sense of a teaching that is hidden from the generality of the followers of that group and others).

There are many terms used in this book for which there is not an exact English equivalent. To avoid defining such words every time, I have generally defined them in the text the first time they appear. They are also listed and explained in the glossary at the end of this book, to which the reader can refer. In this book, the capitalised word 'Tradition' is used to translate the word '*hadith*' or '*khabar*' (plural '*akhbar*'), a transmitted oral report of the words or actions of the Prophet Muhammad or one of the Imams. The word 'cleric' is used as the equivalent of '*'alim*' (plural '*'ulama*'), used to designate one who is learned in the religious sciences. The transliteration system used in this book roughly equates to the system used in the *Encyclopedia Islamica* and the *International Journal of Middle East Studies*, except that no diacritical marks are used in the text. The letter '*ayn* is designated by the mark "'" and the *ta marbutah* ending by '*-ah*' (the Persian pronunciation of this is closer to '*-eh*'). The transliteration follows the Arabic pronunciation rather than Persian, although for frequently-used words that are pronounced very differently in Persian (for example, Arabic *rawdah*, Persian *rowzeh*), the Persian pronunciation is given in the glossary and on the first occasion of use in the text. A few words that are predominantly used in their Persian form are given in that form (for example *imamzadeh* and *velayat-e faqih*).

Words and names that have acquired a usual English spelling, such as Ayatollah and Khomeini, are given in that form.

A bibliography at the end of the book gives the main general sources used. Since most of the quotations used in this book are also to be found in my longer work, *An Introduction to Shi'i Islam: the history and doctrines of Twelver Shi'i Islam*, the specific references can be found there.

1
The succession to Muhammad

The Prophet Muhammad was born in the town of Mecca to a family of the clan of Banu Hashim of the tribe of Quraysh and, according to Shi'i Traditions, on 9 May 570 CE (17 Rabi' I). His father, 'Abdullah, died before Muhammad was born; his mother when he was six years of age. Muhammad was then brought up first by his grandfather and later by his uncle Abu Talib, the head of the clan. When Muhammad grew up, he was employed by Khadijah, a wealthy Meccan widow, to trade on her behalf. In about 596 CE, Muhammad married Khadijah and set up house. Although Abu Talib was an important person in Mecca, he was not a rich man and when his eldest son 'Ali (born in about 600 CE) was five or six years old, Muhammad took him into his own house and brought him up.

According to Shi'i Traditions, it was on 26 June 610 (27 Rajab), when Muhammad was 40 years of age, that he experienced what he would later describe as the appearance of the Angel Gabriel, who ordered him to recite verses. The first to believe in him were his wife Khadijah and his cousin 'Ali, who was about ten years old at this time. The next to believe was Zayd, Muhammad's adopted son. The first to believe from outside the family, and the first adult male to believe, was Abu Bakr. Soon there was a small group of believers, including

'Uthman and later 'Umar (after a period when he opposed Muhammad).

When, in about 613 CE, Muhammad began to preach his message publicly, he faced intense hostility. The prosperity of Mecca depended on the fact that during an annual festival the surrounding tribespeople came to Mecca and worshipped their gods in the shrine called the Ka'bah. Muhammad's message that there was only one God and that the worship of idols was wrong threatened the prosperity of Mecca and the livelihood of the Quraysh tribe. Although Muhammad himself was to some extent protected by his prestigious family connections, many of his followers, who were mostly of low social status, faced perse-cution and even torture at the hands of most of the leaders of the tribe of Quraysh, led by Abu Lahab, Muhammad's uncle, and Abu Sufyan, the head of the Umayyad family. Since the Umayyad family will feature greatly in the later history, this is perhaps the best place to say a few more words about them. Abu Sufyan was a third cousin of Muhammad (they had a common great-great-grandfather 'Abd Manaf). Muhammad's clan was a senior clan in Quraysh, being responsible for taking care of the pilgrims who came to the shrine of the Ka'bah, but other clans within Quraysh such as the Banu Umayyah (Umayyads) and Banu Makhzum had prospered much more from trade and therefore wielded great influence.

By 615 CE, the persecution of the Muslims had become so intense that Muhammad ordered a group of his most vulner-able followers to migrate to Ethiopia and seek the protection of its Christian sovereign (the Negus). The following year, the leaders of Quraysh ordered a boycott of the Banu Hashim clan. However, led by their chief Abu Talib, the Banu Hashim continued to support their family member, Muhammad, even though most were not Muslims. For a time, the clan blockaded itself in a defile to defend itself against a potential attack. This boycott failed to shake the resolve of Abu Talib and was abandoned in 619 CE. But in that year, two events occurred that severely undermined Muhammad's position: his wife Khadijah and his uncle Abu Talib, his two most powerful supporters, both died. Muhammad's uncle, Abu Lahab, who had been antagonistic to Muhammad from the beginning, now became head of the Banu Hashim clan. He soon found a pretext to withdraw the family's protection from Muhammad. This placed Muhammad's life in danger since, according to tribal law, he could now be killed with impunity by anyone (withdrawal of clan protection meant that neither blood revenge nor blood money would be exacted for his murder). Muhammad was forced to leave Mecca and try to find a protector. At the nearby town of Ta'if, he was ridiculed and rejected. Finally, he found protection with the chief of the Banu Nawfal, a clan of Quraysh, and suffered the humiliation of returning to Mecca under the protection of a clan that was not his own and a chief who was an idolator.

Just at this time, when Muhammad's fortunes were at their lowest ebb, an event occurred that presaged the turn of the tide. At the annual pilgrimage and festival in Mecca in the summer of 620, Muhammad met six men from the tribe of Khazraj of the town of Yathrib, some 300 kilometres north of Mecca, and converted them to his teachings. The following year, five of them returned and together with another seven, received instruction from Muhammad at secret meetings at a pass called al-'Aqabah, near Mecca. They pledged to follow his teachings but did not pledge to take up arms on his behalf. When it was time for them to return to Yathrib, Muhammad sent one of his Meccan disciples with them. Muhammad's teaching spread in Yathrib and the following year, 622 CE, seventy-two men and three women came from there to Mecca to pledge their allegiance to Muhammad, again at al-'Aqabah. Since these represented prominent members of both Aws and Khazraj, the two major rival tribes of Yathrib, and they now promised to protect Muhammad with arms if necessary, Muhammad decided to move to Yathrib. He instructed his followers to leave secretly until only Muhammad himself, 'Ali, Zayd and Abu Bakr were left in Mecca. The Meccan leaders were alarmed at the departure of the Muslims and dismayed at the disregard they showed for kinship ties. They decided that Muhammad must be killed. That night, however, Muhammad slipped away from the town with Abu Bakr and hid in a nearby cave. To fool the assassins, 'Ali slept that night in the Prophet's bed. Muhammad managed to reach Yathrib, which was henceforward called Madinat an-Nabi, the City of the Prophet, or just Medina for short. This move of the Prophet from Mecca to Medina signalled the turnabout in his fortunes and that year, 622 CE, the year of the Hijra (Hegira, Emigration), is the starting point of the Islamic calendar. Muhammad was 52 years old by this time.

Although his followers were at first a minority, Muhammad greatly improved his position when he was called upon as an outsider to arbitrate in an ongoing dispute between the two main tribes of the town, Aws and Khazraj. His successful resolution of this problem, through a series of treaties creating a confederation of all the tribes in the town, gave him a position of great power and influence. As the number of converts to his religion increased, Muhammad became the *de facto* ruler of Medina.

There were, however, two groups of people who created problems for Muhammad within Medina. An important faction of the people of the town resented his rule. Under the leadership of 'Abdullah ibn Ubayy, this faction, known to later Islamic history as the *munafiqun* (the hypocrites), sought to undermine Muhammad's leadership and create alliances among his opponents. Although the Jews of Medina had originally welcomed Muhammad, who was preaching a monotheism not dissimilar to their own religion, they soon fell out with him and some

16 months after his arrival in Medina, Muhammad signalled his displeasure with the Jews and strengthened the new Islamic identity by changing the direction of Islamic prayer from Jerusalem to Mecca.

Externally, Muhammad also faced problems. Relationships with Mecca, which were already bad, deteriorated further after a number of raids upon their caravans. The Meccans came out towards Medina with an army in 623 but Muhammad defeated them at the Battle of Badr. Some time after this battle, Muhammad besieged and then expelled from Medina one of the three main Jewish tribes of the town, Banu Qaynuqa'. The reasons for this expulsion are a matter of debate but may have included their contacts with the Meccans (thus breaking the above-mentioned treaty of confederation) and with the *munafiqun* leader 'Abdullah ibn Ubayy. In 625, at the Battle of Uhud, Muhammad's army was successful at first, despite the desertion of the *munafiqun*. But the Muslim army broke up, seeking booty, which allowed the Meccans to reverse some of their losses and no side was the clear winner. After this battle, Abu Sufyan, the leader in Mecca, tried to form an alliance of Arab tribes against Muhammad. Muhammad attacked some of these tribes and expelled from Medina another Jewish tribe, Banu Nadir, which had expressed hostility towards him. The final battle was in 627, when a large Meccan army came to Medina. Although Muhammad was outnumbered three to one, one of Muhammad's followers, Salman the Persian, suggested the tactic of digging a trench (hence the battle became known as the Battle of the Trench). This novel form of defence discomfited the attackers and after an inconclusive siege they withdrew. During the siege, Banu Qurayzah, the last remaining Jewish tribe in Medina, leagued themselves with the Meccans. After the battle, they agreed to surrender and Muhammad appointed the chief of the Aws tribe of Medina to judge them. Everyone expected a lenient judgement, as Aws had been allies of Banu

Qurayzah in former years, but the chief of Aws decreed that the men of Banu Qurayzah be killed and the women and children sold into slavery.

In 628, Muhammad decided to perform a pilgrimage to Mecca during the traditional two months of truce for religious observances there (Dhul-Qa'dah and Dhul-Hijjah). A Meccan force blocked his approach at Hudaybiyyah, just outside Mecca. After negotiations, a truce was signed, allowing Muhammad to perform the pilgrimage the following year. So in 629, in fulfilment of the Treaty of Hudaybiyyah, Muhammad was able to perform the pilgrimage to Mecca. Towards the end of this year, however, the Treaty was broken when some allies of the Meccans attacked some allies of the Medinans. In early 630, Muhammad decided to march against Mecca. The Meccans were unable to mobilize an army that could match that of Muhammad and so they surrendered. Many of them, including Abu Sufyan also accepted Islam at this time. As soon as he entered Mecca, Muhammad went into the Ka'ba with 'Ali and together they destroyed all the idols there. The year 631 is remembered as the year of delegations, when tribes across Arabia sent delegations to Muhammad, accepting his authority, and most also accepting Islam and asking to be sent Muslim teachers. In 632, Muhammad performed what came to be known as the Farewell Pilgrimage to Mecca. Shortly after his return he fell ill, dying on 25 May 632 (28 Safar 11 AH), according to Shi'i Traditions.

Events after the death of the Prophet

When the Prophet Muhammad died in Medina, his daughter Fatimah and her husband 'Ali occupied themselves with preparing his body for burial. Meanwhile, in another part of the town, a gathering was taking place of the leading Ansar (the Medinan followers of Muhammad) in the portico (*saqifah*) of the hall of the Banu Sa'idah, a clan of Khazraj, one of the Ansar tribes. Hearing of this meeting, and of the fact that the Ansar were probably going to give their allegiance to Sa'd ibn 'Ubadah, one of their chiefs, the Muhajirun (the Meccans who had migrated to Medina with the Prophet Muhammad), headed by Abu Bakr and 'Umar, hurried to the meeting of the Ansar.

At this meeting, first, one of the Ansar spoke up, saying that since the Ansar had given victory to Islam and the Muhajirun were only guests in the town, leadership of the Islamic community should go to one of the leaders of the Ansar. Abu Bakr replied that, while the Ansar had assisted Islam at a critical point, nevertheless it was Quraysh (the Meccan tribe of which the Prophet was a member) who had been the first to accept Islam, they were nearer in kinship to the Prophet and they were the only clan whose nobility was universally acknowledged among the Arabs, and so the Arabs as a whole would only accept the leadership of one of the Quraysh tribe. The meeting became tumultuous as various proposals were put forward, including a voice raised in favour of 'Ali's claim. But then 'Umar proposed Abu Bakr as leader of the Islamic community and everyone present, both the Ansar and Muhajirun, pledged their loyalty to him and he became the successor (*khalifah*, caliph) to the Prophet.

The meeting dispersed and 'Umar with a body of armed men went to the house of 'Ali, where the Prophet's body was being prepared for burial, to demand that 'Ali should also pledge allegiance to Abu Bakr. It is said they even threatened to burn down 'Ali's house if he did not do as they demanded. It fell to Fatimah to make a personal appeal and disperse the crowd. Some accounts state that the crowd entered the house and some Shi'i accounts say that 'Umar struck Fatimah during this episode.

The claim of 'Ali

Shi'i Islam formally starts at the time of the death of the Prophet Muhammad, when there was a difference of opinion about who would succeed him as leader of the Islamic community. The majority accepted the acclamation of Abu Bakr as the leader of Islam; this acclamation had been made at a gathering of the senior figures in the Islamic community within a few hours of the Prophet's death. Abu Bakr was a senior figure who had been a Muslim from the earliest days and whom Muhammad had honoured in various ways (including marrying Abu Bakr's daughter 'A'ishah and appointing him to lead the ritual prayers in his absence). There was, however, a minority that thought that leadership should have gone to 'Ali, who was the Prophet's cousin and son-in-law. It was this minority that would eventually lead to the emergence of Shi'i Islam.

Shi'is point out that, with regard to the above speech by Abu Bakr at the Saqifah, in which he refuted the claims of the Ansar to the leadership and advanced the claims of Quraysh, 'Ali fulfilled the criteria given in the speech much better than Abu Bakr. Thus if Quraysh were closer in kinship to the Prophet than the Ansar, then 'Ali was closer than Abu Bakr. If Quraysh were first to accept Islam, then 'Ali accepted Islam before Abu Bakr. If Quraysh were more entitled to leadership among the Arabs than the Ansar on account of its nobility, then 'Ali and the house of Hashim were the noblest clan within Quraysh. And 'Ali's services to Islam and his close personal companionship with the Prophet, were at least equal, if not superior, to Abu Bakr's. Moreover, if selection of the leader was to have been by consultation and consensus, then why was the house of Hashim, the house of the Prophet, not consulted?

In general, Shi'is feel that the succession to Muhammad was decided hurriedly and by political manoeuvring, rather than as a result of religious considerations and justice. Jealousies among the clans of Quraysh had played a part; they did not want the Banu Hashim, who had already had prophethood in their house, also to have the caliphate. Abu Bakr belonged to an insignificant clan. The Ansar had been contemplating choosing Sa'd ibn 'Ubadah, the chief of Khazraj, as their leader and so when Abu Bakr was put forward as a candidate, the Aws tribe which had been the great rival of Khazraj in Medina, was only too eager to have this alternative. Shi'is maintain that it was the way 'Umar expertly played the crowd gathered at the Saqifah that resulted in what they consider to have been an outcome disastrous for Islam.

Those who thought that leadership should have gone to 'Ali pointed to the great honours heaped upon 'Ali by the Prophet and to some of the episodes in the life of Muhammad which indicated that the Prophet wanted 'Ali to succeed him as leader. Although only ten years old in 610 CE when the Prophet Muhammad first began to confide his message to others, 'Ali had immediately accepted this claim and thus was the first male to become a Muslim, after the Prophet's wife Khadijah but preceding Abu Bakr. 'Ali had been present about two years later when the Prophet had invited his relatives to a meal and made an open announcement of his claim (called by Shi'is the Feast of the Close Relatives or the Day of the Warning, on account of the event having been precipitated by the revelation of Qur'an 26:214: 'Warn your close relatives'). 'Ali had been the only one who stepped forward and accepted Muhammad's claim on that day and Muhammad had responded by announcing: 'This is my brother, my trustee and my successor among you, so listen to him and obey him.' When the night came for the flight from Mecca to Medina, it was 'Ali who slept in the Prophet's bed, risking his life to fool the assassins who had been sent to murder the Prophet.

Shortly after their arrival in Medina, Muhammad paired off each of the Meccans who had come with him with one of his Medinan followers, declaring them to be brothers to one another, as a way of cementing bonds between these two factions of his followers. At this time, Muhammad chose 'Ali to be his 'brother'. During the Medinan period, 'Ali acted as Muhammad's secretary and deputy, for example writing the significant treaty of Hudaybiyyah and carrying out important duties such as reading the Surah of Bara'ah (Surah of Disavowal), in the year 631 to the people of Medina, announcing that henceforward only Muslims would be allowed to perform the pilgrimage to Mecca. When Abu Bakr complained, asking why he had not been asked to perform this last task, Muhammad told him that this important task could only be undertaken by the Prophet himself or a member of his family. 'Ali married the Prophet's daughter, Fatimah; the children of this marriage, Hasan and Husayn, were the only grandchildren of the Prophet to survive into adult life. All the millions who now claim descent from the Prophet Muhammad do so through this line of descent. 'Ali's life was intimately intertwined with that of the Prophet Muhammad. He was the Prophet's cousin by birth, his foster-brother because the Prophet was fostered by Abu Talib, his foster-son, when he went to live with the Prophet after the latter's marriage and his son-in-law, when he married Fatimah.

'Ali was also one of the most courageous and able men in the Muslim army. He was appointed the standard-bearer at the battles of both Badr and Khaybar. When the Prophet left to go on his longest expedition, to Tabuk, 'Ali was left in charge in Medina. When 'Ali protested about being left behind, the Prophet was reported to have said to him: 'Are you not content to be with respect to me as Aaron was to Moses?', implying that 'Ali was Muhammad's deputy and successor, just as Aaron had been to Moses. Then there was an episode in which a delegation of Christians from Najran came to Medina in 631 CE to engage Muhammad in debate. Muhammad went out to meet them accompanied by his daughter Fatimah, 'Ali and their two sons Hasan and Husayn, all covered by Muhammad's cloak. The Christians are reported to have recognized this as a sign from God that had been predicted in their holy books and agreed to pay tribute. Thus it is considered that the words in verse of the Qur'an 'And God only wishes to remove all abomination from you, O Members of the Family, and render you pure and spotless (33:33)' apply only to these four people, the People of the Cloak (Ahl al-Kisa').

Most significant of all, however, was the Episode of Ghadir Khumm, which is considered so important that it is commemorated by Shi'is all over the world and is a national public holiday in Iran today. As the Prophet was returning to Medina from the Farewell Pilgrimage to Mecca a few months before his death, the caravan stopped at a place called Ghadir Khumm, where the Prophet made a significant statement that whoever regarded the Prophet as his master (*mawla*) should also regard 'Ali as his master.

Lastly there was the Episode of Pen and Paper, which occurred as the Prophet lay dying. He called for pen and paper, saying that he wished to write instructions so that the Muslims would not be led into error after him. But 'Umar prevented this, saying: 'The illness has overwhelmed the Prophet. We have the Book of God [the Qur'an] and that is enough for us.' Shi'is claim that had Muhammad been allowed to do this, he would have made his appointment of 'Ali clear.

THE EPISODE OF GHADIR KHUMM

The following is the account given in Ibn Hanbal, a Sunni collection of Hadith:

We were with the Apostle of God (blessings and peace be upon him) in his journey and we stopped at Ghadir Khumm in order to perform the obligatory prayer together and a place was swept for the Apostle under two trees and he performed the mid-day prayer. And then he took 'Ali by the hand and said to the people: 'Do you not acknowledge that I have a greater claim on the believers than they have on themselves?' And they replied: 'Yes!' And he said 'Do you not acknowledge that I have a greater claim on each one of the believers than he has on himself?' And they replied: 'Yes!' And he took 'Ali's hand and said: 'Of whomsoever I am master [*mawla*], then 'Ali is also his master. O God! Be Thou the friend [*wali*] of whoever befriends 'Ali [*walahu*] and the enemy of whoever opposes him.' And 'Umar met him ['Ali] after this and said to him: 'Congratulations, O son of Abu Talib! Now morning and evening [i.e. forever] you are the master of every believing man and woman.'

There were a number of other statements which both Sunnis and Shi'is agree were made by the Prophet Muhammad and which point to a prominent position for 'Ali and his family:

1. Hadith of the Two Weighty Matters (al-Thaqalayn). This is a very widely-reported statement of Muhammad, occurring even in Sunni collections of Traditions about the Prophet Muhammad, such the one by Ibn Hanbal: 'The Apostle of God said: "I have left among you two weighty matters which if you cling to them you shall not be led into error after me. One of them is greater than the other: The Book of God, which is a rope stretched from Heaven to

Earth and my progeny, the people of my house. These two shall not be parted until they return to the pool [of Paradise on the Day of Judgement].'''

2. The Hadith of the Safinah (Noah's Ark). 'My family among you are like Noah's Ark. He who sails on it will be safe, but he who holds back from it will perish.'

3. On one occasion when four of the Muslims complained to the Prophet concerning something that 'Ali had done, the Prophet grew angry and said: 'What do you want from 'Ali? 'Ali is from me and I am from 'Ali. He is the guardian (*wali*) of every believer after me.'

4. And in another context, the Prophet said: to 'Ali: 'You are my authorized representative (*wali*) in this world and the next.'

5. The Prophet is reported to have said: 'No one may execute my affairs except myself and 'Ali.'

6. The Prophet said: 'As for 'Ali, Fatimah, Hasan and Husayn, I am at war with whoever fights against these and at peace with whoever is at peace with these.'

7. 'There is no more chivalrous youth (*fata*) than 'Ali.'

8. 'No one but a believer loves 'Ali and no one but a hypocrite (*munafiq*) hates 'Ali.'

9. 'The truth circulates with him ('Ali) wherever he goes.'

10. 'I am the City of Knowledge and 'Ali is its Gate (Bab).'

11. On one occasion, the Prophet called 'Ali and began whispering to him. After a time those present began saying: 'He has been a long time whispering to his cousin'. Later, the Prophet said: 'It was not I that was whispering to him but God.'

12. The Prophet took the hand of Hasan and Husayn and said: 'Whoever loves me and loves these two and loves their mother and father, will be with me in my station on the Day of Resurrection.'

Shi'is point to these episodes and statements by the Prophet Muhammad as being evidence of the Prophet's desire that 'Ali should succeed him. Sunnis do not dispute that these episodes occurred and such statements were made (almost all are recorded in Sunni Traditions as well as Shi'i) but they give a different interpretation to these episodes and they also point to the great honours that were laid upon Abu Bakr and 'Umar by the Prophet and the statements made about them. Part of the problem arises from the subtleties of the meaning of words such as *mawla* and *wali*, as indicated in the translations above. These two words come from the same root, meaning to be near to someone, to be friends with someone or to have authority or guardianship over someone. Thus *mawla* can mean both master and friend, and was the word used both for the head of a tribe and for a non-member who was protected by a tribe but would have had a low status. This range of meanings makes it difficult to be certain what Muhammad meant when he gave the speech at Ghadir Khumm. Shi'is understand the meaning of *mawla* to have been 'master' (thus indicating that 'Ali should be the successor of Muhammad), while many Sunnis assert that the meaning is of 'friendship' and that 'Ali used this statement of the Prophet in later debates as evidence of his spiritual excellence, not of his successorship to the Prophet.

In addition, there are numerous statements made by and about 'Ali that are only recorded in Shi'i sources. For example:

1. The Fourth Imam is reported to have said: 'The Apostle of God taught 'Ali a matter (*harf*, literally: a letter) which opened up one thousand matters each of which in turn opened up a thousand matters.'
2. 'Ali said: 'I am Muhammad and Muhammad is I.'
3. 'Ali said in the Hadith al-Nuraniyyah: 'Muhammad is the

warner (*al-mundhir*) and I am the Guide (*al-hadi*; see Qur'an 13:7) ... Muhammad is the one with revelation (*al-wahy*) and I am the one with inspiration (*al-ilham*) ... Muhammad is the Seal of the Prophets (*khatam al-anbiya*) and I am the Seal of the Successors (*khatam al-wasiyyin*).'

2

The life and times of the Twelve Imams

The Shi'ah as a whole were a persecuted minority for most of the early years of Islam. They were not a cohesive or united group. They followed different, often rival, Imams and had different attitudes towards and expectations of them. Twelver Shi'i Islam is so named because it accepts a series of twelve Imams as successors of the Prophet Muhammad. Other Shi'i sects accept other lines and other numbers of Imams.

One way of thinking about the history of Shi'i Islam is to consider it as having formed from a coalescence of two major trends. Firstly the political trend, which was perhaps largely a movement of the underdogs, the downtrodden, trying to assert themselves against the powerful elites of the Islamic Empire. Secondly, there was Shi'i Islam as a religious movement, which was at first much smaller than the political protest movement, but became larger as it increasingly focused on the Prophet and his family with the suffering and martyrdoms that occurred. This religious movement largely eschewed political involvement, and especially revolt against the established order. While there was tension between these two wings of the movement, they interacted and were often not clearly distinguishable.

By the time of 'Ali's caliphate, the Islamic world extended from Central Asia to north-west Africa. During the period of the Imams after 'Ali, it was ruled by two successive dynasties of caliphs:

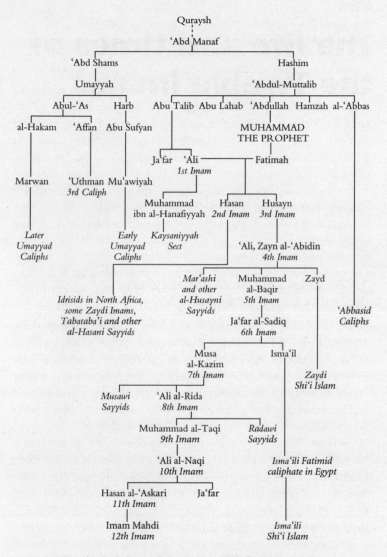

Genealogical chart of the Imams and their relationships

the Umayyads (ruled 661–750) with their capital at Damascus; and the 'Abbasids (ruled 750–1258) with their capital mainly at Baghdad. During the period that we are concerned with in this chapter, 656–941, these two dynasties of caliphs had political control of the Islamic world and were able to appoint governors and collect taxes. The Shi'i Imams of the Twelver line, however, only held religious authority over a minority of Muslims, who had to carefully conceal their beliefs to avoid persecution; while paying their ordinary taxes to the government of the caliph, these Shi'is also paid the religious tax of *khums* (see pp. 189–90) to the Imam, secretly, through intermediaries and agents. In this chapter, we look first at the lives of the Twelver Imams and then try to disentangle what was happening among the Shi'ah during this period.

1. 'Ali ibn Abi Talib, the First Imam (Imamate 632–61, caliphate 656–61)

After Abu Bakr's acclamation as leader (caliph), at first there was a group who rejected this and urged 'Ali to challenge him for the leadership. Abu Sufyan even offered to fill Medina with armed men to enforce 'Ali's leadership. But 'Ali was not one to create disunity in the community that his beloved Muhammad had spent so much time uniting, particularly since, shortly after Abu Bakr assumed the caliphate, a large number of Arabs apostatised from Islam and a campaign had to be waged against them. Shortly after the Prophet's death, Fatimah approached Abu Bakr to claim valuable lands in Fadak, which she believed her father had left her. Abu Bakr refused, saying that this land belonged to the Islamic community. Fatimah was angry at this and withdrew to her home, where she died six months after her father. According to Shi'i accounts, the attack upon her and her house after the death of the Prophet (see pp. 13–14) caused Fatimah to miscarry, which weakened her and led to her death.

Abu Bakr's caliphate lasted only two years (632–4) and, before his death, he appointed 'Umar as his successor. During 'Umar's caliphate (634–44), the Muslim armies achieved remarkable victories against both the Persian and Byzantine Empires, extending Muslim rule from Tunisia to the Oxus river in Central Asia. The succession to 'Umar was decided by a council of six appointed by the caliph. Both 'Ali and 'Uthman of the Banu Umayyah family (the Umayyads) were on this council, but one of the members of the council hated 'Ali and another's sister was married to 'Uthman. The caliphate was offered to 'Ali on condition that he rule in accordance with the rulings already made by the preceding caliphs. 'Ali was known to disagree with some of these rulings and would not compromise his principles. 'Uthman, however, accepted these terms and was made caliph. 'Uthman ruled for twelve years (644–56) but became very unpopular towards the end of his life, due to his nepotism; he appointed members of his own Umayyad family to governorships, despite the fact that most of them had opposed the Prophet Muhammad until the final defeat of the Meccans.

While Sunni accounts describe these first three caliphs as epitomes of Islamic piety and paragons of wise rule, Shi'i sources regard them as usurpers of the rightful position of 'Ali. While Sunni sources describe 'Ali as having supported the three first caliphs, Shi'i sources depict him as secluding himself from the caliph's circle of advisers. What is clear, however, is that under these three caliphs, 'Ali neither advanced his claim openly, nor did he actively participate in social and political affairs or in the campaigns of the Muslim armies, despite the fact that he had been most active in both roles during Muhammad's lifetime.

The *Nahj al-Balaghah* (The Peak of Eloquence) is a collection of the orations and letters of 'Ali. Although it is a late compilation (tenth century) and some have expressed doubts as to its reliability, many, including some prominent Sunni scholars, accept its authenticity. The following oration, known as the Shiqshiqiyyah (Oration 3), reveals, for example, the smouldering resentment that 'Ali felt at the usurpation of what he considered to be his rightful position by the first three caliphs:

By God! Ibn Abi Quhafah [Abu Bakr] dressed himself with it [the caliphate] and he well knew that my position in relation to it was the same as that of the axis in relation to a grinding–mill. The flood–water [of learning and grace] flows down from me and the bird [Abu Bakr] could not fly up to me. I lowered a curtain to separate me from it [the caliphate] and kept the matter concealed within my bosom.

Then I began to consider whether I should take the offensive when I did not have the means of attaining my goal [literally, attack with an amputated hand] or should I endure in patience the blinding darkness [of error and ignorance], in which adults become aged, the young grow up and the believers toil until they meet their Lord [on their death]? I considered that patient endurance was the wisest and proper [course of action]. So I was patient, although it was like having a particle of dirt in the eye or a bone stuck in the throat. I watched as my inheritance was plundered, until the first one [Abu Bakr] went his way [died]. And he handed it [the caliphate] over to the one after him ['Umar] ...

How strange it is that during his [Abu Bakr's] lifetime, he wished to be released from it [the caliphate] but then he imposed it upon the other one ['Umar] after his death. Greatly indeed did these two milk the udders [of the caliphate, i.e. took advantage of it for themselves]. He ['Umar] made it [the caliphate] his own well-fortified property; he made its language harsh and its impact severe. Many were the errors he made during it [his caliphate] and many the excuses he made [for these errors].

To go along with it [his caliphate] was like riding an untrained and unruly camel. If it is pulled up by its reins, its nostrils would be slit, but if the reins be let loose, it would plunge headlong forwards. And so, by the everlasting existence of God! people were tried by the pounding of the hooves on the ground and the refusal to be ridden; he was variable in his disposition and veered from the straight path.

And so, I remained patient despite the length of time and the severity of the trying affliction, until, when he ['Umar] went his way [died], he put the matter [of the caliphate] to a group [of six] and regarded me as one of them. But by God! what had I to do with this assembly of consultation? When did any doubt arise concerning me with regard to the first of them [Abu Bakr], that I had now become linked to the like of these? However, I swooped low when they swooped low and flew high when they flew high. One of them was influenced by hatred of me [Sa'd ibn Abi Waqqas] and another because of his in-law relationship ['Abdul-Rahman ibn 'Awf whose sister was married to 'Uthman] and so on and so forth, until the third of these people ['Uthman] arose, filling his belly between his dung and his fodder. And there arose with him the Banu Umayyah [his relatives], devouring the wealth of God like a camel devours the foliage of spring, until his rope became undone, his actions brought about his death and his greed brought him down prostrate.

'Uthman was assassinated in 656 and 'Ali was proclaimed caliph by popular acclamation. It has been pointed out that 'Ali did not have the backing of the majority of Quraysh, whom Abu Bakr had considered entitled to decide on the caliphate, nor was he chosen after a consultation among the most eminent companions of the Prophet, which 'Umar had stipulated as the condition for valid succession. However, 'Ali never considered himself bound by the decisions of these previous caliphs. After twenty-four years, he had come to the position that he had considered to be rightfully his from the start. But it was already too late. 'Uthman's nepotism had placed members of the Banu Umayyah clan in powerful positions throughout the expanding Islamic Empire, even though most of them had led the Meccans in opposing the Prophet. They were led by Mu'awiyah, whose father Abu Sufyan was the Prophet's greatest enemy and whose mother, Hind, had eaten and spat out the heart (or according to another account the liver) of the Prophet's uncle Hamzah, the Prince of Martyrs, after the Battle of Uhud. Mu'awiyah was governor of Syria and refused to submit to 'Ali, accusing him of giving shelter to 'Uthman's assassins and hence of being guilty of complicity in the murder. On another front, two senior Muslims, Talhah and Zubayr (who had been on 'Umar's council of six that chose 'Uthman to be caliph), sought to grasp the caliphate for themselves. They withdrew to Mecca and aligned themselves with the Prophet's wife 'A'ishah and many of the Quraysh nobility. 'A'ishah's hatred for 'Ali went back to the lifetime of the Prophet, when she had been implicated in a scandal and 'Ali had advised the Prophet to divorce her. This group went to Basrah and raised an army there, in the name of avenging the death of 'Uthman.

'Ali was, however, a great military leader and undaunted by these revolts. With most of the elite of Quraysh either gathered around Talhah and Zubayr in Mecca or with Mu'awiyah in Syria, 'Ali naturally went to Kufah in Iraq, where the Yemeni tribesmen, who resented the primacy that the Quraysh had assumed for themselves, gathered around him. Other residents of Kufah were attracted to his teaching. Even before the advent of Islam, Iranian-controlled Iraq had been at war with Byzantine-controlled Syria for generations. With Mu'awiyah ruling in Damascus in Syria, it was natural for the people of Iraq to support his rival.

'Ali first went to Basrah and, at the Battle of the Camel,

defeated Talhah, Zubayr and 'A'ishah. Then in 657, 'Ali turned his attention to Mu'awiyah and advanced towards Syria. The two armies met at Siffin. Again 'Ali's military prowess was set to triumph, but the wily Mu'awiyah, at the instigation of his general, told his men to lift copies of the Qur'an on their lances and cry: 'Let the Qur'an decide between us.' 'Ali urged his men to fight on and complete the victory but they refused.

'Ali was forced to accept arbitration and cease fighting. This disaster for 'Ali was followed by a second, since 'Ali was pressured by his army into accepting an unskilled negotiator to represent him. 'Ali's negotiator was duped into accepting a decision that 'Ali was bound to find unacceptable: that both 'Ali and Mu'awiyah be deprived of the caliphate and a new caliph be elected. There then followed a third disaster for 'Ali. The very people who had pressured 'Ali into accepting arbitration now rejected it, saying that: 'arbitration belongs to God alone'. They separated from 'Ali's army and were therefore called the Kharijites (the Seceders).

THE EVENTS AT SIFFIN

In an oration delivered to the Kharijites and recorded in the Nahj al-Balaghah *(Sermon 121, or in some editions 122), 'Ali gives his thoughts about what went on at Siffin:*

These are his ['Ali's] words to the Kharijites when he had gone out to their camp and they were still insisting on rejection of the Arbitration. The Commander of the Faithful [Amir al-Mu'minin, i.e. 'Ali] said:

Were all of you with us in Siffin?

They replied that some of them were but some of them were not. And so he ['Ali] said:

Then divide yourselves into two groups: those who were in Siffin and those who were not, so that I may address you appropriately.

Then he shouted to the people:

Stop talking, be silent and listen to what I say. Turn your hearts to me. And whomever we ask for testimony, let him say what he knows about the matter.

Then he spoke with them at length, among the things he said being:

When they had raised the Qurʾan by way of deceit, artifice, trickery and beguilement, did you not say 'They are our brothers and the people who accepted our invitation [to become Muslims]. They want us to desist and they ask for peace in the name of the Book of God, praised be He. And our opinion is to accept what they say and relieve their distress'.

Then I said to you, 'In this affair, the outer appearance is faith but the inner reality of it is enmity. It begins with pity [for them] but will end in regret. And so remain steadfast in your task and undeviating on your path. Cleave firmly to Holy War (*jihad*) and pay no heed to the shouts of the shouter. If he is answered he will mislead, but if he is left [unanswered], he will be brought low'.

And so this matter [the Arbitration] was concluded and I saw that you gave it to them. By God! If I refuse it, its conditions would not be obligatory on me, nor would God lay it on me as a sin. And by God! If I accept it, I verily am the rightful person who should be followed, for the Book [the Qurʾan] is with me [and the arbitration was to be decided according to the Qurʾan]. I have never forsaken it since I first began to go along with it. We have been with the Messenger of God, when there was killing of one another by fathers, sons, brothers and relatives. Every misfortune and hardship only served to increase us in our belief, in our pressing on upon the right path, in our submission to [Divine] command and in our endurance of the pain of our wounds.

But now we have come to fighting our brethren in Islam on account of the deviation [from the truth], the distortion, the doubts and the [wrong] interpretations that have entered into it [Islam]. However, if we strive for a means by which God may put our unsettled affairs in order and through which we may come closer to the others in what we have in common [i.e. Islam], then we strongly desire this and would cleave to it, forsaking all else.

'Ali was in a perilous position. The break in hostilities gave Mu'awiyah an opportunity to regroup and strengthen his position, even as the Kharijites were causing dissent among 'Ali's forces. In Egypt, 'Ali's governor was overthrown through Mu'awiyah's machinations and the province came under Mu'awiyah's control. Then the Kharijites began committing atrocities close to 'Ali's capital in Kufah and posed a serious threat. 'Ali acted decisively, attacking and defeating the Kharijites at the Battle of Nahrawan.

After the Battle of Nahrawan, 'Ali returned to Kufah and was contemplating what to do about Mu'awiyah when he was attacked, while praying in the mosque, by 'Abdul-Rahman ibn Muljam, who is said to have been a Kharijite. He died of his wounds two days later, on 28 January 661.

'Ali has become something of a legendary figure, not just for Shi'is but also for many other Muslims. He became regarded as a paragon of virtues and is revered for his piety and righteousness, adherence to justice and principle, and knowledge of the Qur'an and the Sunnah of the Prophet. His magnanimity towards his defeated opponents, his sincerity and straightforwardness and his eloquence are all noted in the historical records of both Sunnis and Shi'is. He is also credited with having been the founder of the study of Arabic grammar through his disciple, Abul-Aswad al-Du'ali, and the source for the correct method of reciting the Qur'an. The *Nahj al-Balaghah*, a collection of his discourses and letters, is a masterpiece of Arabic eloquence and style and is considered by many Muslims, especially Shi'is, as second only to the Qur'an in importance. Through disciples such as Rabi' ibn Khaytham, he is considered to have given the initiative to Sufism in Islam and the majority of the chains of transmission in Sufism go back to him. He was regarded even by people such as the second caliph, 'Umar, as the 'best of judges' and his judicial decisions are highly regarded both by Sunni and Shi'i experts in religious law. 'Ali participated in almost all the early battles and expeditions, during which his leadership, chivalry, bravery and skill as an expert swordsman were well-regarded and posthumously took on legendary proportions. Stemming from 'Ali's bravery in battle, his virtues of forbearance and justice, and his protection of women and the weak, he is regarded as having been the archetypal chivalrous youth (*fata*), and the role model for the various brotherhoods that arose in Islam, under the names of *futuwwah* in the Arabic world, *akhi* in the Turkish-speaking world and *ayyar* and *javanmardi* in the Persian-speaking world. From these traditions, the moral ideal and codes of conduct of many Islamic guilds, societies and orders of warriors are derived. These codes were also influential in popular social institutions such as the *zur-khanihs* (gymnasia) of Iran. It may even be that these moral ideals and codes of conduct passed over to Europe through the early Crusaders and influenced the European concept of chivalry.

For Shi'is the brief period of his caliphate is looked upon as a Golden Age, when the Muslim community was directed as it always should be directed, by the divinely-chosen Imam. Especially for Isma'ili Shi'is (see pp. 200–6), and also many other Shi'is, Muhammad was responsible for the revelation (*tanzil*), while 'Ali was responsible for its interpretation (*ta'wil*); Muhammad expounded the *zahir* (outward form) of Islam while 'Ali explained the *batin* (inner reality).

There are differing accounts regarding what happened to 'Ali's body and where he is buried but the majority of Shi'is consider that he was buried near Kufah; a large town, Najaf, has grown around his shrine, which is surrounded by some of the foremost centres of Shi'i religious education. There is also a shrine in the city of Mazar-e Sharif in north Afghanistan that is claimed to be the shrine of 'Ali.

2. Hasan ibn ʿAli, the Second Imam (Imamate 661–70)

ʿAli's caliphate lasted less than five years. He was unable to put right the wrongs that he perceived had seeped into Islam and died at a time when his position was weak. His eldest son Hasan (given by Shiʿis the title al-Mujtaba, the chosen) was proclaimed caliph at Kufah in 661. He was the elder of the two grandsons of the Prophet Muhammad and many could still remember the great love that the Prophet had for them. Hasan was 37 years old when he became caliph but his position was very weak. He soon found himself facing an advancing Syrian army, with his troops vanishing as a result of the false reports and liberal bribes of Muʿawiyah's secret agents. Although some historians have regarded Hasan as weak for abdicating in favour of Muʿawiyah, Shiʿis point out that it would have been a futile waste of lives to have committed his few remaining troops to battle. Once again, as after the death of Muhammad, power and political manoeuvring, rather than religious considerations, had decided the leadership of Islam. The old Meccan nobility of the pre-Islamic era had triumphed over the new Islamic order that gave seniority to those closest to the Prophet. The Prophet's grandson was being forced to give way in favour of the son of the Prophet's greatest enemy.

Muʿawiyah needed Hasan's abdication to give some semblance of legitimacy to his seizure of power and so he was prepared to be generous to Hasan over the terms of his capitulation. Hasan was allowed to retire to Medina with a large financial settlement. Although some groups came to Hasan in Medina, offering to assist him in an uprising against Muʿawiyah, he refused, because of the treaty he had signed with Muʿawiyah. It is stated in some sources that Muʿawiyah bribed one of Hasan's wives to poison him, as he presented an obstacle to Muʿawiyah's desire to have his own son accepted as his successor. In any case, Hasan died in in 670 CE at the early age of forty-five, and was buried at al-Baqi' cemetery in Medina.

3. Husayn ibn 'Ali, the Third Imam (Imamate 670–80)

Husayn, the younger son of 'Ali, was born in Medina in 626 and was six years old when his grandfather, the Prophet Muhammad, died. He was 43 years old when his brother died and he became the head of the family. He is regarded by Shi'is as the third Imam and has the title Sayyid al-Shuhada (Prince of Martyrs), which was first given by Muhammad to his uncle Hamzah, who was killed in the Battle of Uhud.

The people of Kufah were restive under Mu'awiyah's rule. They revolted in favour of Husayn in 671 but were easily defeated by Mu'awiyah and the leaders executed. Mu'awiyah died in 680, having arranged for his son, Yazid, to succeed him as the second of the Umayyad dynasty. Yazid was a drunkard, who (according to Shi'i and many Sunni historians) openly ridiculed and flouted the laws of Islam. Soon letters and messengers were arriving in Medina from the people of Kufah, urging Husayn to come to Kufah and assume leadership. Husayn had considered himself bound by the treaty that Hasan had made with Mu'awiyah. But with the death of Mu'awiyah, he no longer consider himself bound and he refused to take the oath of allegiance to Yazid. Husayn sent his cousin Muslim ibn 'Aqil to Kufah to assess the situation. In Kufah, large meetings were held for Muslim, at which thousands pledged their support for Husayn. When Husayn received news of this, he set off for Kufah with some fifty armed men and the women and children of his family. He was warned against going and reminded that the Kufans had let down both his brother and his father when they most needed their support, but he decided to press on.

The situation changed even as Husayn was leaving for Kufah. Yazid sent 'Ubaydullah ibn Ziyad to take control of the town. 'Ubaydullah instigated a reign of terror, dealing harshly with any manifestations of revolt. He captured and executed Muslim ibn 'Aqil and threatened anyone who supported Husayn with the same treatment. Then he set military units on all the routes to Kufah from the south, to intercept Husayn. A few of the people of Kufah managed to slip out of the town and join Husayn but most were either intimidated by 'Ubaydullah's sword or over-taken by greed for 'Ubaydullah's money and forgot their pledges of support for Husayn.

Husayn's party was intercepted by a detachment of the Umayyad army led by al-Hurr al-Tamimi. After negotiations, al-Hurr allowed them to proceed, provided they went neither towards Kufah nor Medina. They were shadowed by al-Hurr's men, while he sent for further instructions. The party had reached the plain of Karbala when four thousand men under 'Umar ibn Sa'd arrived with instructions from 'Ubaydullah not to allow Husayn to leave until he had taken an oath of allegiance to Yazid. Ibn Sa'd's men surrounded Husayn's party and cut them off from the river, which was their only source of water. It was the second day of Muharram AH 61/2 October 680.

Husayn tried to negotiate a withdrawal to Medina but Ibn Sa'd would not agree. Time was not on Husayn's side, as he had run out of water. Then 'Ubaydullah sent one of his retinue Shimr (or Shamir) with orders for Ibn Sa'd either to attack Husayn immediately or hand over command to Shimr. The final battle was on 10 Muharram (10 October 680). One by one, Husayn's companions were killed; they numbered, according to tradition, seventy-two men (some having joined since they left Medina, including al-Hurr al-Tamimi, the leader of the Umayyad detach-ment who had first intercepted Husayn). Husayn's half-brother, 'Abbas, was killed as he tried to fetch water for Husayn's party. One of Husayn's sons was killed fighting; his youngest son, an infant, was killed by an arrow. Finally only Husayn himself was left, until he was felled by a blow. The soldiers gathered around him, hesitant to kill the grandson of the Prophet, but Shimr came forward and struck the final blow.

The Umayyad army took the women and children captive, looted the tents and decapitated the bodies of Husayn and all his supporters, raising their heads on lances. Then they returned to 'Ubaydullah's court in Kufah. 'Ubaydullah sent them on to Yazid's court in Damascus. The two leading captives were Zaynab, the sister of Husayn, who spoke out fearlessly before 'Ubaydullah, and 'Ali, the son of Husayn, who had been too ill with dysentery to participate in the fighting and thus survived. Fearing a popular outcry if he executed these remaining members of the Prophet's family, Yazid sent them to Medina.

Shi'is consider that Husayn knew that death awaited him on this journey and he announced this to his companions, urging them to leave the group if they wished. However, he wished to sacrifice himself, as the only way to revitalize the spirit of Islam, which was in danger of being snuffed out by the actions of the Umayyad rulers. He considered that his death would give the jolt needed to bring the Muslims back to a realization of true Islam.

While 'Ali's claim to leadership was understood and accepted by many people, it was Husayn's martyrdom that affected people's hearts and added a distinctive religious dimension to the movement of political opposition, bringing to it a great many supporters. Over the centuries since it occurred, Husayn's martyrdom has been the most passionately commemorated event in the Shi'i calendar. During the first ten days of Muharram every year, the whole Shi'i world is plunged into mourning. Above all, the martyrdom of Husayn has given to Shi'i Islam an ethos of sanctification through martyrdom.

The traditional site of Husayn's grave has become an imposing shrine, around which the town of Karbala has grown, which is also the location of a shrine to 'Abbas and of numerous religious colleges (*madrasahs*), forming a *hawzah* (centre of learning). There is also a shrine in Cairo, built during the time that the Isma'ili Shi'is ruled there, which is believed by them to contain the head of Husayn. Twelver Shi'is believe the head of Husayn is buried with his body at Karbala.

THE MARTYRDOM OF IMAM HUSAYN ON THE PLAIN OF KARBALA

From the popular hagiographic text, Husayn Va'iz Kashifi's Rawdat al-Shuhada *(the foundational text for all ritual recitals of the story of the martyrdom of the Imam Husayn, see pp. 143–4):*
And so he [Imam Husayn] put on his cloak of Egyptian silk and bound the turban of the Apostle of God around his head and hung the shield of Hamzah, the Prince of Martyrs, behind him and donned Dhul-Faqar [the sword of 'Ali]. He mounted his horse Dhul-Jannah and set off for the field of battle.

Those seated in the tent of purity [the women of his family] ran after him calling out: 'Woe unto us! With whom have you left us? In whose care have you left us who have no home or kin?' The Imam (upon him be peace) replied; 'Go back! I have entrusted you to God's care and He is my trustee in all your important affairs. And God is sufficient unto you as a trustee (Qur'an 4:81)'.

And when Imam Husayn (upon him be peace) reached the battle-field, he plunged his lance into the ground and called out to them in verse:
The chosen of God among all of creation was my father
Then after him, my mother, and I am the son of these two chosen ones
Silver cut from gold
And I am the silver and the son of two golden ones
Fatimah the radiant is my mother and my father
Is the heir of Apostles and the Imam of the Two Weighty Matters (see pp. 18–19)

Who is there in the whole of creation who has a grandfather like mine

Or a father? And I am the son of the two people of knowledge (see p. 19)

Gold from gold in gold

Silver from silver in silver

Then he said: 'O people! Fear the great God who changes night to day and causes to die and brings to life ... If you believe in the religion of God and have faith in His apostle, Muhammad the chosen (may God bless him and his family and keep them safe), who is my grandfather, do not wrong me or do me an injustice. Bear in mind that tomorrow you may stand at the judgement seat with my grandfather, father and mother denying you the water of Kawthar [the Stream of Paradise]. You have killed seventy-two of my children, brothers, nephews, family, friends and associates and now you intend to kill me. If it is for the sake of the rule of this territory, let me go to Byzantium, Ethiopia or to the land of the Turks and allow my family and children, who are burning with thirst, to have some water, so that tomorrow you may not face my wrath [after death]. Otherwise then, do what you will and the judgement is with God and we are content with the will of God'.

The Syrians who heard this withdrew from the battlefield and the people of Kufah wept and wailed. When Shimr ibn Dhul-Jawshan and his associates saw that the matter was slipping from their hands and that their troops might turn on their commanders, they approached Imam Husayn and said; 'O son of Abu Turab ['Ali]! Do not draw this matter out! Put aside your pride and come, let us take you to Ibn Ziyad where you can swear allegiance to Yazid. That way you can avoid this being your place of death. Otherwise we will leave you like this until you die [of thirst]'.

[Then Imam Husayn returned to his tents and bade farewell to his family. At this point there is the story of the arrival of other-worldly creatures, offering to assist the Imam and his refusal of their assistance. The Imam then returned to the battle-ground and challenged any of their men to single combat. Tamim, a Syrian commander, stepped forward.]

[Tamim said:] 'O son of Abu Turab! How long will you oppose us? Your sons have tasted death and your family and followers have donned the cloak of the grave. And still you fight on, a solitary individual against an army of twenty thousand men'.

Imam Husayn: 'O Syrian! Did I come to battle against you or did you come against me? Did I block your way or did you block mine? You have killed my brothers and my sons. So now what can there be between you and I except the sword? So do not say any more. Come forward and let us see what you are made of'. With this the Imam let out, as a strategy, a cry that melted the courage of the troops. Tamim froze and his hand became motionless. The Imam struck such a blow to his neck that his head landed fifty yards away. Then the Imam charged the troops and under the blows of his sword, they became afraid and fled.

[After this, one of the commanders of the army faced Imam Husayn and succeeded in wounding him. The Imam made for the river to slake his thirst. He fought his way through three ranks of troops, killing many until he reached the water.]

Just as he was raising a handful of water to his lips, one of the men in the surrounding troops called out to him: 'Do you drink here while armed men are looting the tents of your women [and dishonouring them]?' He let the water fall and ran to the tents like the wind. Finding no men there, he realized that he had been tricked and deceived.

[Once more the Imam said farewell to his family; to his sister Zaynab, to his only surviving son 'Ali, to his wife, and to the rest of the family. Then he faced the troops again.]

Ibn Sa'd said: O people! Know that singly, you are no match for him, but now he is thirsty and near to death, so you should all attack at once'. And so the troops arose and surrounded him. He, like a roaring lion, set about them with his sharp blade, causing the earth to tremble with his cry of 'I am the progeny of the Apostle of God!' And the lightening flash of his blade dazzled the eyes of his enemies.

[The surrounding troops rained arrows upon the Imam and struck him with blows. Greatly weakened the Imam was unable to fight any more and brought his horse to a standstill. At this point a part of the army fell upon the tents of the family to loot them.]

The Imam Husayn (upon him be peace) called out: 'O family of Abu Sufyan! If religion does not move you, are you not restrained by your sense of shame that you molest my women?' Shimr said: 'O Husayn! What do you mean?' He said: 'If your intention is to kill me, then I am here fighting you. I ask that no one should approach my women's quarters as long as I am still alive'.

[Shimr called back his troops that were approaching the women's tents and all the troops concentrated on the Imam. Since no one could approach the Imam without fear overtaking him, they rained arrows upon him. The Imam dismounted so that his horse be not injured and this emboldened his enemies. An arrow pierced his brow and blood poured from this wound. The Imam filled his hands with the blood and smeared it over his face and head. One by one individuals stepped forward and struck blows upon the Imam. But each person who came forward to strike the final blow would retreat in shame after the Imam spoke to them. Until Shimr stepped forward and sat on the Imam's chest. When Imam Husayn observed certain signs upon his body, he said that he had had a dream in which the Apostle of God had told him that a person with those signs would kill him.]

Imam Husayn said: 'O Shimr! The Apostle of God placed his head upon this chest and now you sit upon it. He kissed this throat and you hold a blade against it. I see the spirit of the prophet Zachariah at your right hand and the spirit of John the Baptist at your left hand. O Shimr! Get off my chest for it is time for the evening prayer. So allow me to face the Qiblah and to sit in prayer for it is my inheritance to be wounded while seated at prayer [as my father was]. So when I am seated at prayer do as you wish'.

So Shimr got off the Imam's chest and the Imam got up as best he could and turned towards the Qiblah and began to pray. Shimr did not wait for him to finish his prayer but while he was in the state of prostration, he enabled him to taste martyrdom.

4. 'Ali Zayn al-'Abidin, the fourth Imam (Imamate 680–712)

'Ali was the eldest son of the Imam Husayn, who was too ill to engage in the fighting at Karbala and thus survived. He was sent to Medina by Yazid, together with his aunt, Zaynab. He is usually known by his title Zayn al-'Abidin (the ornament of the worshippers) and also by the titles al-Sajjad (the prostrator) and al-Zaki (the pure). He was born in the year 658 in Medina. According to Shi'i tradition, his mother is said to have been Shahrbanu, the daughter of Yazdigird, the last Sassanian king of Iran, although this is actually a very late tradition that is first recorded some 250 years later. During the period of his Imamate there were a number of developments that were to be very important for the future of Shi'i Islam.

The first of these developments was that a group of Kufah residents began to discuss what they could do to make amends for their failure to come to Imam Husayn's assistance at Karbala. They elected as their leader Sulayman ibn Surad, who became known as Shaykh al-Shi'ah (chief of the Shi'ah). The word 'shi'ah' means faction or party. And so in the time of 'Ali, his supporters were known as 'shi'at 'Ali' (the faction of 'Ali) to distinguish them from 'shi'at Mu'awiyah' (the faction of Mu'awiyah). Thus the designation was at first merely descriptive. With the naming of Sulayman ibn Surad as Shaykh al-Shi'ah, there is the first indication of the emergence of 'Shi'ah' as the name of a group or movement. This movement became known, however, as the Tawwabun (the penitents) and in 684 emerged as an army of 3,000 who, as a token of their remorse, marched to certain death against an Umayyad army of 30,000. Their action set what was to become a dominant ethos of Shi'i religiosity, the idea of repentance and remorse, which is still seen in the chest-beating, self-flagellation and other self-harm that is part of the Muharram commemorations in many parts of the Shi'i world.

Another important development of this period was the arrival in Kufah of Mukhtar al-Thaqafi, who was advancing among the Shi'ah the claim that the rightful successor to Imam Husayn was Muhammad ibn al-Hanafiyyah, the first Imam 'Ali's third son by a woman of the tribe of Banu Hanifah (that is, not by Fatimah, the daughter of the Prophet); they were called the Kaysaniyyah. After the defeat of the Tawwabun, Mukhtar became strong enough in 686 to seize control of Kufah for a time. Given their open proclamation of the Shi'i cause (as opposed to Zayn al-'Abidin's secluded life in Medina) and their control of Kufah, the main stronghold of Shi'i Islam, it seems likely that more of the Shi'ah followed Mukhtar and Ibn al-Hanafiyyah than followed Zayn al-'Abidin.

Imam Zayn al-'Abidin was famed for his piety, and kept himself secluded, avoiding engagement with the various revolts that were going on in his time. Although most of the Shi'i support initially went to the Kaysaniyyah, it seems that after their defeat, the Shi'is rallied around him from about 692 onwards. He was in any case held in the greatest respect by all. He died in about 712 and was buried in al-Baqi' cemetery in Medina. According to Shi'i historians he was poisoned on the orders either of the reigning caliph, Walid, or his brother Hisham.

5. Muhammad al-Baqir, the Fifth Imam (Imamate 712–37)

Abu Ja'far Muhammad, the son of 'Ali Zayn al-'Abidin, known as al-Baqir ('the splitter-open', i.e. of knowledge; also said to mean the 'ample' in knowledge) was born in 677. His mother, Fatimah, was a daughter of the Second Imam, Hasan. Thus, al-Baqir joined the two lines of descent from Fatimah and 'Ali. He was about thirty-five years of age when his father died.

Like his father, Muhammad al-Baqir was politically quiescent and refrained from openly putting forward any claim. As during his father's time with Ibn al-Hanafiyyah, there was a rival claimant for the allegiance of the Shi'is during al-Baqir's time. This was al-Baqir's younger half-brother, Zayd, who advocated a more politically active role for the Imam and was prepared to accommodate to a certain extent the viewpoint of the majority of Muslims, by acknowledging the caliphates of Abu Bakr and 'Umar and accepting their legal practices. From this time, there were a number of revolts under various members of the family of the Prophet. All of them tend to be called Zaydi revolts, since the Zaydis considered that any member of the Prophet's family who rose to power was the legitimate Imam. Abu Hashim, the son of Ibn al-Hanafiyyah was also active at this time, leading a group of the Shi'ah. Also, as in the days of his father, it is likely that the majority of the Shi'ah did not support al-Baqir but rallied around these two more politically active leaders.

The main difference between al-Baqir and his father was that al-Baqir appears to have been more active in giving instructions and guidance to his followers. Consequently, a considerable number of these became incorporated into the body of Shi'i law. Also in view of the rival claimants, he emphasised the importance of *nass*, the specific designation by each Imam of his successor. There is a wide discrepancy in the sources about the manner of his death – Shi'i books state that he was poisoned by the Umayyads; and about its date – dates vary from 732 to 743, so it possible to say that he died in around 737. He was buried at al-Baqi' cemetery in Medina.

6. Ja'far al-Sadiq, the Sixth Imam (Imamate 737–765)

Abu 'Abdillah Ja'far, the eldest son of Muhammad al-Baqir, is known by the title al-Sadiq (the truthful). His mother was a great-granddaughter of the first caliph, Abu Bakr. There are discrepancies about his date of birth but he was born in

about 702 and was therefore about thirty-five years old when his
father died.

The importance of Ja'far al-Sadiq lies in the fact that he was
universally respected throughout the Islamic world for his piety
and learning. Many of his students went on to become renowned
scholars and jurists of Sunni Islam. Abu Hanifah, the eponymous
founder of the Hanafi School of Law in Sunni Islam, is said to
have been one of his students, and Malik ibn Anas, the eponymous founder of the Maliki School of Law in Sunni Islam, was
also evidently closely associated with al-Sadiq and transmitted
Traditions (*hadith* – see Glossary) from him. However, al-Sadiq
did not openly advance his claim to the Imamate. There were
several other Shi'i claimants during this time: Zayd's revolt in
740, the rebellion of 'Abdullah ibn Mu'awiyah (a descendant of
Ja'far, 'Ali's brother) in 744 and the revolt of Muhammad al-Nafs
al-Zakiyyah (the pure soul, a descendant of Imam Hasan) in 762.
But the most important revolt was that of the 'Abbasids, which
began in 747 in the name of 'one who shall be chosen from the
family of the Prophet' – a vaguely-worded phrase carefully calcu-
lated to garner the support of most of the Shi'ah. Throughout
these turbulent events, al-Sadiq followed the policy of his father
and grandfather and remained politically quietist. Even when
Abu Salama, the political leader of the 'Abbasid revolt, reportedly
offered him the caliphate, al-Sadiq declined it. Once the revolt
was successful, it became clear that what the 'Abbasids meant by
the 'one who shall be chosen from the family of the Prophet' was
their leader Abu al-'Abbas. The 'Abbasids claimed at first that the
Imamate was passed on to them from Abu Hashim, the son of
Muhammad ibn al-Hanafiyyah, although they later based their
claim on the fact that the Prophet had died with no male issue
and thus, according to Arab tribal custom, his heir was the most
senior living male member of his clan, and that was his uncle
al-'Abbas, the ancestor of the 'Abbasids. Once in power, they
began to persecute the Shi'ah. Al-Sadiq was summoned to Kufah

and imprisoned for a time. Most authorities agree that al-Sadiq died in 765. Shi'i historians have attributed his death to poisoning, on this occasion by the 'Abbasid Caliph al-Mansur.

During his Imamate, al-Sadiq emphasized the two doctrines of *nass* (the specific designation by one Imam of his successor) and *'ilm* (the special knowledge of the Imam), perhaps as a way of distinguishing his claims from those of rival Shi'i claimants. He also emphasized the doctrine of *taqiyyah* (religious dissimulation) as a way of protecting his followers in the increasingly hostile environment created by the 'Abbasids. It was probably during al-Sadiq's Imamate that the idea was consolidated that the Imam was a descendant of the Prophet Muhammad through the line of 'Ali and Fatimah, and was the infallible and authoritative interpreter of the Islamic revelation. In other words, the foundations of the doctrine of the Imamate were laid.

7. Musa al-Kazim, the Seventh Imam (Imamate 765–99)

The Seventh Imam of the Twelver Shi'is was Abul-Hasan or Abu Ibrahim Musa, the son of Ja'far al-Sadiq. He was known as al-Kazim (the forbearing). He was born in about 745, his mother being a Berber slave, Hamidah. He was about twenty years of age at the time of his father's death. The succession of al-Kazim marks an important division in Shi'i Islam. It appears that during his lifetime, al-Sadiq had appointed his eldest son Isma'il to be his successor as Imam. But Isma'il died while al-Sadiq was still alive, and Twelver Shi'is say that al-Sadiq then appointed Musa al-Kazim. Upon al-Sadiq's death, however, the succession was disputed, with both 'Abdullah al-Abtah, al-Sadiq's eldest surviving son, and Muhammad, the son of Isma'il, denying that al-Kazim had been appointed, and each pressing his own claim. 'Abdullah died only seventy days after al-Sadiq and most of those who had followed al-Sadiq drifted towards al-Kazim. The latter departed a little from the policy of non-involvement in political affairs pursued by his father and grandfather: he had participated in the revolt of Muhammad al-Nafs al-Zakiyyah in 762 while his father was alive. He is also credited with having started the network of agents (*wikalah*) that later became a prominent part of the organization of the later Imams of the Twelver line.

Musa al-Kazim faced intense hostility from the 'Abbasid caliphs, especially after Harun ar-Rashid became caliph in 786. The caliph is reported to have had hundreds of 'Alids (descendants of 'Ali) killed. Al-Kazim was arrested and brought from Medina to Baghdad, and imprisoned several times. During his last imprisonment, he is said to have been poisoned, on the caliph's orders, in about 799. The caliph had to make a public display of his body, as a significant number of his followers refused to believe that al-Kazim had died, since many thought that the seventh Imam would be the last Imam and the Mahdi. Many of these followers formed a group called the Waqifiyyah, which claimed that al-Kazim had gone into hiding (occultation) and would return as the Mahdi. A smaller group with similar beliefs, the Nawusiyyah, had formed after the death of al-Sadiq. Al-Kazim was buried in the Quraysh cemetery on the west bank of the Tigris river, a short distance north-west of Baghdad. In later years, a shrine was built over this grave and that of his grandson the ninth Imam, and a small town called Kazimayn grew around it. The shrine and town are now part of greater Baghdad.

8. 'Ali al-Rida, the Eighth Imam (Imamate 799–818)

Abul-Hasan 'Ali, the son of Musa al-Kazim, was known as al-Rida (the approved or acceptable, pronounced 'Reza' by Persian speakers) and was born in Medina in 765. It is known that his mother was a Berber slave but her name is given differently in the various sources. He was about thirty-four years old when his father died. Although at first the Waqifiyyah were more numerous than his supporters, with time he managed to win many of them over and to gain control of the network of agents established by his father. When the caliph Harun al-Rashid died there was a civil war between his two sons, with al-Ma'mun eventually winning. At this time, al-Ma'mun unexpectedly summoned Imam al-Rida to his capital at Marv, in central Asia, and had him proclaimed his heir-apparent in 817. It is not at all clear why al-Ma'mun should have done this. Some have suggested that it was to take the wind from the sails of several Shi'i revolts that were going on, mainly in Iraq, at a time when the 'Abbasid state was weak after the civil war. The decision was probably also influenced by al-Ma'mun's powerful chief minister (vizier), al-Fadl ibn Sahl, who had Shi'i proclivities.

At this time, al-Rida's sister, Fatimah, known as Ma'sumah (the immaculate), set out from Medina to see him in Marv. She died *en route*, at Qom in Iran; her shrine is the religious focus of the city of Qom. Towards the end of the eighth century, Qom became predominantly Shi'i, when members of the powerful al-Ash'ari clan there converted. An imposing shrine was later built over the grave of Fatimah and a number of religious colleges were established. The town became one of the leading world centres for Shi'i studies in the tenth century, and again from the twentieth century to the present day.

In 818, al-Ma'mum set out with al-Rida towards Iraq, where some of the 'Abbasid family had revolted against al-Ma'mun's appointment of al-Rida as his successor. On the way, at Tus, al-Rida suddenly became ill and died. Shi'i sources usually state that al-Ma'mun poisoned him, but it is equally possible that it was the work of the rebel members of the 'Abbasid family, who rejected his nomination as heir-apparent. Al-Rida was buried near Tus and later a town, Mashhad ('place of martyrdom'), grew around the shrine. It is an important place of pilgrimage for Shiʻis and has become a centre for religious studies (a *hawzah*).

9. Muhammad al-Taqi (al-Jawad), the Ninth Imam (Imamate 818–835)

Abu Jaʻfar Muhammad ibn ʻAli, known by the titles al-Taqi (the God-fearing) and al-Jawad (the generous), was born in 810. Most sources say that his mother was a Nubian slave. Muhammad al-Taqi was born in Medina and remained there when his father went to join Maʼmun in far-off Marv. He was only about eight years old when his father died and he succeeded to the Imamate. His youth was a source of controversy among the Shiʻah, some asking how a boy could have the necessary knowledge to be the Imam. This caused Shiʻi writers to emphasize the doctrine of *ʻilm*, the (innate) knowledge of the Imams, where for the previous Imams they had emphasised how much each Imam had learned from close association with his predecessor. This claim of supernatural transfer of knowledge must to some extent have lent credence to claims by the leaders of some Gnostic Shiʻi groups that the Imamate had been transferred to them (see p. 57).

The caliph al-Maʼmun continued to be friendly towards the family of the Imams and al-Taqi went to Baghdad where he was respectfully received and given the daughter of al-Maʼmun in marriage. Al-Maʼmun died in 833 and was succeeded by his brother, al-Muʻtasim, who in 835 summoned Muhammad al-Taqi back from Medina to Baghdad, where he died later that same year. Since it has become almost a doctrine among Twelver Shiʻis that each of the Imams was martyred, Shiʻi writers have claimed Taqi was poisoned by his wife, but the stories about this differ and one early prominent Shiʻi scholar, al-Shaykh al-Mufid, dismissed this rumour. As mentioned above, this Imam was buried close to his grandfather in what has become the shrine of Kazimayn.

10. 'Ali al-Naqi (al-Hadi), the Tenth Imam (Imamate 835–68)

Abul-Hasan 'Ali, the son of Muhammad al-Taqi, is known by the titles al-Naqi (the pure) and al-Hadi (the guide) and was born in about 828 in Medina. His mother was a Moroccan slave, Samanah. He was about seven years old when his father died and once again the Shi'is were faced with the problem of a child Imam.

When al-Mutawakkil became caliph, the persecutions of the Shi'is began again. Al-Naqi was summoned to Samarra, the new 'Abbasid capital north of Baghdad, in 848 and thereafter, although treated respectfully, he was in effect the prisoner of successive caliphs. He was given a house in the military quarter, which was known as al-'Askar (the army), and so both al-Naqi and his son are known as al-'Askari. During his time, the network of agents set up under the previous Imams became very much more effective under the leadership of 'Uthman ibn Sa'id al-'Amri and was able to gather large sums of money from the Shi'is as religious taxes (khums). Its effectiveness allowed a great growth in the number of the Imam's followers at a time when Islam was expanding rapidly from conversions among the conquered peoples of Iraq and Iran. This period was also marked by a split among Shi'is over the nature of the Imamate. One group, the Mufawwidah, maintained the Imams were the agents to whom God had delegated His powers of creation and command, a belief that the other group declared to be heresy. 'Ali died in Samarra in 868; many Shi'i writers state he was poisoned by the caliph al-Mu'tazz, but the early Shi'i scholar al-Shaykh al-Mufid, in his account of the Imam, does not say this. 'Ali al-Naqi and his son Hasan al-'Askari were buried in Samarra and a large shrine built over their graves in later centuries.

11. Hasan al-'Askari, the Eleventh Imam (Imamate 868–74)

The Eleventh Imam was Abu Muhammad Hasan, the son of 'Ali al-Naqi. He was born in about 846 in Medina and was therefore only about two years of age when his father was summoned to Samarra. Both remained there in detention for the rest of their lives. He is thus known as Hasan al-'Askari. His mother was a slave, who is named as Hadith.

The death of the tenth Imam had caused something of a crisis in Shi'i ranks. The tenth Imam had originally appointed his son Muhammad as his successor, but he died. The Imam's next son Hasan was considered unsuitable by some of the learned among the Shi'is because of his lack of religious knowl-edge and they turned to the tenth Imam's youngest son, Ja'far. However, 'Uthman al-'Amri, the head of the network of agents (*wikalah*) remained loyal to Hasan and this proved decisive. The outcome greatly strengthened the authority of the network of agents among the Shi'ah – something that was to become criti-cal after the death of Hasan. The period of Hasan's Imamate was brief – only six years. During both his and much of his father's Imamate, pressure from the 'Abbasids was severe and access to the Imam was restricted, increasing the importance of the network of agents to enable communication with the Shi'ah. Hasan al-'Askari died on either 25 December 873 or 1 January 874. The Shi'i histories maintain that he was poisoned by the caliph al-Mu'tamid.

12. Muhammad al-Mahdi, the Twelfth Imam

After the death of Hasan al-'Askari there was a great deal of confusion among the Shi'ah. The histories say that the Shi'i followers of Hasan al-'Askari split up into at least fourteen sects. Many accepted the word of Ja'far, the brother of Hasan, that the Imam had had no children. Some of these considered the Imamate had stopped with Hasan, some said Hasan had gone into occultation and would re-emerge as the Mahdi, some accepted Ja'far's claim to be the Imam (with various justifications) and some said that although the Imamate had ceased with Hasan, the Mahdi would arise from among the descendants of the Imams in the last days. Those who were eventually to become the main body of the Twelver Shi'ah believed that Hasan had had a son, Muhammad, by a slave-girl who is usually identified as Narjis or Saqil, and that he was the true Imam and had gone into occultation through fear of his enemies. He is thus Abul-Qasim Muhammad ibn Hasan, known as al-Mahdi (the guided), al-Muntazar (the awaited), al-Hujjah (the proof), al-Qa'im (the one who stands as the present Imam and will arise as the Mahdi), and the Baqiyatullah (the remnant of God).

It is not at all clear to which group the majority of the followers of Hasan adhered after his death, but 'Uthman al-'Amri, who had been the head of the Imam's network of agents, headed the group that maintained that Hasan had had a son, Muhammad, who was the Imam and had gone into hiding. 'Uthman claimed that he himself had been appointed the agent of this Hidden Imam. The believers could continue to send their supplications and monies to the Imam through him and the Imam would reply through him. This was effectively what had happened under the two previous Imams, so it may be that most of this group of Shi'is thought that there was nothing very different about the Twelfth Imam. When 'Uthman died, the position of agent was taken over by his son Abu Ja'far Muhammad; Husayn ibn Ruh al-Nawbakhti became the agent in 917 and 'Ali ibn Muhammad al-Samarri in 938. He held office for only three years and died in 941.

Just before his death, the fourth agent, al-Samarri, brought this written message from the Hidden Imam:

In the name of God the Merciful, the Compassionate! O 'Ali ibn Muhammad al-Samarri, may God magnify the reward of your brethren upon you! There are but six days separating you from death. So therefore arrange your affairs but do not appoint anyone to your position after you. For the second occultation has come and there will not now be a manifestation except by the permission of God and that after a long time has passed, and hearts have hardened and the earth become filled with tyranny. And there will come to my Shi'ah those who claim to have seen me, but he who claims to have seen me before the emergence of the Sufyani and the call [of the caller from heaven; these are two signs of the return of the Hidden Imam, see pp. 186–7] is assuredly a lying imposter. And there is no power nor strength save in God the Almighty, the All-High.

Thus the Shi'ah passed in 941 from the period that became known as the Minor or Lesser Occultation, during which communication with the Hidden Imam was possible through his agents, into what became known as the Major or Greater Occultation, the period of time when there is no agent of the Hidden Imam on Earth. This has lasted to the present day. For further details on the doctrine of the Twelfth Imam and the Occultation, see pp. 185–8.

The Shi'ah during the time of the Imams

The story told by each generation of Shi'i historians has largely been (as most history writing always has) a reconstruction of the past in the image of the present. This makes a reconstruction of what actually occurred very difficult. Under severe repression and with a number of individuals claiming the Imamate, the Shi'ah were a fragmented, underground movement. From this

Table 1 The Twelve Imams

	Name	Titles and epithets	Dates of birth, start of Imamate and death	Place of burial	Contemporary Caliphs
I	ʿAli ibn Abu Talib	Amir al-Muʾminin, al-Murtada, Abu Turab, Abul-Hasan	600–632–661	Najaf	Abu Bakr, ʿUmar, ʿUthman
II	Hasan ibn ʿAli	al-Mujtaba, Abu Muhammad	625–661–670	Medina	Muʿawiyah
III	Husayn ibn ʿAli	Sayyid al-Shuhada, Abu ʿAbdillah	626–670–680	Karbala	Muʿawiyah, Yazid I
IV	ʿAli ibn Husayn	Zayn al-ʿAbidin, al-Sajjad, Abu Muhammad	658–680–712	Medina	Yazid I, ʿAbdul-Malik, Walid I
V	Muhammad ibn ʿAli	al-Baqir, Abu Jaʿfar	677–712–737	Medina	Walid I–Hisham
VI	Jaʿfar ibn Muhammad	al-Sadiq, Abu ʿAbdillah	702–737–765	Medina	Hisham–Yazid III, al-Saffah, al-Mansur
VII	Musa ibn Jaʿfar	al-Kazim, Abul-Hasan	745–765–799	Kazimayn	al-Mansur–Harun al-Rashid
VIII	ʿAli ibn Musa	al-Rida, Abul-Hasan	765–799–818	Mashhad	Harun al-Rashid, Amin, Maʾmun
IX	Muhammad ibn ʿAli	al-Taqi, al-Jawad, Abu Jaʿfar	810–818–835	Kazimayn	Maʾmun, al-Muʿtasim
X	ʿAli ibn Muhammad	al-Hadi, al-Naqi, Abul-Hasan	828–835–868	Samarra	al-Muʿtasim–al-Muʿtazz
XI	Hasan ibn ʿAli	al-Askari, Abu Muhammad	846–868–874	Samarra	Al-Muʿtazz–al-Muʿtamid
XII	Muhammad ibn Hasan	Al-Mahdi, al-Muntazar, Abul-Qasim	869–874–?		

distance in time and the sources available, it is almost impossible to determine how many of them there were, what proportion of them followed each of the rival Imams, what station (political and metaphysical) they gave to their Imam and what were the exact relationships among the different Shi'i groups. The story told in the Twelver Shi'i history books, of an orderly succession of Twelve Imams each with a large following and believing the same doctrines as present-day Twelver Shi'is, is largely a backward projection of the final stage; the past reconstructed in the image of the norms of the present. In so far as we can reconstruct that past, it was probably very different and much more complex than the simple picture told by the later Shi'i historians.

Although recent research indicates that the Zaydi community split to some extent from the other Shi'is in Kufah during the early second century, in all likelihood, Shi'i Islam during the first 120 years of Islamic history was more of a sentiment than a clearly-defined movement. It was perhaps largely a sentiment of the underdogs, the downtrodden, trying to assert themselves against the powerful elites that ran the Islamic Empire. Thus at one time we see them as the Arab tribesmen from Yemen and the south contending with the Umayyads, the 'Abbasids, the other elites of Quraysh and the northern Arabian tribes. Then again we see them as the people of Iraq struggling against their historical rivals the people of Syria, who had gained the upper hand through the establishment of the capital of the Umayyad Islamic Empire at Damascus. Then, with the rising of Mukhtar, we see them as the Iranian converts to Islam, resentful of their lower status as clients (*mawali*) of the Arab tribes. All these lower-status groups saw the family of 'Ali as being, like themselves, downtrodden, unjustly treated and cast aside by the elite. These people, protesting against their low status in a wealthy empire, were joined by those pious individuals who were disgusted by the irreligious nature of most of the rulers of the Umayyad dynasty, many of whom openly drank alcohol and were disdainful towards Islam. Although some such individuals joined the Kharijite movement, many were attracted to Shi'i Islam. Finally there were those who thought that leadership of Islam belonged to the family of Hashim. The family of 'Ali became a rallying point that united these elements against their common foe. The cause of the family of 'Ali became their cause. At first for many, it did not even have anything to do with descent from the Prophet of Islam.

This sentiment of protest that was early Shi'i Islam would from time to time congeal around a specific figure as a figurehead, the Imam. At any one time, there were often two or three different such figures claiming the loyalty of the Shi'ah; all being descendants of 'Ali or of other figures from the Prophet's family. When one of these Imams died or was killed, the following around him would become divided into sects for a time and then either melt away or turn to another Imam, often the son of the Imam who had just died. This pattern started as early as the death of Imam Husayn and the split among the Shi'is between the Kaysaniyyah and the followers of Imam Zayn al-'Abdidin, and continued with each succeeding Imam. Although this movement of protest was at first largely political, later it became increasingly religious, especially with the martyrdom of Husayn.

After the martyrdom of Husayn and the Tawwabun episode, the largest group of Shi'ah appear to have flocked to Mukhtar and the Kaysaniyyah, who were promoting the cause of Muhammad ibn al-Hanafiyyah. There are a number of features of this movement that are of great importance in the study of Shi'i Islam. Firstly, Mukhtar appealed strongly to the *mawali*. These were non-Arabs who had become Muslims but, because it was considered that, as well as making a religious declaration of faith, they needed to become clients of one of the Arab tribes, they occupied an inferior position to Arabs who were full members of the tribes. Secondly, it tells us that at this time, being a descendant of the Prophet Muhammad was not a primary consideration, since Muhammad ibn al-Hanafiyyah was not a descendant of the Prophet, but of 'Ali, and yet he succeeded in rallying the majority of the Shi'ah in Kufah, the most important Shi'i stronghold. If lineal descent from the Prophet Muhammad was not important to the majority of the Shi'ah, then what does this say about the Shi'ah movement? It provides the strongest indication that most of the Shi'ah at that time formed not so much a religious movement as a political protest movement – a protest by the southern Yemeni tribes and the *mawali* against the elite of Quraysh that formed the ruling aristocracy of Islam. It was not so much descent from the Prophet Muhammad and the religious claims of the Imams that attracted these people, as the sense of betrayal and injustice that they shared with 'Ali and the Imams.

The Kaysaniyyah was also important because when Muhammad ibn al-Hanafiyyah died in 700, one group of his followers considered that he had not died at all but had gone into occultation (*ghaybah*) and would return (*raj'ah*) as the Mahdi. Among his followers, there also emerged the idea of the allegorical interpretation of the Qur'an, the idea that beneath the *zahir* (the exoteric, or plain meaning), there is a *batin* (esoteric meaning). This is also the group that is said to have introduced the concept of *bada'* (God changing his mind) after Mukhtar claimed that it had been revealed to him that they would win a battle and they then lost it. This group of the Shi'ah were thus the first to bring into prominence a number of key religious ideas that have played an important role in Shi'i Islam up to the present day. For the purposes of this book, the Saba'iyyah, followers of 'Abdullah ibn Saba, who are said to have made similar claims about 'Ali after his death, are ignored, as it is almost impossible to be certain what this group believed or whether it even existed. Thus, although I have divided the Shi'ah into a political wing and a religious wing, and ascribed the Kaysaniyyah to the political wing, it is clear that the two wings intermingled, interacted and influenced each other greatly.

The next important figure around whom Shi'i sentiment congealed was Zayd, a son of 'Ali Zayn al-'Abidin. He may have had less legitimacy than his half-brother Muhammad al-Baqir, who was the oldest son of Zayn al-'Abidin and thus entitled to primacy, but because Zayd was willing to come out in open opposition to the Umayyad caliphate, many of the Shi'ah flocked to him in preference to his half-brother. From this there came into existence a branch of Shi'ism called Zaydi Shi'i Islam or the Zaydiyyah (see pp. 196–200) and there followed a number of Zaydi Imams who rose in rebellion. The evidence seems to indicate that, during the Umayyad period, there were many more Shi'is willing to follow these activist, political Imams than the more pacificist, quietist Imams that became the Twelver line, who were willing to submit to the Umayyad caliphs at Damascus and later the 'Abbasid caliphs in Iraq.

Apart from the varying political trends among the Shi'ah, there was also much religious speculation. A wide variety of people were part of this cloud of Shi'i sentiment. Many were not yet firmly wedded to the idea that the Imam had to be a descendant of Muhammad. We have seen how Muhammad ibn al-Hanafiyyah and 'Abdullah ibn Mu'awiyah, who were from the family of Hashim but not descendants of the Prophet Muhammad, claimed the Imamate. But there were others, who were not even Hashemites, but claimed that the Imamate had been transferred to them; for example Abu Mansur, who is said to have claimed the Imamate had been passed to him by al-Baqir (he formed the Mansuriyyah sect of Shi'is) and Abul-Khattab, who is said to have claimed the Imamate had passed to him from Ja'far al-Sadiq (he formed the Khattabiyyah sect).

From the description of various Shi'i groups that existed, it appears that a number of ideas were circulating among those with Shi'i sentiments, such as *tanasukh* (transmigration of souls), *ghaybah* (occultation), *raj'ah* (return), *hulul* (descent of the Divinity into a human being), *imamah* (Imamate, divinely-inspired leadership and guidance), *tashbih* (anthropomorphism with respect to God), *tafwid* (delegation of God's powers to other than God), *bada'* (alteration in God's will) and the coming of prophets and messengers after Muhammad. Some of these concepts, such as the Imamate, occultation and return, entered into the mainstream of Twelver Shi'i thought in later years, while others were condemned by later orthodox Twelver Shi'is as extremism (*ghuluww*) and heresy. However, it is clear that in this early period, they were all discussed in Shi'i circles and it is unlikely that they were thought of as being extremist. Indeed, as the eminent American scholar, Marshall Hodgson, has pointed out, there is nothing inherently extremist in these ideas. There is nothing inherently extremist in claiming that someone other than one of Muhammad's descendants could be an inspired or messianic figure; one might equally say the extremist is the one who exalts people purely on account of their birth. Nor is there anything more extreme in expecting a man to return whom others regard as dead (as some Shi'i groups did with respect to some of the Imams) than in what became the later orthodox Twelver Shi'i position, that a man will return whom some doubt was ever born (the Twelfth Imam). Furthermore, several of the leaders of these Shi'i groups claimed to be prophets, for example Bayan ibn Sam'an, the leader of the Bayaniyyah, and al-Mughira ibn Sa'id, the leader of the Mughiriyyah. This should not surprise us for, as Western scholars such as Marshall Hodgson and Montgomery Watt have pointed out, the idea that Muhammad was the last prophet from God is not explicitly stated in the Qur'an and there was no consensus on this point until quite late in the evolution of orthodox Muslim theology; it is not mentioned, for example, as a fundamental Islamic belief in the Shi'i creed, *al-Bab al-Hadi 'Ashar*, compiled by 'Allamah al-Hilli in the thirteenth century, or in the section on the foundations of Islamic belief in the encyclopædic compilation of Islamic knowledge, the *Ihya 'Ulum al-Din* by Muhammad al-Ghazali, the leading Sunni scholar of the twelfth century.

Moreover, even if we look at the group of Shi'ah that surrounded the Imams of the Twelver line, we find that they do not conform to the ideal picture painted by later Shi'i historians. Many held to beliefs that later Twelver Shi'is would find heretical. Indeed it is difficult for Shi'i writers to find eminent religious figures of this period who can be claimed to be Shi'i but who did not hold to some of the views that were later condemned as extremist. For example, the two leading Shi'i theologians of Imam al-Sadiq's time were Hisham ibn al-Hakam (who laid the foundations of the Shi'i theory of the Imamate) and Muhammad ibn Nu'man Mu'min al-Taq. The first is credited with believing that God has a three-dimensional body, that He does not know things before they come into being, and that parts of the Qur'an have been suppressed and corrupted; while the latter is accused of anthropomorphism towards God. All these opinions are contrary to the positions later adopted by the Twelver Shi'i theologians and are condemned by them as extremist. It would seem, therefore, that these 'extremist' ideas were in fact part of the discourse in the main body of the Shi'ah at this time, including among the followers of al-Sadiq. Thus it is only retrospectively that some of the beliefs of these Shi'i circles came to be labelled as extremist by later Muslim writers, who compared these ideas and beliefs with the fully-evolved orthodox position. While the main body of the followers of the Imam discussed these ideas, some groups of Shi'is, often led by a charismatic figure, focused on these ideas, elevating the Imams to a divine or quasi-divine status. As indicated in the Introduction, I will call these groups Gnostic Shi'is, to avoid calling them *ghulat* (extremists), the designation given to them by their enemies. They would probably have said that their only extremism was in their love and regard for the Twelver Imams. Indeed, they called their Shi'i opponents, the *muqassirun* (those who fall short [in their regard for the Imam]).

The Traditions ascribed to al-Sadiq specifically refuting Gnostic views may well be later inventions, for it is doubtful whether men such as Hisham ibn al-Hakam would go against the explicit teachings of their Imam. It is possible however that al-Sadiq did act against those who considered the Imams as incarnations of the Divinity (hulul). He is reported to have expelled Abul-Khattab, who made this claim about him, from among his supporters. Indeed, this particular belief appears to have died out among the Shi'ah in the generations succeeding al-Sadiq and is not in the list of Shi'i beliefs compiled by the later historians of the sects of Islam. Thus, with Ja'far al-Sadiq, we may begin to see the development of a separate proto-Twelver Shi'i identity. Abul-Khattab, the leader of a Shi'i group called the Khattabiyyah, is said to have been close to Ja'far's son, Isma'il, and some of Abul-Khattab's doctrines, such as the esoteric (batini) interpretation of the Qur'an, may have entered Isma'ili thought in this way.

For many of those who had Shi'i sentiments, the success of the 'Abbasid revolt was the fulfilment of their aspirations. For the Kaysaniyyah and the Zaydiyyah, a member of the Hashemite clan was now the caliph ruling Islam; for the Iraqis, the centre of power had shifted from Syria to Iraq; for the non-Arab mawali, there was an improvement in their situation and many rose to high positions in the 'Abbasid state. The 'Abbasids therefore almost certainly brought with them, into what was evolving into Sunni orthodoxy, large numbers who had previously been members of the political wing of Shi'sm (particularly those in the Zaydi and Kaysani camps). These people rejoined the mainstream of Islam after the 'Abbasid revolution. Iraq, the population of which had previously been predominantly Shi'i, now became a bastion of what would become orthodox Sunnism, although there were still considerable numbers of Shi'is there. Likewise, the Hijaz is reported to have been predominantly Shi'i before the 'Abbasid revolution and yet one hundred years later, it is predominantly Sunni. On the individual level, one example of this change is Abu Hanifah, who studied under Imam al-Sadiq and supported a number of Shi'i uprisings of this period, such as that of Zayd ibn 'Ali against the Umayyads, and yet went on to lay the foundations of Sunni jurisprudence and is the eponymous founder of the Hanafi school of Sunni law. Malik ibn Anas, the eponymous founder of the Maliki School of Law in Sunni Islam, appears to have followed a similar trajectory. It is almost certainly this influx of people with Shi'i sentiments into the ranks of the evolving Sunni orthodoxy that led to the presence among the Sunni collections of *hadith* of many Traditions that are clearly favourable to the Shi'is (see examples of these on pp. 18–19).

However, although the 'Abbasid revolt was based on Shi'i sentiment, as soon as they seized power, the 'Abbasid caliphs realized that they had to broaden the base of their power. They quickly suppressed the Shi'i elements in their propaganda and adopted a line that brought them into line with the majority of their subjects, who accepted the first three caliphs (Abu Bakr, 'Umar and 'Uthman), and who honoured the early companions of the Prophet. Despite, or perhaps because of, their closeness to Shi'i Islam, the 'Abbasids were much fiercer in their persecution of the Shi'is than the Umayyads. Those of the more politically active Shi'i groups who were not absorbed into the 'Abbasid state were heavily persecuted and their leaders killed. The remnants of the more politically active Zaydis were pushed to the geographical margins of the Islamic world, remaining strong only in Mazandaran and Gilan in Iran, in Yemen and in north-west Africa (Morocco). Paradoxically then, because the 'Abbasids drained away many from the political wing of Shi'i Islam, and because they persecuted groups such as the Zaydis, the rise of the 'Abbasids may have resulted in a relative strengthening in the position of the Twelver line of Imams within Shi'i Islam. It may be that, for a short time at the end of the ninth century, the majority of Shi'is were followers of the Twelver line of Imams, who were relatively apolitical. Certainly the quietist line of the Twelver Imams may well have been more appealing to those who wanted to accommodate the state and benefit from it; some rose to high positions in the 'Abbasid state, including becoming vizier (chief minister) to the caliph. The main Shi'i rivals to the Twelver line of Imams became the Isma'ilis, who were rapidly growing in numbers at this time and would soon overtake the Twelvers. They had established a state in al-Ahsa and Bahrain and were spreading their propaganda in North Africa preparatory to making a bid for power there.

By the end of the ninth century, a distinctive Twelver Shi'i community was beginning to emerge. It appears that at this time they referred to themselves as the Imamiyyah, while their opponents called them the Rafidah (the Rejectors). The term Rafidah is said to relate to those who rejected Zayd ibn 'Ali when he began to compromise Shi'i tenets in an effort to win support from non-Shi'i Muslims. More probably it refers to the rejection by these Shi'is of Abu Bakr, 'Umar and most of the companions of the Prophet. This latter rejection was of fundamental importance, since it implied a rejection of the body of oral Traditions (*hadith*), transmitted by these companions, on which the structure of what was gradually evolving into Sunni Islam was based. It was probably this point that was decisive in causing the Twelver Shi'is and the evolving Sunni community to start seeing each other as distinct and mutually exclusive communities. The Twelver Shi'is were strong in Kufah, the Karkh or West Bank quarter of Baghdad, Basrah and south Iraq, Qom, and to a lesser extent in Rayy (near present-day Tehran), Kashan and the cities of Khurasan. Gnostic Shi'i Islam appears to have been confined to Kufa, Baghdad and Basrah, in Iraq.

Although for later Shi'is the number of Imams had been completed and the Twelfth Imam had begun his Occultation by the end of the ninth century, this was not how contemporary Shi'is saw matters. Shi'i books from that period, such as al-Saffar al-Qummi's *Basa'ir al-Darajat* and al-Barqi's *Kitab al-Mahasin* show no consciousness of the idea that the number of Imams was to be limited to twelve, that there would be two occultations, or even that the occultation was anything more than a temporary manoeuvre by the Imam for security reasons, much as the previous Imams had secluded themselves. It is quite clear that even as late as the fourth decade of the eleventh century, a century after the Greater Occultation, many Shi'is were in doubt and confusion over these matters, and Shi'i scholars such as Ibn Babuyah were forced to write books in explanation. Furthermore, well into the tenth century there appear to have been considerable numbers of the Waqifiyyah (those who believed that the seventh Imam al-Kazim had gone into occultation and would return) and those who adhered to the Imamate of Ja'far, the brother of the eleventh Imam.

The change in Twelver Shi'i Islam, from a religious sentiment interwoven with Gnostic Shi'i ideas to a more closely defined religious movement rejecting the Gnostic ideas, appears to have occurred gradually. The beginnings of this process may have occurred as early as the time of the sixth Imam, Ja'far, and his expulsion of Abul-Khattab for teaching the doctrine of divine incarnation (hulul), as described above. However, even at the end of the ninth century, writers such as al-Khayyat and al-Ash'ari still stated that the majority of the Shi'ah held to such doctrines as anthropomorphism with respect to God, that God willed every act of sin and disobedience, and that the Qur'an has been altered; all doctrines rejected by later Twelver Shi'is. These writers do, however, report that a small school of Mu'tazilis existed among the Shi'ah. The Mu'tazilis were a school of rationalist theologians, widespread in the Islamic world at this time. This small Mu'tazili stream among the contemporary Shi'is eventually evolved into what is now the orthodoxy of Twelver Shi'i Islam.

Later Shi'i histories make it appear that, during the period of the Lesser Occultation, the Shi'ah were led successively by the four agents described above. It is possible, however, that the importance of these four individuals has been overstated in the later histories because they were the leaders of the Mu'tazili faction amongst the Shi'ah; the faction that eventually became the majority position of the Shi'ah but was at this time a minority. The majority of the Shi'ah at this time may well have been under the leadership of other figures, some of whom claimed to be agents of the Twelfth Imam and some of whom held Gnostic Shi'i views and claimed an independent leadership. Even during the lifetime of the eleventh Imam, there were individuals with Gnostic Shi'i views, such as Muhammad ibn Nusayr al-Numayri (or Namiri, died after 868) in Basrah, who claimed to be the true agent of the Imam. After the death of the eleventh Imam, there was Husayn al-Hallaj (executed 922) who claimed to be the agent of the Hidden Imam in about 912 and later Muhammad al-Shalmaghani, who at first laid claim to the position of being the rightful agent of the Hidden Imam and later in 926 denounced the whole concept of the Occultation as a lie. This put him at odds with the Nawbakhti family, who led the Mu'tazili faction among the Shi'ah and one of whose members, Husayn ibn Ruh, was the third of the four agents. The Nawbakhti family held high positions in the 'Abbasid court, including that of vizier (chief minister) of the caliph, and its members were able to engineer the execution of al-Shalmaghani in 935. While the Twelvers use the terms *safir* (ambassador, plural *sufara*) and *na'ib* (deputy, plural *nuwwab*) for the four successive agents of the Hidden Imam, the more general term among the Shi'ah for the agent of the Hidden Imam appears to have been the *bab* (gate, plural *abwab*).

Yet another indication of a split between the proto-Twelvers and the Gnostic Shi'is comes from an earlier episode of about 869, when Ahmad ibn Muhammad al-Ash'ari, who is described as the Shaykh of Qom, expelled a number of Shi'is who held Gnostic views from Qom in Iran (a town that had a majority of Shi'i inhabitants). Thus, the period of the Lesser Occultation can be pinpointed as the time when the proto-Twelver Shi'is separated themselves from the Gnostic Shi'i groups.

To summarise, after the martyrdom of the Imam Husayn, the political wing of Shi'i Islam focussed on Mukhtar and the Kaysaniyyah, who promoted the cause of Muhammad ibn al-Hanafiyyah. Later it moved to the Zaydi Imams, who rose in revolt against the Umayyad caliphs. Also rising fast was the 'Abbasid movement, which advanced the claims of the descendants of an uncle of Muhammad, al-'Abbas. Finally in about 744, these political strands coalesced into a general anti-Umayyad movement that agreed to join together to overthrow the Umayyads and defer the decision regarding who would become the Imam in place of the Umayyad caliph. The 'Abbasids eventually seized control of the movement and placed their candidate on the throne of the caliphate once the Umayyads were defeated. Thus, this political Shi'i Islam eventually led to the 'Abbasid revolution and once the goal of removing the Umayyads and placing one of the family of Hashim in power had been achieved, most of its members probably merged back into the mainstream of Islam that was evolving into Sunnism.

Initially, the main manifestation of the religious movement in Shi'i Islam was the Tawwabun episode. But the leaders of the religious movement of the Shi'ah during this period, the Twelver Shi'i Imams, resolutely refused to engage with the revolutionary Shi'i movements. Their followers were to be found in small numbers in the towns of the central part of the Islamic Empire. Everywhere, except perhaps in Qom, they were a minority among what was evolving into Sunni Islam, the followers of the Umayyad and later 'Abbasid caliphates, and they kept their beliefs secret to avoid persecution. At this time, the followers of the Twelver line of Shi'i Imams included elements that would in later years, during the Lesser Occultation, separate off as Gnostic Shi'i movements. Straddling the political and religious wings of the Shi'ah was the Isma'ili movement, whose propaganda emerged in the mid-ninth century. They combined esoteric beliefs about the Imamate with a strong political campaign that resulted in their seizure of power in north Africa at the beginning of the tenth century and their eventual control of north Africa, Syria and the Hijaz region of Arabia (where Mecca and Medina are located).

3
The political leadership of the Shi'ah

This, and the next two chapters, cover the same period of time, 950–1900. In this chapter, we will look at the political leadership of the Twelver Shi'is, through a survey of the more important Shi'i dynasties that have ruled over various parts of the Islamic world. This political survey then acts as a framework for the next two chapters, which look in more detail at Shi'i scholarship and mysticism (Chapter 4) and popular religion (Chapter 5).

The Shi'i century (950–1050)

According to later Shi'i orthodoxy, the Twelfth Imam is said to have communicated with the Shi'i faithful through four successive representatives, ending with the Greater Occultation in 941. Even before this, in 935, a Shi'i dynasty, the Buyids, had come to power in central Iran; just four years after the Greater Occultation, in 945, they captured Baghdad. The next hundred years has been called the 'Shi'i century', because most of the Islamic world was under the control of Shi'is of one sect or another. The Buyids (935–1062) controlled central and western Iran and most of Iraq. The Hamdanids ruled over northern Syria for the first half of this period (944–1003). The Isma'ili Shi'i dynasty of the Fatimids (909–1171) controlled Egypt and much of north Africa, southern Syria and the Hijaz (western Arabia, including Mecca and Medina). Although Mecca and Medina were under Fatimid rule, the local ruler (*amir*) in Mecca from 964 was Ja'far al-Musawi, a descendant of Imam Hasan, who was probably a Zaydi Shi'i. His descendants were (with a few breaks) sharifs of Mecca, although not Shi'is, until 1925. There was also a semi-independent Shi'i emirate in Medina under the Banu Husayn (descendants of the Imam Husayn), who were probably Twelver Shi'is, and this extended into the Ayyubid period. The Qarmati Isma'ilis controlled Bahrain and al-Ahsa (north-west Arabia, 899–1067). There were Zaydi Shi'i rulers in Yemen (896–1066) and central Arabia (Banu al-Ukhadir, 867 to around 1050). The Idrisids were a Zaydi dynasty who ruled in Morocco (788–985), until they were finally defeated by the Fatimids. Although these were all Shi'i dynasties, this did not mean they were allies. The Fatimids fought the Buyids, the Hamdanids, the Qarmatis and the Idrisids, Zaydi Imams in Yemen fought the Isma'ili rulers in central Arabia and the Buyids fought the Hamdanids. Moreover, although Shi'is ruled in these areas, they did not succeed in obtaining the religious allegiance of the masses under their control. Consequently, after the fall of these dynasties, Shi'i Islam almost completely disappeared from many of these areas, such as in north Africa, or remained as a minority, such as in Syria and Iran.

The Buyids (935–1062)

The Arabs, and Islam, came late to the areas in north Iran called Daylam or Daylaman (today's Gilan) and Tabaristan (today's Mazandaran), probably because the Arabs were at a disadvantage in the high mountains and dense jungle of this area. This terrain also made it the ideal refuge for Shi'is, and particularly for descendants of 'Ali, fleeing persecution from the Umayyads and 'Abbasids. From the 860s onwards, this region saw many Shi'i converts to the Zaydi sect of Shi'i Islam and brief periods of rule by Zaydi Imams, descended from the second Shi'i Imam, Hasan. The three brothers who established the Buyid dynasty came from Daylam and it is likely, therefore, that they were initially Zaydis. When they came to power, however, Zaydi doctrine would have required them to make a descendant of 'Ali the leader of the state. It is likely, for this reason, they became attracted to Twelver Shi'i Islam, which, with its occulted Imam, made no such demands on them. Evidence that they favoured Twelver Shi'i Islam comes from the fact that they patronized Twelver Shi'i scholars and built or greatly extended the shrines of the seventh and ninth Shi'i Imams at Kazimayn and the shrines of the tenth and eleventh Imams at Samarra (these Imams were Twelver Imams, not accepted by the Zaydis).

Although they were Shi'is, the Buyids did not oppose Sunni Islam, made no attempt to force Shi'i Islam on the population under their control and kept the 'Abbasid caliph as a figurehead. Nonetheless, under their leadership, Twelver Shi'i Islam flourished, both in its scholarship and popular religious practices. The Buyids were, however, riven by strife among the descendants of the three brothers who had seized power and this seriously weakened their grip on power. One of their centres, Rayy (present-day Tehran), fell to the Sunni Ghaznavids in 1029, the Seljuks occupied Baghdad in 1055 and finally Fars (south Iran) fell in 1062, ending the dynasty.

The Hamdanids (905–1003)

The Hamdanids rose to power as emirs of Mosul and northern Iraq, appointed by the 'Abbasid caliph in 905. In 944 they captured Aleppo and came to control north Syria. However they were under attack from all sides; from the east, the Buyids (who took Mosul in 978) and from the south, the Fatimids. A Byzantine attack from the north finally ended the dynasty, in 1003. The best-known member of this dynasty is Sayf al-Dawlah, who gathered to his court in Aleppo some of the period's foremost philosophers and literary figures. The exact nature of the Hamdanid's Shi'ism is not clear; they may have been Twelver Shi'is but it seems more likely that they were Nusayris ('Alawis). Since this movement of Gnostic Shi'i Islam also reveres the Twelve Imams, Twelver Shi'is seem to have found the Hamdanid areas congenial and Aleppo became an important centre of Twelver scholarship from this time, and especially in the twelfth century.

The Medieval period (1050–1500)

The Shi'i century was brought to an end in the eastern Islamic world by Sunni Turkish tribesmen. The Seljuks captured Baghdad from the Buyids in 1055 and remained in power until the end of the twelfth century. They were at first fiercely anti-Shi'i and there was extensive persecution of Shi'is, as well as damage to the shrine of Husayn at Karbala. However, after the assassination of the powerful anti-Shi'i minister Nizam ul-Mulk in 1092, the Seljuk rulers moderated their position and there were even a few Shi'is in high government positions in the twelfth century. The end of the twelfth century and early thirteenth century also saw a brief resurgence of the 'Abbasid caliphate under the caliph al-Nasir, who ruled from 1180–1225. Several of his ministers were Shi'is.

In the western Islamic world, the Fatimid dynasty declined in the twelfth century and was finally extinguished in 1171, when Salah al-Din (Saladin), the founder of the Ayyubid dynasty, took power in Egypt. Even before that, they had lost effective power in Syria to the Zangid dynasty of Sunni Turks, who took Aleppo in 1128 and instituted a persecution of Shi'is. Salah al-Din took Aleppo in 1183.

In the confused situation of the decline of the Seljuks in the east and the Fatimids in the west, a number of minor Shi'i emirates came to power in Iraq and Syria.

The Mazyadids

The Mazyadids were first recognized as emirs in central Iraq by the Buyids, in 956. The greatest of the dynasty, Sayf al-Dawlah Sadaqah (1086–1108), founded the town of Hillah, which lies between Karbala and Najaf, on the banks of the Euphrates, as his capital in 1102. He ruled over an area that included both Najaf and Karbala. From the first, Hillah was an important centre for Shi'i Islam and in the thirteenth century it became the foremost seat of Shi'i scholarship. The dynasty continued precariously in power until 1150, juggling the different claimants for power among the Buyid and Seljuk dynasties and the 'Abbasid caliphate.

The Mirdasids and other clans

When the Hamdanid power in north Syria faded, the Fatimids took control. But in 1024, Aleppo was captured by another Shi'i clan, the Mirdasids, who controlled the city on and off until 1080. Increasing Seljuk domination of the region by 1070, however, compelled the Mirdasid emir, Rashid al-Dawlah, to convert to Sunni Islam if he wanted to keep his rule. Control of Aleppo was finally wrested from the clan in 1080, when a Seljuk army led by an 'Uqaylid emir took the city. There is some evidence that the 'Uqaylids (990–1096), who first came to power under the Buyids and ruled from Mosul, were also Shi'is. In Tripoli, the Shi'i Banu 'Ammar threw off Fatimid rule in 1070 and controlled the city until it was captured by the Crusaders in 1109.

The Mongol invasions and their aftermath (1220–1380)

The Mongol invasions began in 1220 and led to the fall of Baghdad and the killing of the last 'Abbasid caliph in 1258. Although a great blow to Sunni Islam, the Mongols were not so much of a blow for Shi'i Islam. The great cities of the eastern Islamic world were devastated and Baghdad pillaged but Hillah, Najaf and Karbala escaped relatively lightly. The Sunnis were severely affected by the loss of the caliph, the apex of the Sunni hierarchy and the main pillar of Sunni constitutional theory, but for Shi'is there was no such constitutional crisis since the equivalent position in their hierarchy, the occulted Imam, was in no danger from the Mongol depredations. The Sunni dominance imposed by the Seljuk dynasty was removed and Sunnis and Shi'is treated alike. The Mongol leader, Hulagu Khan, took the eminent Shi'i scholar Nasir al-Din Tusi into his inner circle of advisers. The first Mongol (Ilkhanid) ruler to become a Muslim, Ghazan (reigned 1295–1304), showed marked Shi'i sympathies and the second, his brother Oljeitu (reigned 1304–16), who took the Muslim name Khudabandah, was converted to Shi'i Islam in 1309 by the Shi'i scholar 'Allamah al-Hilli, and for a short time Shi'i Islam was proclaimed the official religion of the realm.

The Mongol invasions reached as far as Aleppo and many Shi'is died in a massacre in that city in 1260. For most of the twelfth and thirteenth centuries, the whole of Syria was a confused battleground, in which Ayyubids, Mamluks, Byzantines, Crusaders, Mongols and various local rulers contended for supremacy. During this period, the Shi'is of this area, in particular the Isma'ilis, often made alliances with the Crusaders against Sunni forces. And so when, at the end of the thirteenth century, the Crusaders were driven from Syria by the Mamluks of Egypt, there was a massacre of Shi'is in retaliation. The Mamluk Sultans Baybars (reigned 1260–77), who turned back the Mongols, and al-Ashraf Khalil (reigned 1290–3), who in 1291 took Acre, the last Crusader stronghold, were particularly severe on the Shi'is. The former ended Shi'i rule in Medina (although some of the descendants of Imam Husayn remained emirs until the seventeenth century), while the latter forced the Druze and Nusayris to conform to the outward forms of Sunni Islam. The Isma'ili fortresses were reduced one by one, and many of the Twelvers were driven out of Kisrawan (an area north of Beirut) in 1305 and sought refuge in the Beqaa (Biqa') valley of central Lebanon, where they remain to this day.

Minor Shi'i states

From about 1335, the Mongol state gradually disintegrated and as with other periods when great empires declined, this gave minor Shi'i states the opportunity to emerge. At Sabzivar in Khurasan, Iran, Hasan Juri, the head of the Shaykhiyyah-Juriyyah, a Shi'i-Sufi order, helped the Sarbardarids to establish a small republic, with a strong emphasis on expectation of the Hidden Imam, that lasted from 1337 to 1386. There were many religious influences on this state and Twelver Shi'i Islam was only firmly established as the religion of the state with the rule of Ali Mu'ayyad (reigned 1361–86). Mir Qavam al-Din Mar'ashi (died 1379), known as Mirza Buzurg, the head of another branch of the Shaykhiyyah order, founded a Shi'i state centred on Amul in Mazandaran in 1359. His son, Sayyid Kamal al-Din (died 1417), was defeated by Timur in 1391 but was confirmed in his governorship and the line continued as semi-independent rulers until the Safavid era. These small Shi'i states were examples of the emerging phenomenon of Sufi orders combining Shi'i Islam with military characteristics; the same combination that more than a century later was to bring the Safavid order to power in Iran and have a decisive influence on the fortunes of Shi'i Islam in Iran. The Shi'ism of these states was similar to the Shi'ism of the Safavid order, having a large element of Gnostic Shi'i Islam. The Sarbardarids also had a further parallel to the Safavids in their later turn to orthodox Twelver Shi'i Islam.

The Timurid Period (1380–1500)

In 1370, Timur (known in Europe as Tamerlane, 1336–1405) captured Samarkand and made it his capital. From there he launched the second wave of Mongol invasions of the eastern Islamic world, beginning in 1380. He conquered Iran in the 1380s and, after a campaign that took him almost to Moscow and included the conquest of Delhi, he captured most of Syria and Anatolia between 1399 and 1402. Timur was a Sunni but had Shi'i sympathies. The attitude of his son and successor, Shahrukh (1377–1447), was ambivalent but he visited the shrine of the eighth Imam in Mashhad and his wife Gawharshad built a magnificent mosque (completed in 1418) adjacent to the shrine. The last of the Timurid rulers, Sultan Husayn Mirza Bayqara (1438–1506), who was based in Herat, had some Shi'i sympathies, as shown by his construction of a shrine over the reputed grave of Imam 'Ali at Mazar-e Sharif in Afghanistan.

To the west, Sultan Husayn's main opposition was the Qara-Quyunlu Turkomen rulers (1375–1468) whose capital was Tabriz. The poetry of their leader, Jahan Shah (ruled 1438–67), shows a tendency to Shi'i Islam, albeit of a Gnostic nature, and his brother Ispand, governor of Baghdad, is reported to have been converted to Twelver Shi'i Islam in 1436 by the scholar Ibn Fahd. The Qara-Quyunlu were succeeded by the Aq-Quyunlu, who were Sunnis, and carried out some anti-Shi'i measures but, on the other hand, the sister and daughter of the Aq-Quyunlu leader, Uzun Hasan, were married to successive shaykhs of the Safavid order, respectively Junayd and Haydar (the Safavid order being Shi'i by this time). South of the

Qara-Quyunlu territories, the Musha'sha' was a harshly intol-
erant Gnostic Shi'i movement started by Muhammad ibn Falah
when he proclaimed himself the Mahdi in 1436. With a number
of tribes allying themselves with him, he soon controlled an
area centred on Huvayzah (near present-day Ahwaz) in south-
west Iran. From here his forces attacked Najaf and Hillah and
even (in 1456) Baghdad. His descendants ruled the area until
overcome by the Safavids in 1508.

Although there may have been individual Twelver Shi'is in
India from the time of early Islam, it is likely that they only
came in appreciable numbers among those fleeing the Mongol
invasions. Large numbers of Shi'is flocked to the capital of the
Bahmani dynasty (ruled 1347–1527) at Bidar in the Deccan
region of central India. The kings of this dynasty showed favour
towards the Shi'is and incorporated many of them into their
armies. This led to Sunni-Shi'i rivalry and on one occasion to the
killing of some 2,500 Shi'is, half of them Sayyids. The mosques
built by the Bahmanid kings, as well as their graves, show that
they were strongly influenced by Shi'i Islam and one or two
may have been Shi'is. Shah Ni'matullah Wali (see p. 95), a Sufi
shaykh with marked Shi'i leanings, was invited to come to India
by Ahmad I of this dynasty in about 1430, but sent his grandson
instead; his son settled there later.

The modern period (1500–1900)

The dawn of the sixteenth century saw a major change in the
fortunes of Twelver Shi'i Islam. Until then, the Shi'i states that
had existed had either not been Twelver (as with the Isma'ili
Fatimid Empire), were minor states (for example the Mazyadids),
or had not actively promulgated Twelver Shi'i Islam (as with
the Buyids). All this was to change with the establishment of the
Safavid state.

Safavid Iran (1501–1722)

The Safavids were a family of Kurdish origin with a strong admixture of Turkish and Greek-Byzantine blood, who moved to Azerbaijan and were Turkicized. They headed a Sunni Sufi order (for the earlier history of this order, see pp. 93–4), which, with the passing of time, gradually became more oriented towards Shi'i Islam, albeit of a Gnostic nature, and increasingly militant until in 1501, its then leader, Isma'il (reigned 1501–24), defeated the Aq-Quyunlu and proclaimed himself shah at Tabriz. In the next ten years, he conquered all of Iran and much of Iraq. In his lineage, his poetry and his policies, Isma'il variously appealed to Gnostic Shi'i Islam, to orthodox Twelver Shi'i Islam, to Iranian nationalism, to Turkic shamanism, to Sufism, and even to Christianity (he was of Greek descent on his mother's side and, in his poetry, claimed to be Christ). The polyvalency of Isma'il's identity must have contributed to attracting the loyalty of his subjects and his success in establishing the foundations of a dynasty that was to last more than two hundred years.

Although both Isma'il and the core units of his army, the Qizilbash (red head, i.e. red hatted), were clearly of Gnostic Shi'i orientation, once installed in power, Shah Isma'il proclaimed orthodox Twelver Shi'i Islam to be the official state religion. It is probable that among the reasons for Isma'il's adoption of orthodox Twelver Shi'i Islam as the state religion was that he could see that the fanaticism engendered by the Gnostic Shi'i Islam of the Qizilbash, while it may have been crucial to his military success, was not a stable basis for the administration of an expanding empire. He probably understood that there was no chance that the sophisticated urban populations of Iran would be attracted to the ecstatic, shamanistic practices of the Qizilbash and the Safavid Order. The only chance of converting Iran's Sunni majority was to present them with a Shi'i Islam that could command the same level of scholarly legitimacy as the Sunni Shafi'i school that most espoused, and that was the Shi'i Islam of the orthodox Twelver clerics. Orthodox Twelver Shi'i Islam both gave him the stability and order he needed for his state and bound his subjects to his newly-founded state rather than to the surrounding Sunni enemy states, the Ottomans and the Uzbeks. Although scholars have debated this point over the years, it seems likely that the Safavid genealogy that gave them descent from the Shi'i Imams was faked before the time of Shah Isma'il, to enhance their Shi'i legitimacy.

The move towards orthodox Twelver Shi'i Islam was, however, slow. Gnostic themes, including implicit claims of being the Imam, were present in the official documents and coinage throughout Isma'il's reign. The agents of the Safavid order spread these Gnostic Shi'i teachings with great success among the Turkoman tribes of Anatolia and the Shi'is of Syria. The Ottoman sultan, who had given himself the title of caliph and thus the protector of Sunni Islam, and in whose lands the Safavid agents were promulgating their doctrines, became greatly alarmed. Large numbers of people in the Ottoman domains were attracted by these teachings. There was even a danger of a collapse of support among the Janissaries who formed the core of the Ottoman army, since the Bektashi order that most followed was derived from the same Gnostic Shi'i roots as the Safavids, and Isma'il's poetry was circulating among them. There was a pro-Safavid revolt in the province of Tekke (Antalya) on the Mediterranean coast of Anatolia in 1511. When Sultan Selim I acceded to the Ottoman throne in 1512, he determined to act decisively against the Safavid danger. He began by massacring thousands of Shi'is in Anatolia and in 1514, he marched against Shah Isma'il. The two armies met on the plain of Chaldiran in Adharbayjan. The Ottomans greatly outnumbered the Safavids and had the advantage of gunpowder artillery, which decided the day. Instead of pressing home the advantage and overthrowing the Safavid state, however, Selim withdrew. This decision may have been due to the difficulties of the Ottomans' extended lines of communication and the scorched earth policy of Isma'il, or the sultan may have feared the effects that a prolonged campaign in Iran might have had on his Janissary troops, whose loyalty was already under question because of their religious affinities with the Safavids.

The Battle of Chaldiran was, nevertheless, decisive. Its most important effect was that it broke the back of the Safavid propaganda that had claimed that Shah Isma'il was infallible and invincible. Safavid support in the Ottoman domains evaporated. After Chaldiran, Shah Isma'il was a broken man and withdrew from active involvement in the affairs of state. He died in 1524.

Shah Isma'il's successors continued the movement away from the Gnostic Shi'i roots of the Safavid order towards orthodox Twelver Shi'i Islam. The second Safavid ruler Tahmasp (or Tahmasb) I (reigned 1524–76), who moved his capital from Tabriz to Qazvin, suppressed Gnostic Shi'i Islam among the Qizilbash troops, and their tendency to regard him as a divine being. He also moved, in 1573–4, against a combination of Isma'ilis and Nuqtavis, a Gnostic Shi'i movement linked to the Hurufis, who had gathered at Anjudan near Mahallat in Iran. The third Safavid ruler, Isma'il II (reigned 1576–88), tried, unsuccessfully, to revert the country to Sunnism.

The Safavid dynasty reached its peak with the reign of Shah 'Abbas I (reigned 1588–1629). He completed the movement away from the Safavid's origins in Gnostic Shi'i Islam by violently suppressing the Qizilbash. During his reign, the Nuqtavis came to the fore, under their leader Darvish Khusraw. Eventually this came to pose a threat to the shah and he started to move against them, but when they and the court astronomer predicted the death of the shah on a particular day in 1594, Shah 'Abbas abdicated, placing a Nuqtavi on the throne for three days, until the danger was past. He then had the Nuqtavi pseudo-shah, and large numbers of other Nuqtavis throughout the realm, killed. He extended the empire into the Caucasus and, in 1598, moved his capital to Isfahan, where he built an array of magnificent buildings. He greatly embellished the holy shrines at Qom and Mashhad and performed several pilgrimages, on one occasion walking the entire distance from Isfahan to Mashhad on foot.

During much of the latter part of the seventeenth century, however, the Safavid dynasty was in decline and it was only because the empires on its borders had their own concerns that it lasted as long as it did. The last Safavid monarchs imposed an orthodox legalistic Shi'i Islam on the population, part of which involved repudiating the Safavid's own Sufi roots. In the end it was a revolt from within the borders of the empire that terminated the dynasty. In 1722, Sunni Afghans rose at the harsh suppression of Sunnism. They found the Safavid forces melting away in front of them, so were able to advance until they captured Isfahan.

India (1500–1900)

The Shi'i proclivities of the Bahmani dynasty of the Deccan were mentioned above. One piece of evidence for these proclivities is the fact that as the power of this dynasty waned and its territories were broken up by local leaders, it gave rise to a number of smaller Shi'i states:

> Ahmad Nizam Shah was the first ruler, in 1490, of a Shi'i kingdom centred on Ahmadnagar. The Nizam Shah dynasty ruled until overrun in 1636 by Aurangzeb, while the latter was the Mughal governor of the Deccan.
>
> Yusuf 'Adil Shah proclaimed his independence of Bahmani rule in 1489 and, following the Safavid proclamation in Iran, made Shi'i Islam the official religion of his

state in 1502. The 'Adil Shah dynasty, with its capital in Bijapur (now Vijayapura) lasted until 1686, when it was conquered by the Mughals under Aurangzeb.

Sultan Quli proclaimed his independence of the Bahmani kingdom in about 1512, making Golconda, near Hyderabad, the seat of his government. The Qutb Shah dynasty continued until overrun by the Mughals under Aurangzeb in 1687.

Further north in Kashmir, Mir Shams al-Din 'Iraqi, from Gilan, in Iran, arrived at Srinagar in 1492. He was a follower of Muhammad Nurbakhsh and propagated a strongly pro-Shi'i Sufi doctrine. A number of the notables of Kashmir converted, in particular the Chak family. This family was very powerful and ruled intermittently until 1540, when Mirza Haydar Dughlat, at the head of a Mughal army, occupied Kashmir. He was defeated and killed in 1551 by Ghazi Chak, who proclaimed himself king in 1561. In 1586, the Mughal emperor Akbar overran Kashmir and ended the dynasty. Although the dynasty did not rule for long, they promoted Shi'i Islam aggressively and by the end of their rule, much of the peasantry in large areas of Kashmir were Shi'is. The Afghans, who ruled from 1751 to 1819, severely persecuted the Shi'is.

The kings of the Mughal (Mogul) dynasty, although posing for the most part as champions of Sunni Islam, were not without Shi'i influences. The first Safavid monarch, Isma'il I, assisted the first Mughal emperor, Babur, on the condition that he accepted Shi'i Islam. His troops wore the red, twelve-pointed hat of the Qizilbash, which was, in those days, a symbol of being Shi'i. Humayun, the second of the Mughal dynasty, was at one time driven from India and sought refuge in Iran, where Shah Tahmasp gave him assistance to recapture his throne, on the condition he accepted Shi'ism and his troops wore the Qizilbash cap. Although some of the Mughal rulers, such as Aurangzeb, persecuted the Shi'ah, they continued to use Iranian immigrants as soldiers and administrators; even some princes and ministers were Shi'is. During much of the Mughal period, the court was divided into two factions: the Irani, which was in effect the Shi'i faction of Iranian origin, and the Turani, which was the Sunni faction of Turkic origin.

In 1722, Mir Muhammad Amin Musawi (died 1732), who was descended from the seventh Shi'i Imam and came from Iran, was appointed governor (nawwab) of the Mughal province of Awadh (Oudh, now part of Uttar Pradesh) with its capital at Lakhnau (Lucknow). The descendants of this man became known as the Nawabs of Awadh and, by 1819, had become sufficiently independent of Mughal rule to be crowned as kings. Lakhnau consequently became the leading centre of Twelver Shi'i Islam in India. Awadh, however, increasingly fell under British domination and the last king of Awadh was forced by the British to abdicate in 1856. As a result, the status of the Shi'is moved from being the ruling elite of Awadh to being a minority among the Muslims, who were themselves a minority among the total population.

When the Isma'ili leader, Hasan 'Ali Shah the first Agha Khan, arrived in Mumbai (Bombay, India) in 1846 (see p. 205), a number of the Isma'ilis there (who were called Khojas) refused to accept his leadership. Some subsequently became Twelvers, especially those Khojas who had migrated to East Africa.

Shi'i Islam in the Arab lands (1500–1900)

While Shi'i Islam was on the rise in Iran, it was declining politically in most Arab lands for much of this period; the conquest of most Arab countries by the Ottoman Empire ensured an anti-Shi'i environment. Aleppo, which had been an important

centre of Twelver scholarship in previous centuries, lost most
of its Twelver population, although Twelver Shi'i Islam clung
on in some of the villages of north Syria and there was a large
'Alawi population in north Syria. In Lebanon, control largely
remained in the hands of powerful local families, some of them
Shi'i, such as the 'Assaf (in Kisrawan, north of Beirut, for most
of the sixteenth century), Hamadah (in the areas north and east
of Beirut, seventeenth century), and Harfush (around Baalbek,
seventeenth to nineteenth century) families. But by the late
sixteenth century, the Ottomans were increasing their control
over the area and with this came the oppression of the Shi'ah.
In the Lebanon, during the eighteenth and nineteenth centuries,
the migration of Shi'is from the west side of Mount Lebanon to
the Beqaa (Biqa') valley continued, while Christians migrated
in the opposite direction. The Shi'ah in the south (Jabal 'Amil)
suffered greatly after their defeat by al-Jazzar, the ruler of Acre,
at the end of the eighteenth century; Shi'i scholars were killed
and their libraries burned.

The capture of Bahrain by Safavid forces in 1602 allowed the
Shi'ah of that area the freedom to practise their religion openly
and to build up centres of scholarship on the island. After the fall
of the Safavid, and a period of instability in the eighteenth century,
Bahrain was conquered in 1782 by the Sunni al-Khalifah tribe,
who have remained in control of the island up to the present,
although they were defeated on several occasions by the Imam
of Muscat and the Wahhabis. They brought in Sunni Arabs from
other regions who soon formed the majority of the urban population, leaving the Shi'is as the peasantry. Between 1788 and 1793,
fiercely anti-Shi'i Wahhabi forces conquered the neighbouring Shi'i area of al-Ahsa on the Arabian mainland, deposing the
ruling Shi'i Banu Khalid tribe, killing many Shi'is and destroy-
ing Shi'i shrines. In 1801, they overran Karbala and stripped the
shrine of Husayn of its gold and ornaments. In 1803 and 1806,
they attacked Najaf but were repulsed. The Wahhabi threat

continued until 1811, when they turned their attention to an attack from Egypt. In 1831, the Ottomans reasserted their control over Iraq. But Karbala and Najaf maintained a semi-independent status and defied Ottoman control until Karbala was stormed, with great loss of life, in 1843 and Najaf was conquered in 1852. In 1871, the Ottomans captured al-Ahsa from the Wahhabis, bringing relief to the Shi'i population of that area.

Iran (1722–1900)

The eighteenth century was a chaotic period, during which the Safavid dynasty fell (in 1722) to an invasion by Sunni Afghan forces, followed by a brief period of rule under Nadir Shah (reigned 1736–47), who favoured Sunnism, probably as a way of uniting his army, which included Sunni Afghans and Uzbeks. He replaced the twelve-pointed Safavid hat with a four-pointed one, signifying the first four caliphs. He also attempted – unsuccessfully – to have Shi'i Islam accepted by the Sunni world as a fifth Sunni school of law (see p. 110).

In the second half of the eighteenth century, Iran was divided between two competing Shi'i tribes: the Zands in the south, with their capital in Shiraz, and the Qajars in the north. At first the Zands, under Karim Khan Vakil (reigned 1760–79), were victorious. Karim Khan Vakil is remembered as a ruler with a genuine regard for his subjects. After his death, the Qajars gained the upper hand and eventually Agha Muhammad Shah Qajar (1742–97) extended his rule to the whole of Iran, was crowned shah in 1794, and established his capital in Tehran.

The Qajars (reigned 1794–1925) were pious Shi'is and, partly to buttress their legitimacy with the people, deferred greatly to the Twelver clerics. During the reign of Fath-'Ali Shah (reigned 1797–1834), there were two disastrous wars against the Russians, in which Iran lost all of its Caucasian provinces. The third Qajar monarch, Muhammad Shah (reigned 1834–48) was inclined to Sufism, but his successor Nasir al-Din Shah (reigned 1848–96) restored the religious dominance of the clerical class. Towards the end of the nineteenth century, there were increasing pressures for political reform and an end to the authoritarian rule of the shah.

4

The intellectual and spiritual history of Shi'i Islam

A number of scholars gathered around each of the Twelver Imams, especially Ja'far al-Sadiq, who attracted many students who were not Shi'is. The home of the Imams continued to be Medina, although the later Imams were frequently summoned to Baghdad by the 'Abbasid caliph and the tenth and eleventh Imams were detained in the new 'Abbasid capital at Samarra. Kufah was at first the principal stronghold of Shi'i Islam and the main cauldron in which the ideas of the various Shi'i groups fermented. When at the end of the eighth century the 'Abbasid caliphate moved to the new capital, Baghdad, and Kufah went into decline, many Shi'is, including their scholars, also moved there.

The separation of the Twelver Shi'is from the Gnostic groups had occurred by the middle of the tenth century (see Chapter 2). But there was great confusion among the emerging Twelver Shi'is about the identity of the Imam, his Occultation and whether the Lesser or Greater Occultation would be the longer. There were even rumblings of discontent among the Shi'is. It was now more than seventy years since the Imam had gone into occultation, the normal lifespan of a man. A contemporary

Shi'i author, Muhammad al-Nu'mani, reports that most of the Shi'is were now asking questions about the Occultation: '"Where is he? ... How long will he remain concealed? How much longer will he live? ..." Some of them began to believe he was dead, while others began to doubt that he was ever born or existed and mocked those who believed in him'. Al-Nu'mani states that in this period, the majority of the Shi'is stopped believing in the Hidden Imam. It was at this time, in 941, that the Greater Occultation was said to have occurred, putting the Imam completely beyond the reach of his followers. Shi'i scholars, such as al-Nu'mani, quickly brought out books explaining it and asserting that the Twelfth Imam would be the Imam Mahdi. Although the doctrine of *Ghayba* (Occultation) had been present in various forms among Shi'i groups since the time of the Kaysaniyyah, the crystallisation of it in the form in which Twelver Shi'is currently adhere to it occurred at this time, the mid-tenth century. Before then, Twelver Shi'i books make no reference to this doctrine (see pp. 62–3). A short while later, however, books appear with all twelve Imams listed and the Occultation stated as a fact, although it took longer for the Twelver Shi'is to realize that the Greater Occultation was going to extend for much longer than the Lesser Occultation.

In the period immediately after the Greater Occultation began, there was a division among Shi'i scholars between the Traditionist school of Qom and a rationalist school based in Baghdad:

1. The Traditionist scholars considered the most important occupation of Shi'i scholars to be the collection of Traditions (*hadith*). The main focus of this activity was at Qom, although the first major figure, Muhammad al-Kulayni, moved to Baghdad, where he died in 940 just before the beginning of the Greater Occultation. He collected what some regard as the most important collection of Shi'i Traditions, *al-Kafi fi*

'*Ilm al-Din* (The Sufficient in the Science of Religion). After him, Abu Ja'far Muhammad, known as Ibn Babuyah (Ibn Babuwayh) or al-Shaykh al-Saduq (born about 918, died 991) was the leading scholar of a group of Traditionists. He travelled throughout the Islamic world collecting *hadith*, for his books such as *Man La Yahduruhu al-Faqih* (He who has no Jurist present). He also wrote books resolving some of the issues that perplexed the Twelvers (such as the nature of the Imamate and the Occultation). In his writings, Ibn Babuyah gradually moved towards Mu'tazili positions on issues such as believing that those statements in the Qur'an which speak of God having human features, such as a face or hands (anthropomorphism), are only figurative, but he bases his arguments on proofs from the Traditions (*hadith*) rather than rational proofs. As the recording of Traditions became important, so too did the compilation of books giving biographical data about the transmitters of the Traditions.

2. The Rationalist scholars were more interested in theological (*kalam*) issues and were strongly influenced by the rationalist school of Mu'tazili theology. This group of Shi'is was based in Baghdad and initially centred on the Nawbakhti family. After the death of Ibn Babuyah, the central focus of Shi'i scholarship shifted back to Baghdad under the leadership of Muhammad al-Shaykh al-Mufid (born about 949, died 1022, also known as Ibn al-Mu'allim). The Traditionist school was criticized, doctrines about God and His Justice, derived from rationalist Mu'tazili teaching, became central to Shi'i teaching and earlier Shi'i Twelver contentions that the text of the Qur'an had been altered were gradually marginalized. The Shi'i discipline of *kalam* differed from the standard Sunni Mu'tazili *kalam* in that, in addition to deriving proofs regarding such areas as God and the Resurrection, it also derived rational proofs for areas of Shi'i concern, such as the Imamate and the Occultation. It is of interest to note that

al-Shaykh al-Mufid was shifting the Shi'i community towards
this rationalist Mu'tazili theology at exactly the same time
that the Sunni community under the leadership of the caliph
al-Qadir (died 1031) was officially abandoning Mu'tazilism.
The doctrine of the Imamate underwent rapid evolution at
this time with the Imam becoming regarded as having been
infallible (Ibn Babuyah had considered that it was possible for
the Imams to err). From this time the theology of Twelver
Shi'i Islam was based on rational proofs, with the Qur'an and
the Traditions being cited only as supplementary evidence.
Al-Shaykh al-Mufid also strengthened the movement towards
having reason added to the other three foundations of Shi'i
jurisprudence, the Qur'an, the *hadith* and consensus (*ijma'*).

While al-Shaykh al-Mufid followed the Baghdad school of
Mu'tazili thought, his successor Sayyid 'Ali al-Sharif al-Murtada
('Alam al-Huda, 966–1044) followed the more radically rationalist Basran school. Thus while al-Shaykh al-Mufid used reason to
defend and justify doctrine, for al-Sharif al-Murtada reason itself
was the starting point for theology. Al-Sharif al-Murtada's brother,
al-Sharif al-Radi, was responsible for the compilation of the talks
and letters of Imam 'Ali, known as *Nahj al-Balaghah* (the Path of
Eloquence), which many Shi'is regard as second only in importance to the Qur'an. The next leading scholar of the Twelvers,
Muhammad Shaykh al-Ta'ifah Tusi (995–1067), while following
the doctrines of the Basran school in theology, gave a renewed
emphasis to the Traditions with his composition of two important collections of *hadith*, *Tahdhib al-Ahkam* (The Rectification
of Judgements) and *Al-Istibsar* (The Perspicacious), and a book
of biographies of the transmitters of the *hadith*, *al-Rijal*. During
the lifetime of Shaykh al-Ta'ifah, conditions changed drastically
for the Shi'ah, with the overthrow of the Shi'i Buyid dynasty
and the capture of Baghdad by the Sunni Seljuks in 1055. The
following year Shaykh al-Ta'ifah's house was attacked and his

library burned by a mob. He left Baghdad and settled in Najaf, where he died.

The resurgence of Sunni power (the Seljuks in the east and the Ayyubids in the west) led to a decline in Shi'i scholarship. For a time Najaf was the foremost centre of Shi'i scholarship, under the son and grandson of Shaykh al-Ta'ifah. Then, for a period of about half a century (1145–93), Aleppo rose in importance with the presence of Ibn Zuhrah (1127–89) and Ibn Shahrashub (1096–1192). Probably the most important book to appear in this period was the Qur'an commentary (*tafsir*), *Majma' al-Bayan* by Fadl ibn Hasan al-Tabarsi (at-Tabrisi, died 1153), who lived in Khurasan. This book remains important to the present day. The period of Aleppo's predominance marks an important turning-point in Shi'i history. It ended a period of just under three hundred years when Iranian scholars had been the leading Twelver scholars and began just over four centuries of the predominance of Arab scholars.

Hillah

The last decade of the twelfth century saw the emergence of Hillah, in southern Iraq, as the foremost centre for Shi'i scholarship with the presence of Ibn Idris al-Hilli (1149–1202). While Shaykh al-Ta'ifah had retreated from rationalism and towards the Traditions, Ibn Idris reversed this and formally introduced the idea that rationality (*'aql*) should be one of the sources (*usul*) of Shi'i jurisprudence (although this was implicit in the writings of earlier scholars, such as al-Shaykh al-Mufid and al-Sharif al-Murtada). He was followed by Muhammad (died 1239 or 1248) and his son Ja'far (died 1281), both known as Ibn Nima, and Sayyid Radi, known as Ibn Tawus (died 1266). The Mongol invasion and the fall of Baghdad left Hillah relatively unscathed and the school of Shi'i scholars at Hillah continued.

The leading Shi'i scholar at the time of the fall of Baghdad (1258) was the Iranian Nasir al-Din Tusi (1201–73). He was a polymath, who made important contributions to the Islamic world in the fields of astronomy, mathematics, medicine, ethics, history and geography. From the point of view of Shi'i Islam his most important achievement was the introduction of philosophical methodology into Twelver theology. Until this time, philosophy had been viewed with suspicion, as it was closely associated with Isma'ili thought; indeed, Tusi had spent many years in the Isma'ili stronghold of Alamut (many consider that he may have been an Isma'ili during this period).

The next major figures in Hillah were Ja'far ibn Hasan, known as al-Muhaqqiq al-Hilli or al-Muhaqqiq al-Awwal (1205–77) and his nephew Hasan ibn Yusuf 'Allamah al-Hilli (1250–1325). These two had studied under Sunni as well as under Shi'i scholars and brought into Shi'i scholarship some of the methodology that had been established in Sunni Islam, such as the critical study of the *hadith* literature (*dirayah*) and the concept of *ijtihad*. Al-Muhaqqiq al-Hilli authored the *Shara'i' al-Islam* which remains one of the foremost works in Shi'i jurisprudence to this day. 'Allamah al-Hilli established the Shi'i concept of *ijtihad* as the basis of Shi'i jurisprudence and can be considered as the founder of the Usuli School (see below).

After 'Allamah al-Hilli, his son Muhammad Fakhr al-Muhaqqiqin (died 1370) taught at Hillah, and it was he who taught the first of the great scholars from the Jabal 'Amil region of what is now Lebanon, Muhammad al-'Amili, known as al-Shahid al-Awwal (the First Martyr, killed 1384). The latter went on to establish himself as a *qadi* (judge) in Damascus. Because of the strongly anti-Shi'i climate maintained by the Mamluks, he was forced to maintain dissimulation (*taqiyyah*) and would give rulings on Sunni law while secretly leading the Shi'i community. He was eventually arrested, imprisoned and executed. He wrote his most famous book, *al-Lum'ah al-Dimashqiyyah*, for 'Ali

Mu'ayyad, the Sarbardarid ruler in Khurasan (see p. 73), while in prison. Having been trained in Hillah, al-Shahid al-Awwal and other scholars established the methodology of the Usuli school among the clerics of the Jabal 'Amil. Other prominent scholars from Hillah were al-Miqdad al-Hilli (died 1422) and Ibn Fahd al-Hilli (1356–1437), but Hillah was in decline. Its decline was complete when, in 1453, it was taken by Musha'sha' forces, looted, and burned to the ground. This ended the period when Hillah was the foremost centre of Shi'i scholarship; the Jabil 'Amil in modern Lebanon took over the role, although for some fifty years after the death of Ibn Fahd there were no major Twelver scholars. Hillah remained under the control of the Musha'sha' until 1467.

The Usuli School and the concept of *ijtihad*

It was al-Muhaqqiq al-Hilli and 'Allamah al-Hilli who reorganized Shi'i jurisprudence and made the changes that can be said to have created the Usuli School and thus cast Twelver Shi'i jurisprudence in a form that is recognizably the same as the school that predominates in Shi'i Islam today. Just as reasoning had been made the central feature of Twelver theology (*kalam*) three centuries previously, 'Allamah al-Hilli made reasoning (*'aql*) the central feature of Twelver jurisprudence. In the methodology he advocated, the jurist uses *'aql*, usually supported by the other three sources of law, the Qur'an, the *hadith* (Traditions) and *ijma'* (consensus), to weigh up opposing arguments and arrive at legal decisions. This process is called *ijtihad* and may be defined as the process of striving to arrive at judgements on points of religious law using these principles of jurisprudential reasoning (*usul al-fiqh*). Hence, the school that 'Allamah al-Hilli brought into being became known as the Usuli School. The process of *ijtihad* may also be thought of as striving to uncover (through rational processes supported by transmitted sources) knowledge of what the Imams would have decided in any particular legal case. It is recognized that the process of *ijtihad* is not infallible and produces only a valid conjecture (*zann*) rather than certainty. But it is considered that even if the wrong result is produced through the process, the *mujtahid* who carries it out and the one who obeys its result have committed no sin.

Although theoretically the process of *ijtihad* may appear to give *mujtahids* a great deal of latitude for innovative thinking, in practice the concurrent attitude of *ihtiyat* (prudence and caution, lest one stray from the path of the Imams) and, from the Qajar period until the Islamic Revolution, the pressure created by the fact that much of the income of the *mujtahid* came from the bazaar and other conservative sources severely limited initiatives outside traditional avenues of thought and practice.

From the time of 'Allamah al-Hilli, all Shi'is have in theory been divided into two groups: those who have the training and the skills to practise *ijtihad* to arrive at legal decisions, who are called *mujtahids*, and those who do not have this training and skill and are required to turn to a *mujtahid* and follow his rulings; they are called *muqallids*. The qualifications to be a *mujtahid* include: maturity, being of legitimate birth, and having faith, intelligence and justice (the word 'justice' here means one whose words and deeds are strictly controlled by the *shari'ah*). *Mujtahids* are over-whelmingly male. Although a few women have been *mujtahidahs* (female *mujtahids*), they have catered only to women followers. The person must have pursued a course of studies at one of the religious colleges and received a certificate (*ijazah*) from a recognized *mujtahid* that states that he is capable of exercising *ijtihad*. The mere possession of a certificate does not, however, guarantee that one becomes a functioning *mujtahid*. It is only when people start to refer to a person for legal judgements that he can be said to have become a *mujtahid*. Currently, this is often more dependent on one's family connections and social networks than one's learning.

Although the idea of the *mujtahid* was enthusiastically taken up by clerics such as al-Muhaqqiq al-Karaki in the early Safavid era, there was also opposition in the form of the Akhbari movement (see below), so it was not until the second half of the eighteenth century that the Usuli School became the predominant school in Iraq, Iran and the Lebanon, and later in other areas.

Sufism and Shi'i Islam

An important trend in the period after the Mongol invasions was the interaction between Shi'i Islam and Sufism. From about the twelfth or thirteenth centuries, many Sunni Sufi orders became closer to Shi'i Islam in their high regard for Imam 'Ali and many of the Sunni Sufi orders that came into existence at this time traced their spiritual lineage back to him. By the fourteenth century, the shaykhs of the Kubrawiyyah Sufi order in Khurasan and India, such as 'Ala al-Dawlah Simnani and 'Ali Hamadani, although they were still Sunnis, showed Shi'i tendencies, such as preferring 'Ali over the first three caliphs.

During the Timurid period (the fourteenth to fifteenth centuries), there was a marked transformation in the Sufi orders in the general area of Iran and Iraq. Several became overtly Shi'i and also displayed a tendency to become militaristic. The most important transformation, from the viewpoint of future historical developments, was in the Safavid order. This order began as an orthodox Sunni order under Shaykh Safi al-Din (died 1334) in Ardabil in north-west Iran and spread into Anatolia, Iraq and north Syria. With the accession of its fourth leader, Shaykh Junayd (died 1460), however, the order changed dramatically. It became political, with Junayd claiming descent from Imam

'Ali and thus having a right to rule. This resulted in him being expelled from Ardabil, and the domains of the Qara-Quyunlu rulers. He gradually moved through Anatolia and north Syria until he finally settled in Diyarbakr and married the sister of the Aq-Quyunlu ruler, Uzun Hasan. These were regions in which Gnostic Shi'i Islam was very widespread and it was probably to increase his following in these regions that Shaykh Junayd moved the order towards Gnostic Shi'i Islam, even encouraging his followers to identify him with the Divinity. The order also became militaristic, launching a series of campaigns (*jihads*) against neighbouring Christian states.

Under the leadership of Shaykh Junayd's son Haydar (died 1488), the order returned to Ardabil and its followers were organized into a body of troops, the Qizilbash (redheads). This name came from their wearing red hats with twelve points that indicated their adherence to the Twelve Imams. In the confused period after the death of Uzun Hasan, Haydar made a bid for power but was defeated and killed in battle, and later his oldest son was assassinated. It was Haydar's second son, Isma'il, who regrouped the Safavid order and then faced and defeated the Aq-Quyunlu, entering their capital, Tabriz, in 1501 and proclaiming the founding of a Shi'i state with him as king. His poetry shows pronounced tendencies to Gnostic Shi'i Islam. He united within himself a claim to both religious and political authority and was even proclaimed as the Hidden Imam Mahdi.

A movement that in many ways paralleled the Safavids was the Musha'sha'. Muhammad ibn Falah, the foster son of the eminent Twelver scholar Ibn Fahd al-Hilli, proclaimed himself to be the Mahdi in 1436. Later, centred at Huvayzah in Khuzistan (south-west Iran), Ibn Falah managed to obtain the allegiance of several of the Shi'i tribes of the area and was soon in control of the whole area from Ahwaz to the Tigris. All who were not his followers were considered infidels and killed.

Despite several defeats, Ibn Falah's descendants ruled the area with Gnostic Shi'i doctrines until overcome by the Safavids in 1508. The descendants of Ibn Falah remained, however, as Safavid governors of the province and, much as the Safavids themselves did, became more orthodox in their Shi'i Islam as time passed, until by the seventeenth century, Huvayzah had become a centre of Twelver Shi'i scholarship and teaching and Ibn Falah's great-great-grandson a respected Twelver Shi'i scholar.

From the Sunni Kubrawiyyah order came further manifestations of Shi'i Islam. Muhammad ibn 'Abdullah, who became known as Nurbakhsh (died 1464), was proclaimed as the Mahdi in a rebellion against the Timurid ruler Shahrukh. He was defeated twice, but spared, and went on to found the Nurbakhshi order. Although a Sunni, Nurbakhsh emphasized his descent from Imam 'Ali, quoted from Shi'i works and visited the Shi'i shrines in Iraq. But he also considered the first three caliphs as Sufi saints. His Shi'i leanings were essentially an expression of his Sufism. In later years, however, his order became overtly Shi'i and was to exert a strong influence on many of the Shi'i scholars of the Safavid period as well as playing a major role in the spread of Shi'i Islam in north India. Also derived from the Kubrawiyyah order was the Dhahabiyyah, which under the Safavids became openly Shi'i.

Yet another Sufi order that moved from Sunnism to Shi'i Islam was the Ni'matullahi order. Its founder, Shah Ni'matullah Wali (died 1430), settled in Mahan near Kirman in south-east Iran. Although a Sunni as far as religious observances are concerned, his writings show a great devotion to 'Ali, from whom he was descended. During the Safavid era, the order became openly Shi'i and is today the largest Shi'i order in Iran, albeit split into a number of sub-groups.

When examining what was going on among the Twelver Shi'i clerics in this period the situation is complicated by the

fact that there is an aversion to Sufism among most orthodox
Twelver scholars and so individuals who were interested in Sufi
themes and incorporated these into Shi'i Islam are usually called
'arifs (mystics), rather than Sufis. Although these individuals
argued against some extreme expressions of Sufism (such as incar-
nationism), this does not mean they were not Sufis, since many
Sufis also argued against such doctrines. The interest in mysticism
began in Bahrain (and may therefore have also been influenced
by Isma'ilism) among a small group of scholars and has been called
the School of Bahrain. They adopted key Sufi doctrines such as
wahdat al-wujud (oneness of being), which they then adapted to
Shi'i Islam; they regarded 'Ali as the Seal of the Saints (khatam al-
'awliya) rather than Ibn al-'Arabi, to whom many Sufis give this
title. They included Ibn Sa'adah al-Bahrani (died about 1245)
and 'Ali ibn Sulayman al-Bahrani (died about 1273) but the
most important of this group was Maytham (or Ibn Maytham)
al-Bahrani (1238–about 1290) who wrote a commentary on the
Nahj al-Balaghah (see p. 31) which interpreted much of its text in
a Sufi manner. Even more important in this respect was Sayyid
Haydar Amuli, who lived until the closing years of the fourteenth
century in Baghdad. He attempted to bring together Shi'i Islam
and Sufism by stating that Sufis were in reality only Shi'is who
were more concerned about the esoteric aspects of religion, while
other Shi'is concentrated on the external aspects such as doctrine
and religious law. In his principal work on this theme, Jami' al-
Asrar (The Compilation of Mysteries), he stresses everything in
Sufi writings that indicates that divine knowledge was purveyed
to the lines of Sufi Shaykhs through the Imam 'Ali, while at the
same time emphasising everything in the writings of previous
Shi'i scholars in favour of Sufism. A further development along
this path was made by Ibn Abi Jumhur al-Ahsa'i (died after 1501),
who integrated philosophy, Mu'tazili and Ash'ari theology and
strands of Sufi thought, such as the existential monism (wahdat al-
wujud) of the school of Ibn al-'Arabi, into Shi'i Islam.

The Safavids

Although Isma'il had proclaimed Twelver Shi'i Islam as the religion of the state when he came to power in 1501, at first there was only a token implementation of this: ritual cursing of the first three caliphs from the pulpit and persecution of those who maintained outward conformity to Sunnism. Many of the elements of Gnostic Shi'i Islam remained, especially among the Qizilbash who held the military positions in the state. They spearheaded the imposition of Shi'i Islam on the populace. The important administrative positions were held by Iranian scholars and nobility, many of whom were sayyids who converted to Shi'i Islam with the advent of the Safavid state, and some of whom were probably cryto-Sunnis. They often clashed with the Qizilbash.

Realizing that he needed individuals with a good knowledge of Shi'i Islam, Isma'il tried to recruit from the pool of scholars that existed in the Jabal 'Amil area of what is now Lebanon, Iraq, al-Ahsa and Bahrain. Although the idea that large numbers of Arab clerics came to Iran in the early Safavid period has been challenged, the importance of those who did come can hardly be disputed. The leading scholar among them was Shaykh 'Ali al-Muhaqqiq al-Karaki or al-Muhaqqiq al-Thani (1465–1533), who was from the Beqaa (Biqa') valley in what is now Lebanon, had studied in Najaf and was brought to Iran by Shah Isma'il. He lived on to the reign of the second Safavid monarch, Shah Tahmasp. He went about Iran supervising the conversion of the country to Shi'i practices, attacking Sunnism and encouraging the cursing of the first three caliphs. He brought with him the methodology of the Usuli School, which he began to spread among the clerics that he trained in Iran. Al-Karaki's eminence was signalled by the designation of 'Seal of the Mujtahids' (*khatam al-mujtahidin*). The early Safavid shahs were already turning against the militant Sufism of their Qizilbash supporters as a matter of state policy (see 78) but al-Karaki supported this trend by writing treatises against Sufism and Gnostic Shi'i Islam. He also issued a *fatwa* condemning the storytellers who recounted stories such as those of Abu Muslim, the military leader of the 'Abbasid Revolution (although these stories were pro-Shi'i, they kept alive a version of Shi'i Islam obnoxious to Karaki, a version in which ideas of the Kaysaniyyah and of Gnostic Shi'i Islam survived).

The fact that al-Karaki had adopted the Usuli School (as opposed to the clerics of Bahrain, al-Ahsa and Najaf) was signifi-cant, in that the tool of *ijtihad* gave him the flexibility to make rulings in the new situations that arose as Shi'i Islam became for the first time a state religion. Thus for example, al-Karaki justi-fied the holding of communal Friday prayers (which had been considered abrogated because of the absence of the Hidden Imam who should have led them, see pp. 100–1). Al-Karaki was strongly challenged by other senior Shi'i clerics on religious grounds, but his innovations suited the needs of the emerging Safavid state and so he was supported by Shah Isma'il and Shah Tahmasp.

Shah 'Abbas I (died 1629) brought about a major change in Shi'i scholarship when he moved his capital to Isfahan in 1597 and constructed a Shi'i religious college (*madrasah*) there. This soon became the most important educational establishment in the Shi'i world and Isfahan the foremost centre of Shi'i scholar-ship.

After al-Muhaqqiq al-Karaki, Shaykh Zayn al-Din al-Juba'i, known as al-Shahid al-Thani (the Second Martyr, born 1506, killed by the Ottoman authorities in 1558), became the lead-ing Shi'i scholar in the Jabal 'Amil (Lebanon) area. Both he and his son, Abu Mansur Hasan Sahib al-Ma'alim (the author of the *Ma'alim al-Din*, died 1602) remained in Syria and maintained its tradition of learning despite varying levels of pressure against Shi'i Islam from the Ottoman authorities. But after 'Abbas I trans-ferred his court to Isfahan, many of the scholars of this region migrated to Iran and it declined in importance as a centre of scholarship. Apart from Iran and the Jabal 'Amil, Najaf resumed its importance as a centre of Shi'i scholarship when Ibrahim al-Qatifi (died about 1540) and Muqaddas Ardibili (died 1585) moved there. Al-Qatifi was a strong critic of al-Karaki and the Usuli School, while Ardibili taught Mulla 'Abdullah Shushtari (Shustari or Tustari, died 1612) who was also critical of the Usulis. He moved to Isfahan and was largely responsible for its establishment as a Shi'i centre of learning.

Following Shushtari, the chief scholar in Isfahan was Shaykh Baha' al-Din Muhammad al-'Amili al-Juba'i, known as Shaykh Baha'i (1547–1621), who had moved from the Jabal 'Amil to Iran with his father in 1554. No Twelver Shi'i scholar, other than Nasir al-Din Tusi, has had the range of knowledge of this scholar. He was an eminent theologian, jurist, philosopher, mystic, astronomer and poet, as well as playing a major role in the planning and construction of Isfahan. Two clerics who moved from Iran to India and helped to establish the Shi'i centres in the Deccan were Shah Tahir of Qazvin (died 1549) who is reported to have converted Burhan Nizam Shah to Shi'i Islam in about 1522 and Qadi Nurullah Mar'ashi Shushtari who reached India in 1585 and was executed for his Shi'ism by the Mughal emperor Jahangir in 1610, becoming known as al-Shahid al-Thalith (the Third Martyr).

By the late Safavid period, the major Twelver clerics had become Iranians again after more than four centuries in which most of the leading Twelver clerics were Arabs. With the decline of Safavid power, they felt secure enough to take an increasingly independent line from that of the state. The two Majlisis, father and son, Muhammad Taqi (about 1594–1659) and Muhammad Baqir (1628–99) dominated the closing years of the Safavid dynasty. Muhammad Baqir exerted great power in his role as the Shaykh al-Islam of Isfahan, the foremost cleric in the Safavid domains. He dominated the last Safavid king, Sultan-Husayn Shah, and managed to persuade him to enforce a number of rulings, such as banning faction-fighting in the towns, pigeon-flying, and the sale of alcohol. Muhammad Baqir Majlisi was particularly antagonistic to Sufis, philosophers and Sunnis and it may well have been his actions that played a part in driving the Afghan Sunnis to the revolt that ended the Safavid dynasty. He also wrote a great deal in Persian (rather than Arabic, the usual language of the clerical class), helping to strengthen the roots of Shi'i Islam among ordinary Iranians.

The development of the concept of the Deputy of the Imam

A process that was developing within Twelver jurisprudence, in parallel with and part of the development of the Usuli School, was the evolution of the idea that the religious jurisprudent (*faqih*), or *mujtahid*, is the deputy of the Hidden Imam. The Imam, by virtue of the line of designation going back to the Prophet Muhammad, is considered in Shi'i theory to have an absolute *walayah* (Persian *velayat*); control over all religious and political matters (for other meanings of *walayah*, see pp. 180–1). During the Lesser Occultation, four successive individuals had each claimed to be the specific deputy (*al-na'ib al-khass*) of the Hidden Imam and to have the authority to carry out all of the religious functions of the Imam in his absence (see pp. 51–2). But with the Greater Occultation, all the communal roles of the Imam fell into abeyance. These roles included leading the Friday prayer, receiving the religious tax of *zakat* and *khums*, putting judicial decisions into effect and imposing legal penalties, leading the Holy War and the division of booty. At first the lapse of these functions was convenient, as it established the Twelvers as being non-revolutionary in sharp contrast with the Isma'ilis who, with their Imam-Caliph present in Cairo, and their active propaganda, were threatening to destabilize and overthrow the Buyids.

Indeed, this consideration may have been one of the principal reasons for the evolution of the doctrine of the Occultation of the Twelfth Imam. As the years went by, however, it became clear that this abeyance of the leadership functions of the Imam could not continue indefinitely as it left the community with no leadership, no organization and no finances.

Therefore, as early as the eleventh century, Shaykh al-Ta'ifah was reinterpreting the doctrine to allow delegation of the Imam's judicial authority to those who had studied *fiqh* (jurisprudence), who are called the *fuqaha* (singular *faqih*). He considered the *fuqaha* as the best people to act as agents of the donor in distributing the religious taxes since they knew to whom it should be distributed. He also allowed clerics to organize the Friday prayers in the absence of the Imam or his special representative. This last point remained controversial, with later figures, such as Ibn Idris and 'Allamah al-Hilli disagreeing. The discussion among the clerical class as to which elements of the *walayah* of the Hidden Imam could be taken on by the *faqih* continued for several hundred years. Al-Muhaqqiq al-Hilli was able to advance these concepts very considerably. He cautiously extended the judicial role of clerics to imposing legal punishments (*iqamat al-hudud*, that is to say, by the clerics themselves rather than the temporal authorities). In his writings, it is possible to see the evolution in his thinking whereby the clerics develop from being deputies of the donor for the distribution of religious taxes in his early writings, to being the deputies of the Hidden Imam for the collection and distribution of the taxes in his later works.

Al-Muhaqqiq al-Karaki was the first to suggest that the clerical class were the *al-Na'ib al-'Amm* (Persian *Na'ib-e 'Amm*, general representative, as distinct from the four agents who were each the *al-Na'ib al-Khass*, the special representative, during the Lesser Occultation) of the Hidden Imam. But he restricted his application of this argument to the assumption of the duty of leading Friday prayers. It was al-Shahid al-Thani (died 1558) who took the concept of *al-Na'ib al-'Amm* to its logical conclusion in the religious sphere and applied it to all of the religious functions and prerogatives of the Hidden Imam. As a result of these developments, the judicial authority of the clerics became a direct reflection of the authority (*walayah*) of the Imam himself and it became obligatory to pay the religious taxes directly to the clerics as the trustees of the Imam, rather than distributing it oneself. Furthermore, al-Shahid al-Thani extended the range of those eligible to receive money from the religious taxes to include the *tullab* (religious students) and the clerics themselves, who thus became the recipients of the money as trustees and were also able to expend the money on themselves and their circle of students. This paved the way, in the post-Safavid era, for the rise of Shi'i *madrasahs* (religious colleges) funded by religious taxes, and also enabled the clerical class to become financially independent of the state. Although the clerics had taken on the religious functions of the Hidden Imam in theory, the Safavid state was too strong for them to put them into practice; not until the Qajar era were the clerics able to do that.

The School of Isfahan

It has been noted above that certain scholars such as the School of Bahrain, Nasir al-Din Tusi, Sayyid Haydar Amuli and Ibn Abi Jumhur brought various streams of Islamic theology, mysticism and philosophy into Shi'i Islam. These preliminary attempts were taken forward by a group of scholars in Shiraz in the late fifteenth to early sixteenth centuries, who are often called the School of Shiraz and whose main representatives were Sadr al-Din Dashtaki (died 1497), Ghiyath al-Din Dashtaki (died 1542), Jalal al-Din Dawani (died 1502) and Shams al-Din Khafri (died

1552). But in Isfahan, at the end of the sixteenth century, a group of mystical philosophers emerged who developed this trend to its fullest extent during the seventeenth century. This movement is known in Iran as the Hikmat-e Ilahi (al-Hikmat al-Ilahiyyah, divine philosophy or theosophy) or Hikmat-e Muta'aliyyah (transcendent theosophy), but is better known in the West as the School of Isfahan.

The School of Isfahan was founded by Muhammad Baqir Astarabadi, known as Mir Damad (died 1631). Its most eminent figure was Sadr al-Din Muhammad Shirazi, known as Mulla Sadra (died 1640). Other prominent names in the movement include Abul-Qasim Astarabadi, known as Mir Findiriski (died 1640), and Mulla Rajab 'Ali Tabrizi (died 1669). A branch of the school centred in Qom and Kashan included Mulla 'Abdul-Razzaq Lahiji (died 1661), Mulla Muhsin Fayd of Kashan (died 1680) and Qadi Sa'id Qummi (died 1691). The School enjoyed the patronage of the court and the government, including such figures as Shah 'Abbas II and his Grand Vazir, Sayyid Husayn Sultan al-'Ulama (died 1654). Some of the most important clerics of the time were also supporters, such as the above-mentioned Mulla Muhammad Taqi Majlisi and Mulla Muhammad Baqir Sabzivari (died 1679) who was Shaykh al-Islam of Isfahan.

The methodology of the School of Isfahan depended on harmonizing and integrating three main sources of knowledge: the transmitted sources (the Qur'an, the Traditions and even the holy books of other religions, such as the Bible); direct intuitive or ecstatic knowledge that arises from the unveiling (*kashf*) or illumination (*ishraq*) that comes from the spiritual world, building on the work of Shihab al-Din Yahya Suhrawardi (killed in Aleppo in 1191) and the Illuminationist (Ishraqi) school (which in turn partly went back to Zoroastrianism); and reason using the method of theology (Mu'tazili and Ash'ari *kalam*) and philosophy (of both the peripatetic and neo-Platonic schools). In addition, the School made use of the insights in the mystical philosophy of Avicenna and Ibn al-'Arabi and the mystical poetry of the great Persian-language Sufi poets, such as Rumi, as well as being closely associated with the Sufism of the Nurbakhshi order.

Briefly, some of the characteristic concepts of the School, and of the writings of Mulla Sadra in particular, are:

1. The integration of the Fourteen Pure Souls (Muhammad, Fatimah, and the Twelve Imams) into Avicennan cosmology where they, in effect, replace the Active Intelligences as the ontological causes of existence.
2. The belief in the reality of an independent world of images (the *'alam al-mithal*) between the intelligible world and the sensible world.
3. The replacement of quiddity (the essence of something that answers the question 'what is it?') as the fundamental basis of metaphysics by the fundamentality of being (*asalat al-wujud*). This development by Mulla Sadra contradicted his teacher, Mir Damad, and Suhrawardi.
4. The doctrine of the substantial motion (*al-harakah al-jawhariyyah*) of being. This doctrine asserts that the being of anything that exists is susceptible to change, intensification and perfection.
5. The essence of individuality is the soul. It is this that is eternal and which experiences the resurrection.

The Akhbari School

The innovation of 'Allamah al-Hilli in bringing *ijtihad* into Shi'i jurisprudence, and thus basing judgements (*fatwas*) not so much on certain knowledge based on the Traditions of the Imams but on valid conjecture (*zann*), eventually brought about a reaction in the form of the Akhbari School. One way of looking at the Akhbari School is to think of it as a reaction by those who thought that the Usuli development was creating a class of clerics that effectively substituted themselves for the position of the Imam in giving legal judgements. The Akhbaris thus sought to return the Imam to his rightful place as the head of the community and to centre the actions of the community on the precedents set by the Imams rather than on the conjecture of the *mujtahids*. While Usulis considered that everyone who is not a *mujtahid* should become a follower (*muqallid*) of a *mujtahid*, Akhbaris consider that all Shiʻis are *muqallids* to the Imams alone. In the Akhbari rejection of the Usuli school, there may also have been an element of reaction against Sunnism in that the methodologies of the Usuli school, such as the critical study of the Traditions and *ijtihad* itself, had been introduced into Shiʻi scholarship from Sunnism.

There has been a great deal of discussion among scholars over whether Akhbarism began with Muhammad Amin Astarabadi (died 1623) and his book *al-Fawaʼid al-Madaniyya* (completed in 1621) in Mecca or whether he merely revived a school that had existed since the early days of Shiʻi Islam. The resolution of this question appears to depend mainly on how one defines Akhbarism. If one considers Akhbarism narrowly as a school of jurisprudence that criticized the Usulism of ʻAllamah al-Hilli, with its accompanying introduction of *ijtihad* and *mujtahids* into Shiʻi Islam, then logically it cannot have predated al-Hilli and indeed Astarabadi can be singled out as the starting point of this school (although a few scholars anticipated him to some degree, see below). If however, one views Akhbarism more generally, then undoubtedly, from the earliest days of Shiʻi Islam there was a tension between those who favoured the Traditions of the Imams (often called *akhbar*, hence Akhbari) as a source of knowledge, regarding them as sacrosanct, and those who gave greater importance to rational thought and were prepared to look critically at the Traditions (see pp. 86–8). This tension was firmly resolved in favour of the rationalists in the area of Shi'i theology in the Buyid period but remained unresolved in the area of jusriprudence (for example in Ibn Idris's criticism of Shaykh al-Ta'ifah, see p. 133). Mulla Muhammad Amin Astarabadi wrote that he was merely reviving a long-standing position that had been present among Shi'i clerics from the earliest days of Twelver Shi'i Islam and doing it only because of the increasing predominance of the *mujtahids*.

The main tenets of the Akhbari school can be summarized by saying that they are against the rationalist methods of the jurisprudence of the Usuli School, in particular rejecting *mujtahids* and the use of *ijtihad*. The Usulis consider that to give *fatwas*, one needs an extensive knowledge of jurisprudence (*fiqh*) and in particular of the rationalist principles on which legal judgements can be made (*usul al-fiqh*) as well as many ancillary Islamic sciences; in other words, one has to be a *mujtahid*. On the other hand, the Akhbaris consider that *fatwas* should only be given on the basis of knowledge that is certain (*qat'*), knowledge that is based on a Tradition of the Imam, whereas the process of *ijtihad* only gives rise to *zann* (valid conjecture) not certainty. In other words, the success of the Akhbari school meant the restriction of the scope of the application of the *shari'ah* and thus a restriction in the ability of the clerical class to intervene in social affairs. Some Akhbaris went further and also rejected the rationalist Mu'tazili basis for Twelver theology that had been established in the tenth century. Also, the Akhbaris greatly developed Shi'i Qur'an commentary. In place of the usual concern of Qur'an commentary with the meanings of words, grammar and the circumstances of the revelation of verses, this Akhbari commentary was concerned with recovering what the Shi'i Imams had said about each verse, and particularly with Traditions that make the verses of the Qur'an refer to the Imams and their authority (*walayah*) by means of metaphor and metonymy (examples of this can be seen on pp. 181-3).

It is possible that Astarabadi was merely giving form to a sentiment that was widespread among the clerical class, as there was no immediate outcry against Astarabadi's attack on *ijtihad* and *mujtahids* and several leading clerics either adopted this position or were at least favourably disposed towards it. In Najaf, the criticism of al-Karaki that had been voiced by al-Qatifi (see above) in the early Safavid period contained many of the elements of the Akhbari position. In Isfahan, the leading cleric Mulla 'Abdullah Shushtari (died 1612) had taught similar ideas and so Astarabadi's students were received enthusiastically by figures such as the above-mentioned Muhammad Taqi Majlisi, Mulla 'Abdullah Tuni (died 1660) and the mystical philosopher Mulla Muhsin Fayd (died 1680), whose book, *al-Wafi*, is an important synthesis and commentary on the four early canonical books of Shi'i *hadith*, while his Qur'an commentary, *al-Safi*, is also highly regarded.

From Astarabadi's residence in Mecca, his School spread to al-Ahsa and Bahrain, where the leading scholars adopted the Akhbari School. Bahrain became predominantly Akhbari and remains so to the present day. It also spread to the Jabal 'Amil, where al-Hurr al-'Amili (died 1692), the author of an important collection of Shi'i hadith, *Wasa'il al-Shi'ah*, was converted; he later took the teaching to Mashhad. The teachings spread to India; they are taught in Hyderabad today. The position of the most powerful cleric of the late Safavid era, Mulla Muhammad Baqir Majlisi, has been a matter of debate. Suffice it to say that, although the uncritical manner in which he collected the *hadith* that went into his main scholarly work, the vast *Bihar al-Anwar*, would signal him as an Akhbari, he also appears to have accepted the role of the *mujtahid*. We cannot be sure of his views since he does not appear to have entered in a substantive way into the Usuli–Akhbari debate.

The success of the Akhbari School was such that Muhammad Taqi Majlisi, writing in about 1655, was able to say that most of the clerics of the shrine cities in Iraq approved of Astarabadi's method. At about this time, 'Ali Naqi Kamarihi Shirazi (died 1650), the chief religious dignitary (*shaykh al-islam*) of the Safavid court, claimed that there were no Iranian or Arab Shi'i *mujtahids* (Usulis) in the world during his time, although that is probably an exaggeration. After the fall of the Safavis, Shaykh Yusuf al-Bahrani (died 1772), the leading scholar in Karbala, travelled widely, embedding the Akhbari school in many towns.

The Akhbari predominance lasted for more than a century, from about 1635 to about 1775. In Isfahan, the Akhbaris remained strong throughout this period although there were a few prominent Usulis clerics resident. In Qazvin, Khalil Qazvini (died 1678), a strong Akhbari, dominated the city's clerics and the city continued to be strongly Akhbari after him; its leading Usuli clerical family (the future Baraghani family – see below) was driven out after a debate with Shaykh Yusuf al-Bahrani in 1751. Yazd, Bihbihan and Nishapur are known to have been predominantly Akhbari and probably most other Iranian cities also. In both Karbala and Qazvin, the predominance was such that it was said that if people wanted to carry Usuli books about the city, they would have to conceal them so that they were not seen. Both Lakhnau and Hyderabad in India were predominantly Akhbari, as were the shrine cities in Iraq.

The eighteenth century and the triumph of the Usuli School

The eighteenth century was a confused maelstrom of events that were of great importance, in that they have shaped Twelver Shi'i Islam's intellectual life to the present day. At the beginning of this century, the Safavid kings were still in power and they in turn were dominated by the clerical class. The Akhbari School was dominant in most parts of the Shi'i world and in Iran, the

Table 2 The differences between Usulism and Akhbarism

USULIS:	AKHBARIS:
Regard the Qur'an, the Traditions, consensus ('ijmah) and the intellect ('aql) as the four authoritative sources of doctrine and Holy Law.	Regard only the Qur'an and the Traditions (akhbar) as authoritative sources for the Holy Law (and for some Akhbaris also for doctrine).
Claim that it is possible to understand the Qur'an through use of the intellect.	Consider that the Qur'an can only be understood through the Traditions of the Imams.
Consider that the Traditions must be examined critically for their reliability and whether they have general applicability or not.	Consider all the Traditions in four 'canonical' collections to be reliable and are willing to accept a wide range of other Traditions.
Give priority to human reason and consider that doctrines and legal decisions drawn from the Traditions must conform to rationality.	Consider that what is derived from the Traditions has priority over what is derived from the use of human intellect.
Consider that all legal decisions must be based on ijtihad and the application of certain principles (usul) of jurisprudence using reason. Where there is not explicit guidance in the Qur'an or the Traditions, a valid conjecture can be given.	Reject ijtihad and the use of human reason and consider that legal decisions can only be given on the basis of a relevant Tradition; and if no such Tradition is available, caution must be exercised.
Consider that since making a legal decision is dependent on knowledge of the wide range of religious sciences, only a mujtahid can give such decisions.	Consider that anyone who knows of a relevant Tradition and knows the terminology used by the Imams can give a legal decision.
Divide all human beings into mujtahid and muqallid (follower); and it is obligatory for anyone who is not a mujtahid to follow the ruling of one as though this were the ruling of the Imam himself.	Consider all human beings are muqallids to the Imams and reject the idea that it is obligatory to follow the rulings of a mujtahid; only the Imam must be followed.
Consider that the use of ijtihad and following the decisions of a mujtahid will result in a heavenly reward even if the ruling is incorrect.	Consider that issuing and following a decision that is not based on an explicit and relevant Tradition is blameworthy.

attack on Sunnism, Sufism and philosophy that had begun under Mulla Muhammad Baqir Majlisi continued.

With the fall of Isfahan in 1722, many of the Shi'i scholars fled to Najaf and Karbala and these two cities became the main centres of Shi'i scholarship. It was in Najaf in 1743 that Nadir Shah convened an assembly of Shi'i and Sunni clerics and coerced them into signing a document in which the Shi'is agreed to recognize the legitimacy of the first three caliphs, and both sides agreed to Shi'i Islam being designated a fifth school of Sunni jurisprudence, named the Ja'fari School. Nadir Shah's scheme failed, however, to win the approval of the Ottoman sultan.

In Karbala, an important drama in the history of Shi'i Islam was played out in second half of the eighteenth century. The pre-eminent scholar of the middle of the eighteenth century was the above-mentioned Shaykh Yusuf al-Bahrani, a moderate Akhbari who sought reconciliation with the Usulis and settled in Karbala. In about 1762, Aqa Muhammad Baqir, known as Vahid Bihbihani (died 1791), who had at first been an Akhbari but switched to the Usuli School, which he took it upon himself to revive, came to live in Karbala. He first began teaching Usulism secretly, in his own home. Then, when he had won over some of the senior students, such as Bahr al-'Ulum, he began to preach his views more openly, challenged Bahrani to debates, and forbade his students from attending Bahrani's lectures. He even declared that the prayer of those who prayed behind Bahrani was invalid, but still Bahrani did not reciprocate. It may be that Bahrani felt that in the face of the threats facing Shi'i Islam from the downfall of the Safavid dynasty and the confused state of affairs in Iran, it was important to try to maintain the unity of Shi'i Islam. Moreover, the Akhbari position was weakened by intellectual differences among the leading Akhbari scholars. The decisive event, however, appears to have been the bubonic plague that swept through Iraq in 1772. Bihbihani ordered his students to leave Iraq, taking his Usuli teachings to Kirmanshah, Isfahan, Mashhad and elsewhere. Shaykh Yusuf al-Bahrani died that year, and probably most of the senior Akhbari scholars and students in Iraq and Bahrain also died in the plague. Bihbihani felt emboldened to issue a declaration of unbelief (*takfir*) against all Akhbaris. He went about the city accompanied by *mir-ghadabs* (executioners) and many Akhbaris probably fled Najaf and Karbala, while others, even senior figures, were forced into silence. For example, Mulla Muhammad Mahdi Shahristani is said to have been inclined towards the school of Yusuf al-Bahrani but kept silent about this and acquiesced in the Usuli takeover of power.

By the time of Bihbihani's death in 1791, he had suppressed all outward expression of Akhbarism in the shrine cities of Iraq. His senior students dominated the teaching in these cities. Students of these senior clerics went out from Najaf and Karbala to all parts of Iran, resulting in the eventual supremacy of the Usuli School there. A few cities, such as Kirman and Yazd, held out for a decade or two and individual Akhbari clerics remained in cities such as Zanjan and Nishapur for several decades more. Sayyid Dildar 'Ali Nasirabadi (died 1820) took the Usuli doctrine back to Awadh in north-east India and established it there. The murder of Mirza Muhammad Akhbari, the last major Akhbari leader, by an Usuli mob in Kazimayn in 1816, marked the final stage of the triumph of Usulism over Akhbarism. Only a handful of Shi'i clerics have remained Akhbari to the present day in a few pockets in south Iraq, Bahrain and Hyderabad in India.

During the late eighteenth century, Shi'i Sufis who had been driven out of Iran to India in the late Safavid period tried to regain a foothold in Iran, but the Usuli clerics under Bihbihani, having seen off the Akhbaris, were in no mood to brook a challenge to their leadership from Sufis. At Kirman in 1792, Mulla 'Abdullah, a *mujtahid*, moved against two Ni'matullahi Sufi shaykhs who were attracting crowds of thousands. He had Mushtaq 'Ali Shah put to death and forced Nur 'Ali Shah to flee. Similarly, Bihbihani's son, Aqa Muhammad 'Ali Bihbihani, had two leading Ni'matullahi Sufi Shaykhs killed in Kirmanshah: Ma'sum 'Ali Shah (in about 1797) and Muzaffar 'Ali Shah (in about 1800). He eventually became known as *Sufi-kush* (Sufi-slayer) on account of the number of Sufis he caused to be killed.

The effects of Vahid Bihbihani's victory were far-reaching. By his *takfir* (declaration of unbelief) against the Akhbaris, Bihbihani continued the work of Majlisi in narrowing the field of orthodoxy in Twelver Shi'i Islam. Majlisi had acted to exclude Sufism and philosophy, which were peripheral to the concerns of most clerics. Bihbihani brought the threat of *takfir* into the central field of jurisprudence, where previously only *ikhtilaf* (agreement to hold differing opinions) had existed. Another development under Bihbihani was his insistence on the right to enforce his own judgements. Previously, clerics depended on the secular authorities to carry out their judgements. Bihbihani, however, surrounded himself with servants who would carry out either corporal or capital punishment immediately, and usually in his presence. These developments paved the way for a great increase in the power and influence of the *mujtahids* in the nineteenth century and the emergence of the concept of *marja'iyyah*, which refers to the need for every Shi'i to choose a living *mujtahid*, who then becomes that person's *marja' al-taqlid* (reference point to be followed in all matters of law). Bihbihani is called Mu'assis (founder [of the Usuli School]), Ustad-e Kull (Universal Teacher), and the Mujaddid (Renewer) of Shi'i Islam for the thirteenth Islamic century (there is a Tradition that states that a renewer would be sent to Muslims at the beginning of each century).

The eighteenth century was a time of turmoil and change in many parts of the world. Enlightenment philosophy was transforming Europe and bringing into existence the modern world, based on rationalism, industrialization and global trade. The efforts of intellectuals and the significance of the word 'science' moved from being primarily centred on theology to being concerned with the investigation of the natural world. At the same time, the experience of the Islamic world was to move in the opposite direction. The old 'Gunpowder Empires' that had dominated most of the Islamic world, the Mughals in India, the Safavids in Iran and the Ottomans in the rest of the Middle East and North Africa, were in decline, leading to a process of decentralization if not complete disintegration. The intellectual reaction to this socio-political turmoil in the Islamic world was to turn away from philosophy and freedom of thought and back to conservative and more rigid interpretations of Islam.

In the Sunni world, the Wahhabi movement started in the Arabian peninsula. Also at this time, Shah Waliullah Dehlavi (the precursor of the Deobandi movement) in India and Ibn Idris (the precursor of the Sanusi movement) in North Africa were urging Muslims to go back to the roots of Islam and moving Sunni Islam, and Sufism in particular, towards a stricter conformity with the *shari'ah*. In the Shi'i world, the Usuli triumph moved the Shi'i world away from the philosophy and mysticism of the mid-Safavid era and towards a legalistic view of Shi'i Islam. Although rationalism was an important element of the Usuli methodology, it was narrowly applied just to the *shari'ah*. The word *'ilm* (science or knowledge), which had previously had a wide range of application to all parts of the religious and natural sciences, was narrowed to the area of religious jurisprudence. The term *'alim* (plural: *'ulama*, the learned), which could previously have been applied to scholars in all fields of knowledge, including philosophy, astronomy and medicine, was now regarded as only properly applicable to the expert in religious law (the *faqih*). Whereas previously all areas of knowledge had been deemed worthy of study in the *madrasahs*, now all other areas took second place to the study of *fiqh* (religious jurisprudence) and *usul al-fiqh* (the methodology of religious jurisprudence). Although all of these movements, the Usuli, the Wahhabi, the Deobandi and the Sanusi, can be described as revival and reform movements, none of them aligned Islam with the emerging modern world.

The nineteenth century and the Qajar dynasty

The Qajar dynasty came to power in Iran in 1794. This marked the return of a strong Shi'i state in Iran. As noted before, in an effort to shore up their legitimacy, the Qajar shahs deferred greatly to the clerical class (see p. 83). The second Qajar ruler, Fath-'Ali Shah (reigned 1797–1834), was particularly anxious to attract the leading Shi'i scholars of the age to his court in Tehran. One or two responded but it appears that the clerics valued the freedom that they had gained after their ties with the Safavid regime were broken, and the centre of Shi'i scholarship remained in the shrine cities of Iraq.

The scholarship of the early part of the nineteenth century was dominated by the students of Bihbihani. Their families, based in Karbala and Najaf, intermarried and formed dynasties of major clerics that have survived to the present day. The most senior after the death of Bihbihani was Sayyid Muhammad Mahdi Tabataba'i Burujirdi, known as Bahr al-'Ulum (died 1797), who was held in great awe and deference by other scholars. Stories of miracles were attributed to him and it was popularly believed that he might be in contact with the Hidden Imam or possibly himself be the Imam. Bahr al-'Ulum moved the centre of Shi'i scholarship from Karbala to Najaf and this remained the world centre of Shi'i scholarship until the middle of the twentieth century (with a brief intermission in the late nineteenth century, see below).

After Bahr al-'Ulum, Shaykh Ja'far al-Najafi (died 1812), known as Kashif al-Ghita on account of his authorship of a manual of jurisprudence, the *Kashf al-Ghita*, was widely acknowledged as the leading cleric. During the first Russo-Iranian War (1804–13), Fath 'Ali Shah's son and heir, 'Abbas Mirza, who was conducting the campaign, turned to the leading Shi'i clerics in 1809 and obtained from Kashif al-Ghita and other eminent clerics in Najaf and Isfahan a declaration of *jihad* against the Russians, thus implicitly recognising their authority to issue such a declaration – one of the functions of the Hidden Imam. Furthermore, Kashif al-Ghita used the opportunity to extract from the state acknowledgement of the clerics' right to collect the religious tax of *khums* – another of the prerogatives of the Hidden Imam. During the same period, another eminent *mujtahid*, Sayyid Muhammad Baqir Shafti (died 1844), known as Hujjat al-Islam (and perhaps the first Shi'i cleric to be given this title), was asserting the right of carrying out the penalties imposed in his religious court (*iqamat al-hudud*). He is said to have executed some seventy people. With these steps, the clerical takeover of the religious functions of the Hidden Imam may be said to have been completed in practice as well as theory. Only the political authority of the Imam remained for Ayatollah Khomeini to claim in the late twentieth century.

After Iran's defeat in the first Russo-Iranian war, it was the Shi'i clerics who clamoured for a renewal of war with Russia and issued a *fatwa* for *jihad*, leaving the shah and 'Abbas Mirza little choice but to renew hostilities. The second Russo-Iranian War (1826–8) proved disastrous for Iran, leading to the permanent loss of all its Caucasian territories and a crippling financial penalty.

After the death of Kashif al-Ghita, there was no clear successor, with a number of individuals being recognized as being of the first rank: Shaykh Musa, son of Kashif al-Ghita (died 1827) and Shaykh Muhammad Hasan al-Najafi (died 1850) at Najaf; Sayyid 'Ali Tabataba'i (died 1815) and Sayyid Ibrahim Qazvini (died 1846) at Karbala; Mirza Abul-Qasim, known as Mirza-ye Qummi or Fadil-e Qummi (died 1816) at Qom; Mulla Ahmad Naraqi (died 1829) at Kashan; Mulla 'Ali Nuri (died 1830), Hajji Muhammad Ibrahim Kalbasi (or Karbasi, died 1845) and Haji Sayyid Muhammad Baqir Shafti Rashti at Isfahan. This list shows that the last of this clutch of senior clerical figures to survive was Shaykh Muhammad Hasan al-Najafi, the author of an important work in Shi'i law, the *Jawahir al-Kalam*, at Najaf. He succeeded in consolidating the authority of *marja' al-taqlid* in one individual for the last four years of his life. After him, there developed a pattern; after the death of each leading scholar, there was a period during which a number of his senior students would all be recognized as *marja' al-taqlids*; then gradually, usually with the death of the others, the authority would consolidate in one person. In this way, within a few years of the death of al-Najafi, Shaykh Murtada al-Ansari (died 1864) came to be recognized as the most import- ant Shi'i cleric. He introduced some major developments in Shi'i jurisprudence, by developing a set of principles to be used in arriving at judgements (*fatwas*) in cases where there is no guidance obtainable from the usual sources and nothing to indicate the probability of what is the correct answer. This greatly extended the ability of the *mujtahid* to make decisions. To the present day, the practice of the Usuli School is basically the same as he estab- lished, with a few modifications by later scholars. He was also an innovator of new methods of teaching in the religious colleges.

After Ansari's death, there was a period of consolidation until, by about 1872, Hajji Mirza Sayyid Muhammad Hasan, known as Mirza-ye Shirazi (died 1895), had become acknowledged as the sole *marja' al-taqlid*. In 1874, he transferred his residence to Samarra, which thus briefly became the main centre for Shi'i scholarship, until his death.

The Shaykhis, Babis and Baha'is

Hardly had the Usulis disposed of the Akhbari threat when a new challenge confronted them. The School of Isfahan had been strongly attacked in the late seventeenth and most of the eighteenth century, along with all other manifestations of mysticism and philosophy, but then re-emerged in two streams. The first was a resurrection of the teaching of the school by Mulla Hadi Sabzivari (died 1878) and a succession of further scholars, continuing to the present day. The second was the Shaykhi School (perhaps more correctly called the Kashfi School), which represents the re-emergence of the main concerns of the School of Isfahan, albeit that its founder, Shaykh Ahmad al-Ahsa'i (1753–1826), was critical of aspects of the teachings of some members of this school, such as oneness of being (*wahdat al-wujud*). Al-Ahsa'i was a cleric from the al-Ahsa region of Arabia (an area with a strong tradition of Akhbarism and mystical philosophy) and trained under the leading scholars of the day in Najaf and Karbala. His approach combined the Imamocentric focus of the Akhbaris and the mystical philosophy of the School of Isfahan. He took forward the work of Mulla Sadra, developing a dialectics of acting and becoming, of essence and existence, indeed a process philosophy that can be compared with that of Alfred North Whitehead in the twentieth century. Al-Ahsa'i tended to explain theological issues in a manner that elevated them from the physical to the metaphysical and this went against the literalist approach taken by most Usuli scholars. He explained such matters as the *mi'raj* (night ascent) of the Prophet and the resurrection as occurring with metaphysical or spiritual, rather than physical, bodies. He considered that through purifying the self, one can be elevated to a station where one gains direct intuitive knowledge (*kashf*) of the truth. This claim to intuitive knowledge was not, however, unusual among the clerics of his time. It was claimed that Vahid Bihbihani's major book was given to him by the Imam Husayn in a dream; Bahr ul-'Ulum was widely considered to be guided by *kashf*; and another senior cleric of the period Sayyid Ja'far was called Kashfi (died 1851) on account of his reputed access to the truth by this means.

Al-Ahsa'i's teaching found acceptance in many parts of Iran and Iraq. He travelled through Iran and settled for a time in Yazd (1806–14) and then in Kirmanshah (1814–22), where he was under the patronage of the powerful prince, Muhammad 'Ali Mirza Dawlatshah. In 1822, al-Ahsa'i was invited to Qazvin by Mulla 'Abdul-Wahhab Sharif Qazvini, a prominent former Akhbari cleric who had become a Shaykhi and now gave al-Ahsa'i his pulpit in the Shah Mosque from which to expound his views. Al-Ahsa'i's popularity in Qazvin did not sit well with Shaykh Muhammad Taqi Baraghani, an Usuli cleric, whose father had been expelled from the town by the Akhbaris seventy years earlier. Baraghani engaged al-Ahsa'i in a debate that he knew would be controversial. Al-Ahsa'i, along with many philosophers and mystics, thought that the Night-Ascent (*mi'raj*) of the Prophet Muhammad was a figurative or spiritual event, rather than a physical one, which was the position of orthodox literalists such as Baraghani. When al-Ahsa'i gave his view, Baraghani promptly issued a declaration of unbelief (*takfir*) against him. Other Usulis, nervous of the threat to their position posed by al-Ahsa'i's school, rallied to Baraghani. Al-Ahsa'i found himself in a difficult position and had to leave Qazvin. After al-Ahsa'i's death in 1826, his successor Sayyid Kazim Rashti (died 1843) was similarly hounded by the Usuli clerics in Karbala where he lived. Although al-Ahsa'i had never intended to form a separate school or sect, the issuing of the *takfir* had the effect of forcing a separation.

After the death of Rashti, the Shaykhi School divided into several factions. One faction, based in Tabriz, was first led by the Hujjat al-Islam family, and later by the Thiqat al-Islam family. Most of the Azerbaijan and Karbala Shaykhis then followed the

Usku'i family, which later took the name Ihqaqi. Their leader, Mirza 'Ali Ihqaqi (died 1967), moved the centre of their activities from Karbala first to Hufuf in al-Ahsa and eventually, in 1960, to Kuwait, where it remains to the present, with adherents in north-west Iran, southern Iraq, Kuwait, and the al-Ahsa region of Saudi Arabia; it has also established a presence in the Sayyidah Zaynab suburb of Damascus. The current leader, Mirza 'Abdullah Ihqaqi (born 1963), lives in both Tehran and Kuwait, but many followers of the Ihqaqi school do not consider him sufficiently learned, and follow other clerics. What was probably the largest faction of Shaykhis after Rashti was led by Shaykh Muhammad Karim Kirmani (died 1871), a Qajar prince, based in Kirman. Leadership of this faction remained with Kirmani's descendants until 1979, when its leader, Shaykh 'Abdul-Rida Ibrahimi, was killed during the Iranian Revolution. After this, the leadership was transferred to Sayyid 'Ali Musawi (died 2015), who lived in Basrah, in Iraq. This group is the predominant Shaykhi group in most of Iran and in Basrah in Iraq.

The offshoot that diverged most from Shaykhi teaching and indeed eventually from Islam itself was the Babi movement, begun in 1844 by Sayyid 'Ali Muhammad Shirazi, known as the Bab (1819–50). In his early writings, the Bab continued the Imamocentric focus of the Shaykhi writings and appeared to be claiming to be an intermediary of the Hidden Imam. But there was also a very clear implication, from the very first work written after he put forward his claim, that this claim was not just that of being an intermediary for the Imam. The Bab claimed his words were Divine revelation and, later in his ministry, he claimed to be the expected appearance of the Hidden Twelfth Imam. Furthermore, he maintained that as the returned Imam, he had not come to bring about the triumph of Shi'i Islam, as Shi'is expected, but to end the Islamic dispensation and begin a new one. Such a claim, coming from a young man who was not even from the clerical class but a mere merchant, rocked the

Shi'i clerical establishment. The six short years between the Bab putting forward his claim in 1844 in Shiraz and his execution in 1850 in Tabriz saw a violent reaction, with the clerical class urging the government to take direct military action against the new movement. After a further wave of persecution in 1852, subsequent to an attempted assassination of the shah, the movement was driven underground.

The Babi movement re-emerged just over a decade later as the Baha'i movement. Its founder Baha'u'llah (1817–92) was first a Babi but later put forward a claim to be the Messianic figure (Him whom God shall make manifest) that the Bab had written about. Later he put his religion on a universal footing by claiming to be the Promised One of every religion, sent to bring into existence a new social order and a new global order that would bring justice, peace and unity throughout the world. The overwhelming majority of Babis became Baha'is, as did a large number of Muslims, and later Jews and Zoroastrians, in Iran. Despite the small number of Baha'is in Iran (their numbers reached a maximum of 3–400,000 during the twentieth century), the Shi'i clerical establishment has always been in great fear of its potential to convert large numbers of their congregations, especially as its global outlook and its modernist teachings (such as the equality of men and women) appeal to many in Iran. This clerical antagonism was increased by the anti-clerical teaching of both the Bab and Baha'u'llah; they decried the legalism and learning of the clerical class as irrelevant to true religion, which they claimed consisted of acquiring spiritual and moral virtues and thus drawing nearer to God. Consequently, there were sporadic persecutions of Baha'is throughout the rest of the nineteenth century and into the twentieth. Since the Shi'i religious establishment gained political power in 1979, this persecution has intensified considerably.

As the Shi'i clerical establishment considered a claim to a revelation after Muhammad to be heretical, putting it outside the pale of Islam, and since the Baha'i community considers that it has a new holy book, a new holy law and new teachings and is outside Islam, it appears that both sides agree that the Baha'i religion is a new religion, independent of Islam. Therefore references to the Baha'i Faith as a sect of Islam should be taken as a statement of historical origins (much as one might say that Christianity is an offshoot of Judaism), rather than a current fact.

The Shi'i clerics and politics

Since Twelver Shi'is hold that all spiritual and temporal power resides in the Imam, it can be, and often is, said that Shi'i Islam regards all rulers as usurpers of the Imam's rightful position and thus illegitimate. In practice, however, Shi'i scholars have adjusted their stance in accordance with the political realities of their situation. As long as there were Imams who could be asked for guidance and they were a persecuted minority in a Sunni state, Shi'i scholars held to a position of rejecting all secular political authority and regarding all secular rulers as illegitimate. But once the Imam was occulted and Shi'i rulers came onto the scene, Shi'i clerics began to moderate this position.

The exact opinion of the Shi'i scholars cannot easily be determined because considerations of *taqiyyah* mean that they did not always write clearly or openly about their opinions on the sensitive subject of political authority or on the legality of working for a temporal ruler (many Twelver Shi'is worked for the 'Abbasid caliphate and for later dynasties). In general, it may be said that, given the need for order in society before the *shari'ah* can be implemented, and the emergence of Shi'i rulers in the Buyid and more particularly in the Safavid and Qajar periods, Shi'i scholars developed a set of conditions under which it was permissible for a Shi'i ruler to rule and for Shi'is to work for that ruler:

the ruler had to be a Muslim; had to be a Shi'i and willing to hand over rule to the Hidden Imam should he appear; had to have the power to maintain order in his realm and defend it; and had to rule in accordance with the Islamic (Shi'i) *shari'ah*. Fulfilment of these conditions rendered a ruler to be *sultan-e mashru'* (a legitimate sovereign) and working for him was allowed. Some Shi'i clerics also allowed that Shi'is could work for a Sunni ruler, in conditions of duress and under the provisions of the doctrine of *taqiyyah*, especially if they used their position to assist the Shi'ah. Association with rulers was always controversial, however. Al-Muhaqqiq al-Karaki, for example, was criticized by the senior clerics in Najaf and al-Ahsa when he migrated to Iran, despite the fact that he was assisting a Shi'i king, Shah Isma'il, to create a Twelver Shi'i state. Much of the controversy came to focus on the question of Friday prayer. The Safavid kings saw the importance of the communal Friday prayer in the creation of a Shi'i identity for their state and were keen to establish it. Thus the question of whether Friday prayer was legitimate in the absence of the Imam became a hotly debated subject among Shi'i clerics.

Since the defeat of the Akhbaris at the end of the eighteenth century, there has been no serious challenge to the clerical appropriation of the religious functions of the Hidden Imam but the clerics have often expressed doubt and antagonism regarding the assumption of political power by temporal rulers on the grounds that this was usurpation of the prerogatives of the Hidden Imam. Over the years, when temporal rulers were strong and acted with justice, many of the clerics cooperated with the government and in their writings found justifications for the temporal state, while others were muted in their opposition or more commonly aloof from political engagement. But when rulers became weak or tyrannical, or threatened the interests of the clerics, the latter emphasized their claim to represent the Hidden Imam and voiced their opposition to the temporal authorities. This was to be the pattern of historical events, particularly in Iran after the emergence of the Safavid dynasty. Sometimes the intervention of the clerics at the national level was invited and welcomed by the king, as with Shah Isma'il and al-Muhaqqiq al-Karaki, or with Fath-'Ali Shah Qajar and the senior clerics of his time. Sometimes, a senior cleric would force his opinion on the ruler. This occurred when Muhammad Baqir Majlisi forced the state to enact a number of anti-Sunni and anti-Sufi policies at the end of the Safavid period. Similarly, the senior Shi'i clerics in the time of Fath-'Ali Shah declared a *jihad* and forced Fath-'Ali Shah into a second disastrous war with Russia (see p. 115).

Following the second Perso-Russian War, the next occasion when clerics intervened in a national matter was when they joined a coalition of reactionary forces who forced Nasir al-Din Shah to dismiss the reforming prime minister, Mirza Husayn Khan Mushir al-Dawlih, in 1873. The leading clerics of the second half of the nineteenth century, such as Shaykh Murtada Ansari and Mirza-ye Shirazi, were steadfast in refraining from any political involvement. But this changed with the episode of the Tobacco Régie in 1891–2. To raise money to fund one of his trips to Europe Nasir al-Din Shah had sold a monopoly for the produc-tion, sale and export of tobacco products within Iran to a British businessman. Many people in Iran were engaged in this trade and were incensed at the shah. Protests erupted in several parts of Iran. Then, at the height of the agitation, a *fatwa* appeared from Mirza-ye Shirazi, then resident in Samarra, prohibiting Iranians from smoking. Although it likely that this *fatwa* was a forgery, Shirazi did not disown it and most Iranians complied with it, forcing an end to the Régie. Even if Shirazi did issue the *fatwa*, this was an exceptional action in a life otherwise aloof from poli-tics. It was to be the twentieth century in which the Twelver Shi'i clerics stepped fully into the political arena, culminating in the 1979 Islamic Revolution in Iran and the clerical takeover of power. At this time, there appeared a new development in

Shi'i political theory, the concept of *Velayat-e Faqih* (govern-ment by an Islamic legal scholar), formulated and put forward by Khomeini (see pp. 127–9).

The power struggle between the secular rulers and the cleri-cal class also happened frequently at the local level in Qajar Iran, when governors and prominent local clerics vied for power in a town. There was only a certain amount of money that could be raised from the inhabitants of a town and whether that went to the governor in the form of taxes or to the local clerics in the form of religious taxes (in particular the *khums*) depended on the relative power and prestige of these two poles of power. Many clerics surrounded themselves with a group of religious students (*talib*, plural *tullab*) and town gangs (*luti*, plural *alwat*) who could be unleashed to cause a disturbance in the town on any excuse. A local cleric might choose a populist issue such as a tax that the governor was trying to raise or a religious issue such as the pres-ence of Sufis or Baha'is in a town to set loose a mob, thereby asserting his power and sending a message to the bazaar and the business community that they had better make sure that they paid their religious taxes in full.

During the Safavid period, the major Shi'i clerics depended on the state for their main source of income. With the fall of the Safavids, this source of income disappeared and most of the major clerics migrated to the shrine cities of Iraq. Both in Iran and Iraq, they developed other means of financial support: the *khums*, which is obligatory, and certain other voluntary payments made by Shi'is after fulfilment of a vow, as a bequest from a deceased person, to purify ill-gotten gains or to support the shrines. In Iran, the clerics also benefited from extensive endowments (*waqf*, plural *awqaf*) left to shrines and religious establishments by pious Shi'is and administered by the clerical class. In Iraq, the clerics benefited from a large bequest made by Ghazi al-Din Haydar, the Nawab of Awadh ('the Oudh Bequest'), which was a major source of income for a number of *mujtahids* in Najaf and Karbala from the mid-nineteenth century onwards and was administered by the British government.

The Shi'i religious college (*madrasah*)

Since Twelver Shi'i Islam lacked open state support in its early years, Shi'i clerics in this period were mainly educated in the private homes of their teachers. Although one or two *madrasahs* may have already existed, it was the building of a religious college by the Safavid Shah 'Abbas in Isfahan that set in train a series of similar works, so that by the end of the Safavid period, there were many such institutions in Iran and Iraq. A collection of *madrasahs* at a centre of learning is called a *hawzah*.

The main features of these institutions is much the same in all areas. Students are expected to have studied the basics of the Qur'an and the Arabic language in their home towns and villages under the tutelage of local clerics, coming to the *madrasah* at between fifteen to twenty years old. They are provided with food and accommodation and a small allowance for other expenses. In the nineteenth century, this allowance was barely enough to live on and there are touching accounts of the hardships suffered by students from a poor background who had no other money to supplement this basic allowance. More senior students could make some money teaching their juniors. Compared to this, since the 1979 Iranian Revolution, the students at Qom have a comfortable life.

Each *madrasah* usually has a senior *mujtahid* as its head, who in Najaf, Qom and Mashhad is often a *marja' al-taqlid*, and several other senior clerics teaching. Teaching at the *madrasahs* tends to be informal, with teachers holding classes at various locations and times, sometimes in the *madrasah* but also in mosques, shrines or even the teacher's home. Since the students' accommodation and allowance comes from the senior *mujtahid* at the head of a school, those with better financial resources tend to attract more students. The teacher and his students sit on the ground in a circle. In advanced classes, teachers often engage in discussions with the senior students, putting questions or hypothetical legal cases to them. The answers given help the teachers to assess how well the students are doing.

The course of study starts at the introductory level (*al-muqad-damat*), ensuring that the students have a good grasp of Arabic and the basics of logic (usually two to three years). After this, students progress to an intermediate level (*al-sutuh*) where they study the Qur'an, books of Traditions, textbooks of jurisprudence where specific areas such as personal life and commerce are studied, and textbooks of the principles of jurisprudence where they are taught how to apply reasoning to the sources of the *shari'ah*. Other subjects such as religious philosophy, Qur'an commentary, theology (*kalam*), mystical philosophy (*'irfan*) and critical examination of the Traditions can also be studied but they tend to be optional (six to ten years). In the final stage (*dars al-kharij* or *bahth al-kharij*), the teaching is done by the principal *mujtahids* and the students are usually free to pick and choose whose lectures they will attend from among all the senior *mujtahids* at their centre of learning. The students consult whatever books they deem necessary, although a few books have become standard texts for this level of study. The subjects are usually jurisprudence (*fiqh*) and the principles of jurisprudential reasoning (*usul al-fiqh*).

The end-point of study is obtaining a certificate (*ijazah*) that states that the student is capable of making independent judgements in matters of Islamic law (*ijtihad*). A person is then entitled to call themselves a *mujtahid*. It is uncommon to have received an *ijazah* before the age of thirty and not uncommon to be forty or fifty years old before achieving it. Students might spend from ten to thirty years at a college and even then not obtain a certificate of *ijtihad*, which is only granted by the senior *mujtahid* if he is satisfied that the student has a thorough grasp of jurisprudence and the principles of jurisprudential reasoning and can reason well enough to make sound judgements. Those who want to progress to become important clerics will usually try to obtain certificates from several leading *mujtahids*. Teachers also hand out certificates (*ijazahs*) that state that the holder is qualified to teach a certain subject or a certain textbook. This allows the holder to teach junior students. Certificates were also given to students stating that the student was authorized to transmit Islamic Traditions from their teacher, although the need for such certificates lessened with the advent and acceptance of printed books. Many drop out of the *madrasah* without a certificate. They may then undertake another occupation or may become clerics at lower levels, perhaps in a village or as a prayer-leader (*imam-jum'ah*) in a small urban mosque.

This description applied to most *madrasahs* for most of Shi'i history. Since the 1979 Islamic Revolution in Iran, however, the Qom *hawzah* has become increasingly formal and more modern in its teaching methods, such that it now resembles a Western university. Najaf, having emerged from its suppression under Saddam Hussain's rule, has partly followed Qom's example, but remains much more traditional in its style of scholarship and teaching.

Velayat-e Faqih

In Shi'i theory (as explained on p. 100), the Imam has *walayah* (*velayat*, rule or governance) over all religious and political functions. Over the centuries, the clerics had taken over all of the religious functions of the Hidden Imam (such as the right to receive the religious taxes and the right to lead Friday prayer) and this was sealed by the Usuli triumph over the Akhbaris in the eighteenth century. This takeover by the clerics of the religious functions of the Imam can be called a limited *walayat al-faqih* (or in Persian *velayat-e faqih*). The innovation that Ayatollah Khomeini introduced was to claim an absolute *velayat-e faqih* – that the Islamic legal expert (*faqih*) has the absolute right to all of the functions of the Hidden Imam – authority over both religious and political affairs. Suggestions along these lines had been made before by Shi'i clerics (such as Mulla Ahmad Naraqi in the nineteenth century) but Khomeini was the first to outline the position unequivocally and openly to challenge the secular authorities. On the one hand, this was a radical departure from the tradition among senior Shi'i clerics of being apolitical. On the other hand, it was the logical culmination of the claim of the clerical class that they were the general deputies (*al-na'ib al-'amm*) of the Hidden Imam and, as such, could move on and claim the only remaining function of the Hidden Imam that they had not yet taken over: the Imam's right to political rule. Indeed, in justifying his stance, Khomeini used the same Traditions that had previously been used by earlier Usuli clerics in justifying their takeover of the religious functions of the Hidden Imam.

Khomeini's concept of *Velayat-e Faqih* was that the Constitution and law of the country is already determined by the Islamic *shari'ah* and only requires interpretation by the *mujtahids* and an executive, which, under clerical control, determines priorities and executes the decisions of the *mujtahid*. There was no place in Khomeini's original scheme for any political parties, parliament or other democratic elements. But there has been no consensus among the clerics that Khomeini's views are correct. At the beginning of the Revolution, Shari'atmadari, Talaqani and others favoured a constitutional democracy, patterned along the lines that Shaykh Muhammad Husayn Na'ini wrote of at the beginning of the twentieth century, with multi-party political activity. Outside Iran also, Ayatollah Khu'i and later Ayatollah Sistani rejected Khomeini's formulation. Khomeini himself, once he had achieved power, made great compromises with the position he had set out earlier when in Najaf (see p. 234).

THE VELAYAT-E FAQIH (RULE BY THE EXPERT IN ISLAMIC LAW) BY RUHULLAH KHOMEINI

Since this is the period of the Occultation of the Imam and the continuation of an Islamic government is needed to prevent chaos and disorder, then it is necessary to establish a government. And reason dictates that organization is needed so that if we are attacked, we can defend ourselves ... The Holy Shari'ah also instructs us that we must ever be prepared to defend ourselves against those who would attack us. A government, a judiciary and an executive force is also needed to prevent some people from abusing the rights of others. These things will not happen by themselves and so it is necessary for a government to be established ...

Since at present, in the absence of the Imam, no person has been decreed by God to establish government, what are we to do? Shall we let Islam go? Do we not need Islam any longer? ... Or is it that government is necessary and, if God has not appointed a specific person to rule during the Occultation, nevertheless the specifications of the ruler which were in place from the beginning of Islam to the time of the Twelfth Imam are also suitable for the period after the Occultation. These qualities that consist of knowledge of the law and justice can be found in any number of the religious legal experts (*fuqaha*) of our time. If they were to get together, they could establish justice for all in the world.

If a suitable individual who has these two qualities (knowledge of Divine law and justice) arises and establishes a government, he would have the same authority (*velayat*) that the Prophet had in his rule over society and it would be obligatory for all to obey him. Those who imagine that the Prophet had greater authority to rule than 'Ali or that 'Ali had greater authority than an expert in religious law (*faqih*) are in error. Of course the virtues and qualities of the Prophet were superior to those of anyone else in the world (and similarly for 'Ali), but a superiority of spiritual virtues does not increase one's authority to rule. God has given the same authority to rule (*velayat*) as he gave to the Prophet and the Imams ... except that it is not to a specific person appointed by God but rather to a person designated as a 'just religious scholar'.

The struggle for the soul of Twelver Shi'i Islam

The intellectual and spiritual history of Twelver Shi'i Islam can perhaps best be seen as a balancing act between three poles. Most individuals and movements within the religion can be seen as focusing on one of the poles, regarding it as the true Twelver Shi'i Islam and themselves as the guardians of this truth, while portraying the other groups as distorted images of the truth. Each group claims to have possession of *'ilm* or *ma'rifah* (*ma'rifat* in Persian). Both words mean knowledge but the latter is often used to designate mystical knowledge. Each group considers that the path that it advocates is the true path of a Muslim. Some individuals and movements can be seen as trying to integrate two of these poles; very rare have been the individuals who have tried to balance all three.

The three poles may be described thus:

1. Imamocentrism–Scripturalism. This represents a focus on the figure of the Imam (and the Prophet Muhammad who as well as being a prophet is also an Imam) as the object of pious devotion and anxious expectation. The pious devotion is because the Imams are seen as the entities that are closest to the Divine (and thus worthy of devotion) and who by virtue of this position are best able to intervene with God for the forgiveness of the sins of the devotee. The anxious expectation revolves around the promise of the coming of the Hidden Twelfth Imam who will come to destroy the enemies of the Shi'ah and bring justice to the world. Since the masses of the Shi'ah have for most of their history been the subject of great discrimination and injustice, this theme of expectation has been a powerful one, often coming to the surface. Imamocentrism has always been at the heart of the popular religion and is manifested as personal prayers

and devotions addressed to the Imams, listening to stories of the lives and martyrdoms of the Imams, the 'Ashura obser- vances and other observances of the births and martyrdoms of the Imams, the practice of visiting the tombs of the Imams and their relatives (*imamzadehs*) and votive offerings (offer- ings made after fulfilment of vows made when praying to an Imam). In the realm of scholarship, this approach is mani- fested in recording and compiling the Traditions about the Imams, sometimes with an emphasis on those Traditions that increase the devotion of the believer: prayers revealed by the Imams, miracles attributed to the Imams and Traditions that affirm the salvific value of devotion to the Imams. The word 'Scripturalism' embraces both the Qur'an and the Traditions. The latter, although not scripture in the sense that they are not Divine revelation, are treated as scripture by Muslims.

2. Legalism-Rationalism. This movement has existed from the early days of Shi'i Islam and has also been called the external- ist or exoteric (*zahiri*) approach. The focus of this approach is on living one's life as closely as possible to the pattern revealed in the *shari'ah*. In the realm of scholarship, it has involved the task of analysing and systematising all that is in the Qur'an and the Traditions that can provide guidance on how to live one's life. Since the written texts can never cover all of the eventualities of life, it has also involved the develop- ment of rationalist methods of applying the framework of the *shari'ah* to the circumstances of everyday life. It is important to appreciate that the word 'rationalism' is here used not in the Enlightenment sense of this word (deriving knowledge through empirical scientific investigation with no *a priori* boundaries), but rather in the sense of medieval scholasticism (deriving knowledge through logic applied within *a priori* boundaries). Its application extends only to jurisprudence and theology, not to other areas of life. Legalism-Rationalism is an approach to Shi'i Islam that can only be carried out by an

individual who is learned and thus is predominantly the form
of Shi'i Islam among the clerical class and the Usuli School
in particular. It has been imposed upon the people as the true
form of Shi'i Islam by the clerical class.

3. Mysticism-Intuition. This approach focuses on the inner or
   esoteric (*batini*) aspects of Islam and the spiritual development
   of the individual and so can also be called internalism. In this
   approach, the Qur'an and the Traditions of the Prophet and
   the Imams are searched for whatever can give guidance for
   the spiritual development of the individual. Often it involves
   discerning the hidden mystical meanings within a single verse
   or passage of the Qur'an. The Imams are seen as spiritual
   guides who have revealed this inner meaning either directly,
   through intuitive understanding or in visions of the Imams,
   or indirectly, passed down through a chain of the transmitters
   of this knowledge. This third trend manifested itself weakly
   in the early history of Shi'i Islam but later came more to the
   fore.

The approach to Shi'i Islam that has been the most successful
throughout the centuries has been rationalism-legalism (externalism). Over the centuries, this group has assumed an ever-
larger claim to determine and control the day-to-day life, both
individual and social, of the ordinary Muslim. The authority for
their position is a rationalist-legalist one, based on the learning
imbibed at their seats of learning. This group has dominated the
public sphere of Twelver Shi'i community life for most periods
of Twelver history and certainly does today. The other two
trends, Imamocentrism and Mysticism-philosophy, have meta-
morphosed more over the centuries, to the extent that some
may doubt the validity of visualizing a continuous thread in
their development. This metamorphosis may be considered to
have been caused by the successive defeats that various groups
representing these two trends experienced at the hands of the

rationalist–legalist clerics; they have been forced to keep re-inventing themselves. The continuity of these two trends can however be traced through families and in particular areas.

The struggle between these approaches can be seen even among the immediate followers of the Imams, some of whom were described as following Mu'tazili rationalism (for example, Abu'l–Hasan A'yan known as Zurarah) and being more interested in the law, while others were focused on a personal devotion to the Imams (which in some groups was taken to an extreme and some of these then split off and were stigmatized as *ghulat*, extremists), and still others of the followers of the Imams were more concerned with mystical and spiritual teachings and are celebrated among Sufis (such as Ma'ruf al-Karkhi). Later, in the period immediately after the occultation of the twelfth Imam, the tension manifested itself mainly between the first two of the above three as the debate between the Qom school of Traditionists (who concentrated on recording the Traditions of the Imams and who regarded Twelver theology as only truly derived from these Traditions), and the criticism of them by the Baghdad school of rationalist (Mu'tazili) Shi'i theologians and legalists. Shaykh al-Ta'ifah al-Tusi tried to create a centrist position between these two groups but this was not accepted by later legalist–rationalist scholars such as Ibn Idris al-Hilli.

It was 'Allama al-Hilli, at the beginning of the fourteenth century who put into place the final pieces of the rationalist–legalist trend that eventually enabled the scholars of that trend to make legal judgements on almost any personal or social issue, thus bringing into being the Usuli School. As a result, tension between the first two of the above three trends moved from being centred on theology to being centred on legal methodology. Al-Hilli's innovation resulted in a backlash by the opposing Scripturalist trend, resulting in the creation, at the beginning of the seventeenth century, of the Akhbari School, that sought to take Twelver jurisprudence back to reliance only on the

Traditions of the Imams, effectively reducing the power of the clerical class to intervene in all areas of life. The next century saw an Akhbari dominance among Twelver scholars. The Safavid period also saw a flowering of concern with the internalist mystical approach, through the development of Shi'i orders of Sufism and of the Isfahan School of mystical philosophy, both of which attracted many of the most important scholars of this period.

The first half of the seventeenth century in Safavid Iran was a rich period for the free development of experimentation with different ways of being Shi'i. One can find many examples of prominent scholars in this period who adopted the different possible combinations of two of these three approaches to Shi'i Islam, although scholars who tried to harmonize all three are rare. Some Shi'is, such as Shaykh Baha'i, tried to balance the legalistic view of the Usuli School and the internalist Sufi approach. Some Shi'is, such as Fayz Kashani and Muhammad Taqi Majlisi, adopted the Akhbari School of jurisprudence as an expression of their Imamocentrism and were attracted to Sufism and to the mystical philosophy of the School of Isfahan as an expression of their desire for the development of the inner spiritual life (internalism). Others, such as Muhammad Baqir Majlisi and al-Hurr al-'Amili, brought together Imamocentrism (in that they both compiled vast collections of Traditions of the Imams) and legalism–externalism (in that both advocated a legalist view of Islam and opposed Sufism and mystical philosophy). This period of experimentation was ended by two attacks, that of Mulla Muhammad Baqir Majlisi on Sufism and philosophy at the end of the seventeenth century and the attack by Vahid Bihbihani on the Scripturalism of the Akhbaris in the second half of the eighteenth century.

The parallels between, on the one hand, the Usuli *mujtahids*, who regard themselves as the deputies (*al-na'ib al-'amm*) of the Imam and therefore the bearers of the Imam's authority (*walayah*) and who are often regarded by their followers as holy persons capable of performing miracles (*karamat*), and, on the other hand, the Sufi shaykhs, who are also said to be the bearers of *walayah* and are regarded by their followers as holy people capable of performing *karamat*, inevitably created conflict between the *mujtahids* and the Sufi shaykhs. The tension between these two poles of Shi'i Islam intensified with Majlisi's attacks on Sufism and continued with the killing of Sufi shaykhs by *mujtahids* in the late eighteenth century (see pp. 111–12).

With Akhbarism, Sufism and mystical philosophy crushed, the tension between these approaches to Shi'i Islam re-emerged at the end of the eighteenth century, with the appearance of the Shaykhi School. The founder of this school, Shaykh Ahmad al-Ahsa'i, is one of the rare scholars who tried to harmonize all three of these approaches to Shi'i Islam. He was a fully-trained and certified expert in religious law and wrote treatises on points of jurisprudence. Thus he did not reject legalism, but rather sought to broaden the concerns of Twelver Shi'i Islam to be more inclusive of non-externalist issues. His approach included Imamocentrism, through its focus on devotion to the Imams, and internalism, through its concern with the spiritual develop-ment of the individual and its revival of mystical philosophy. Where the dispute between the Usulis and Akhbaris was mainly over legal issues, that between the Usulis and the Shaykhis was mainly about philosophical, eschatological and authority issues. Since the Usuli school was now completely dominant in the field of jurisprudence, the Shaykhi School did not seek to challenge it there, but focused on doctrinal matters. Al-Ahsa'i, the founder of the Shaykhi School, bypassed the learning of the Usuli schol-ars and claimed that the authority for his views came not from his vast learning in the sciences prized by the Usulis that he had acquired at the religious colleges of al-Ahsa, Bahrain, Karbala and Najaf, but by the direct authority given to him by the Imams whom he saw in visions. His ideas were declared heretical and his movement crushed by the Usuli scholars.

Out of Shaykhism came the Babi and Baha'i movements. These continued the trend of opposing the legalism and social power of the Usuli clerics and focusing on the inner spiritual life. They also challenged the foundations of the authority of the Usuli clerics by stating that the learning gained at the religious colleges was not a basis for spiritual advancement. The early writings of the Bab also continued the Shaykhi Imamocentric approach, with great devotion to the Shi'i Imams. While al-Ahsa'i had only claimed visions of the Imams as the basis for the authority of his views, the Bab took this further and claimed to be the Imam and later to be of equal station with the Prophet Muhammad, conveying the words of God. Baha'u'llah similarly claimed to be the bearer of a new Divine Revelation and the founder of a post-Islamic religion. The Babi and Baha'i movements were also crushed and only later flourished outside Iran and in a framework outside the religion of Islam.

Thus, with each victory of the legalist-rationalist group, the ground for debate has shifted and the stakes raised. After the defeat of the Traditionists in the area of theology in the medieval period, the contest with the legalist-rationalists shifted with the Akhbaris to the area of jurisprudence. When the Akhbaris were defeated, the ground for debate shifted with the Shaykhis to that of doctrine and mystical philosophy. The stakes were raised by al-Ahsa'i's claim that the authority for his position came from the Imams themselves, in dreams and visions that he had of them. When the Shaykhis were defeated, the ground for debate again shifted, with the Babi and Baha'i religions, to that of the spiritual development of the individual. The stakes were raised still further by claims that the authority for their position was God Himself, in a post-Islamic Divine revelation to the founders of the two movements.

Although all these other movements have been forced to the margins of Twelver Shi'i Islam by the Usulis, there have been echoes of these movements among the scholars in the mainstream. One can discern, in the period from the nineteenth century to the present, hints of the re-emergence of both Imamocentrism and internalism in the re-emergence of mystical philosophy under Shaykh Hadi Sabizvari and other figures down to the present time and the re-emergence of Shi'i Sufi orders among Iranian Shi'is. Even among the Usuli scholars, there have been indications of a desire to incorporate the other two trends. This can be seen in figures such as Shaykh Husayn Tabarsi Nuri (died 1902) who revived the Imamocentrist Traditionist approach by writing an important compilation of Traditions, *Mustadrak al-Wasa'il*, as an addendum to the work of the earlier Akhbari scholar, al-Hurr al-'Amili. Although some may have thought that the 1979 Iranian Revolution was a decisive and irreversible victory for the rationalist-legalist tendency, recent decades have seen a reaction, with the emergence in the Shi'i *madrasahs* (especially Qom) of *'irfan* (mystical knowledge), which consists of mysticism, shorn of the elements that the Usulis found objectionable in Sufism, such as the personal devotion given to the shaykh of a Sufi order, his elevation to a position equivalent to that of the Imam, the doctrine of *wahdat al-wujud* (oneness of being) and the ecstatic practice of *dhikr* (repetitive recitations). More recently there has been the emergence of the *Maktab-e Tafkik* (especially in Mashhad with Mirza Mahdi Isfahani, died 1946), which in many ways parallels the critique of philosophy and rationality advanced by the Akhbari School but focuses on the area of doctrine rather than jurisprudence.

Thus, although with the triumph of the Usuli School, legalism-rationalism became the official religion of the majority of Shi'i clerics, at the level of popular religion and in spiritual enclaves in most Iranian cities, the other two poles, Imamocentrism and mysticism, continue to thrive. Beliefs and practices disapproved of and condemned by the official religion continue.

5
Shiʻi Islam as a lived religion

There are various ways of being a Twelver Shiʻi. There is the way advocated by the Twelver Shiʻi clerics, which can be called the official religion. There is also the mystic path advocated by Sufis, which has been suppressed by the Twelver clerics for the last three hundred years but still exists as an option, although adopted only by a relatively small number. This chapter is concerned with the experience of Twelver Shiʻi Islam by ordinary people, the lived religion (or popular religion) of Shiʻi Islam. While the official religion has a great deal of influence on the people's religion, nevertheless, the ordinary people have always practised Shiʻi Islam in a variety of ways, not all of which have the approval of the official religion. It is much easier to write a history of the official religion since the ideas and actions of its principal figures have been noted in numerous books. For the history of the popular religion, we are dependent on short passages and hints here and there. Thus the picture obtained is much less complete.

A historical survey

The early period

It is in the Buyid period that we obtain the earliest glimpses of Shiʻi popular practices. In 962 the Buyids instituted public

commemorations in Baghdad of two Shi'i events: the martyrdom of the Imam Husayn on 10 Muharram and Ghadir Khumm
(commemorating the Prophet's nomination of 'Ali as his successor) on 18 Dhul-Hijjah. This prompted the start of public mourning ceremonies for the Imam Husayn. Also in this period, shrines
were built for the Imams and some members of their families
(*imamzadehs*) and the custom of pilgrimages to these shrines
was established, especially to the shrines of 'Ali and Husayn at
Najaf and Karbala respectively. Another development during this
period was *manaqib-khans*, poets who recited praise of 'Ali and his
family. By this means, Shi'i ideas such as the succession of 'Ali,
praise of the Imams and stories of their miracles were spread. The
Sunnis countered with celebration of events in Sunni history
and *fada'il-khans*, poets who exalted Abu Bakr, 'Umar and the
companions of the Prophet.

Conversions to Twelver Shi'i Islam in Arab lands

Although the political fortunes of the Shi'is in Syria were in decline
in the eleventh and twelfth centuries (see pp. 70–1), it appears that
there was an increase in the number of Shi'is during this period.
Various travellers in the eleventh and twelfth century note this,
saying that the cities on or near the Syrian coast, Tripoli, Sidon,
Tyre (Sur), as well as Aleppo, Baalbek and Tiberias further inland,
had a Shi'i majority. One traveller, writing in 1184, states that the
Shi'is outnumbered the Sunnis in Syria. Most such accounts do
not, however, state which sect of Shi'i Islam they are referring to:
Nusayris, Druze, Isma'ilis or Twelvers.

The tide of Isma'ili Shi'ism that, in the tenth century, had nearly
engulfed Islam, began to recede in the eleventh century with the
fall of the Qarmati state in 1067. In Syria, also, the Fatimids were
gradually pushed back. In the twelfth century, as noted previously, there were severe persecutions of the Shi'is by the Zangids,

Mamluks and Seljuks. In some areas, such as Bahrain, al-Ahsa and in the Jabal 'Amil and Kisrawan areas of modern Lebanon, there suddenly appeared large communities of Twelver Shi'is where there had been no reports of them before. Although there may have been small numbers of Twelver Shi'is in these areas, they produced no important clerics until the twelfth century and later. It seems likely that as Isma'ili political power ebbed, many Isma'ilis (and possibly some Druze and Nusayris) became Twelver Shi'is. The reasons for such conversions are not hard to discern. After several centuries of negative propaganda from orthodox Sunnis, the Isma'ilis had become feared and hated by the rest of the Muslim world and large numbers were killed whenever the orthodox Sunni community could lay its hands on them. It seems plausible that as the tide of Isma'ili power ebbed, large numbers of Isma'ilis converted to the Twelver form of Shi'i Islam, which was much more acceptable to the Sunni orthodox. An indication of this comes from the fact that the first of the major Twelver Shi'i clerics from the Jabal 'Amil, al-Shahid al-Awwal in the fourteenth century, had to seek his religious education at Hillah in Iraq, indicating there was no tradition of Twelver Shi'i scholarship in the Jabal 'Amil before then. In this way the basis of the present-day Twelver communities in Lebanon, Bahrain and al-Ahsa was formed.

It seems likely that the Syrian coastline from Antakya (ancient Antioch) in the north to Acre in the south had a large Shi'i population from the tenth century onwards, and in parts the majority were Shi'i. In the southern half of this area (as far north as approximately Tripoli), the Shi'is were predominantly Isma'ilis, and from the eleventh century onwards Druze. When the Fatimid dynasty fell in the twelfth century, most of the Shi'is in the coastal areas of this southern half converted to Twelver Shi'i Islam, which was more acceptable to the new overlords of the area. Those who lived in the south Syrian highlands, however, remained Druze. Many of the Twelver Shi'is in the area of

Kisrawan (north of Beirut) were driven inland at the beginning of the fourteenth century and settled in the north Beqaa (Biqa') valley but enough remained in Kisrawan for there to be, at times, Shi'i overlords of this area well into the sixteenth century. In the northern half of the Syrian littoral (from Tripoli to Antakya), Nusayri ('Alawi) Shi'is predominated.

The conversion of the Iranian people to Twelver Shi'i Islam under the Safavaids

From the fall of the Buyids at the end of the eleventh century until the beginning of the sixteenth century, sources tell us of few further developments in popular religion within orthodox Twelver Shi'i Islam itself. The more important developments were within Sunni Islam, which moved it towards a greater sympathy with Shi'i Islam and prepared the ground for the conversion of Iran to Shi'i Islam under the Safavids. When the Safavid rule over Iran was established in the first decade of the sixteenth century, Iran was predominantly Sunni. Up to that time, although an area that formed an inverted triangle with its base along the south coast of the Caspian Sea and its apex in Qom and Kashan, had probably had a majority Shi'i population (albeit that many of these were Zaydi and Isma'ili Shi'is) and there had been Shi'i minorities in some of the urban centres of Khurasan and among the rural populations of west and south-west Iran, the rest of Iran had been predominantly Sunni, in particular the large cities such as Tabriz, Isfahan and Shiraz. And yet the conversion of Iran to Shi'i Islam proceeded remarkably smoothly. A few Sunni clerics here and there resisted but there seems to have been little popular resistance to this great change in religious affiliation, which may appear surprising when one considers the centuries of antagonism and mutual cursing between the Sunnis and Shi'is that had preceded it.

The reasons for the ease with which the people of Iran converted must be sought in a more detailed look at a number of trends that had been going on in the fourteenth and fifteenth centuries, the centuries preceding the establishment of the Safavid state, some of which have been mentioned in previous chapters:

1. Blows to Sunni Islam

   The Mongol invasion, the fall of Baghdad and the overthrow of the caliphate was a major blow to the Sunni orthodox religious leadership, which lost the influence that it had had over the state in previous centuries. This in turn led to an unsettling of the religious *status quo*. As well as overturning the constitutional law of the Islamic state, the fall of the caliphate dealt a severe blow to the Muslim assumptions of religious superiority and the inevitable triumph of Islam. It made many people question the norms of Sunni Islam.

2. Rise of orthodox Sufism

   As a result of this religious unsettlement, many people turned inward, pursuing the inner spiritual life. This was a period in which many Sufi orders came into existence. In Iran in particular, Sufism became very influential, such that the majority of the population of most Iranian cities of this time were followers of one or another of the Sufi orders. When one of the major shaykhs of a Sufi order came to a city, thousands if not tens of thousands would flock to hear him. In Iran several of the most influential Sufi orders, the Kubrawiyyah and Nurbakhshiyyah in the east, the Nimatullahiyyah in the south and the Safaviyyah (the Safavid Order) in the northwest, although Sunni, were gradually moving in a direction that inculcated a greater love for 'Ali and his family and thus made them more open to Shi'i Islam. Most of these Sufi orders claimed that their teaching had been transmitted along a chain of religious authorities going back to Imam 'Ali.

3. Religious toleration

The religious tolerance of most of the rulers of the Ilkhanid and Timurid dynasties allowed a great deal of religious change to occur. Shi'is became free to propagate their religion. Heterodox religious movements that would not have been allowed to grow under the stricter previous Sunni regimes now flourished. Some of the Ilkhanid and Timurid rulers were close to Shi'i Islam or even converts.

4. Shi'i tendencies among orthodox Sunnis

As part of the general atmosphere of religious toleration, the strong antagonism between Sunnis and Shi'is was moderated in this period. With the demise of the Fatimids and Buyids, Shi'i Islam no longer appeared to be a political threat and, although individual Sunni rulers may have attacked Shi'is in this period, there was a lessening of religious tension especially in the literature. The idea that it was acceptable to have a moderate level of sympathy for the Imam 'Ali and his family (who were after all the family of the Prophet) and still be a good Sunni gained ground (*tashayyu'-e hasan*, acceptable Shi'ism). This meant extolling the virtues of 'Ali, having sympathy for Husayn and criticizing Mu'awiyah and Yazid but without going to what was considered by Sunnis to be the extreme of Twelver Shi'i Islam in rejecting the first three caliphs, condemning the companions of the Prophet and exaggerating the position of 'Ali and the Imams. In popular Sunni culture, this resulted in the emergence of recitals of stories of the Imams, especially the martyrdom of the Imam Husayn. Husayn Wa'iz al-Kashifi (died 1504 or 1533), for example, who was a Sunni Traditionist and Qur'an commentator, wrote a book, the *Rawdat al-shuhada* (The Paradise of the Martyrs), eulogizing the martyrdom of the Imam Husayn in such moving terms that the book was enthusiastically adopted by Shi'is. To the present day, Shi'is call the recital by professional storytellers of the martyrdom of Imam Husayn '*rawdah-khani*' (recital of the *Rawda[t al-Shuhada]*). He also wrote a work on the *futuwwah* (see 7 below).

5. The spread of Gnostic Shi'i Islam

Prime among the heterodox religious movements that were increasing in followers, as mentioned in 3 above, was Gnostic Shi'i Islam (or as their enemies called it *ghuluww*, extremism). During this period, numerous Mongol and Turkic people flooded into the Islamic lands and, although converting to Islam, were still influenced by their former shamanism. It appears that the ideas of Gnostic Shi'i Islam were attractive to these people. 'Ali was made the focus of much of their religious life, being elevated to divine or quasi-divine status, often in company with the other eleven Imams of the Twelver line. However, this re-emergence of Gnostic Shi'i Islam (after its prominence in early Shi'i Islam, see pp. 57–9) appears to have originated among Iranian movements such as the Hurufiyyah, which then spread to these Turkic peoples. The Hurufiyyah were a sect started by an Iranian Shi'i sayyid (descendant of the Prophet), Fadlullah Astarabadi (1340–1401), who claimed to be a prophet. Like the Isma'ilis and early Gnostic groups, Fadlullah claimed to be able to reveal the true inner meaning of the Qur'an and of the religious observances of Islam, but in his case, this interpretation (*ta'wil*) revolved mainly around the mystical significance of numbers, letters and the parts of the body. Although the number seven occurs frequently, there is also a clearly Twelver aspect to these teachings, with praise of the Twelve Imams, and Fadlullah even claimed to be the appearance of the Hidden Twelfth Imam. Fadlullah began preaching his doctrine as a result of a vision he had in about 1386. He was executed in 1394 by Miran-shah, the son of Timur but his doctrines continued under his first successor (*Khalifah*), 'Ali al-A'la (executed 1419), who, persecuted by Timur and his successors, fled into Anatolia where he had a profound influence on the evolution of the Bektashi order, which consequently also took on Gnostic Shi'i features (see pp. 213–14). The Nuqtavi movement also derived from the Hurufis. Its founder, Mahmud Pasikhani (died 1427), was a follower of Fadlullah Astarabadi but was expelled from the Hurufiyyah. He proclaimed himself the Mahdi in 1397, shortly after Astarabadi's death. However it was not until Safavid times that the Nuqtavi movement became significant, resulting in a number of uprisings in the sixteenth and seventeenth century.

6. Heterodox Sufism

   Bringing together numbers 2 and 5 above, there arose a number of popular Sufi orders that were heterodox, mixing Sufism and Gnostic Shi'i Islam. These orders took hold among many of these Turkic peoples across much of western Iran, northern Iraq, eastern Anatolia and north Syria. But it was not confined to the Turkic peoples, as the examples of the Musha'sha' movement, among the Arabs of south-west Iran and south Iraq, and the Sarbardarids and the Shaykhiyyah-Juriyyah, among Iranians in Khurasan and Mazandaran respectively demonstrate. The Safavid order can also be counted among these heterodox Sufi orders.

7. *Futuwwah* (chivalric brotherhoods)

   In the cities of the Sunni Islamic world, particularly from the tenth century onwards, fraternities grew among the guilds, merchants and artisan classes of the Islamic cities that held to ideals of courage, comradeship and assistance to the weak. They were known as *futuwwa* (in Persian *ayyar* or *javanmardi* and in Turkish *akhi*) which can be considered to denote 'having the qualities of youthful manliness'. The youth on which they modelled themselves was the Imam 'Ali, based on the Tradition of the Prophet: 'There is no more chivalrous youth (*fata*) than 'Ali'. These *futuwwah* sometimes acted as vocational guilds, sometimes as Sufi orders and sometimes became no more than gangs of street thugs (see also p. 32).

8. Conversion of the cleric class

   While the above factors may help to account for the conversion of the Iranian masses, other reasons must be sought for the conversion of the clerical class in Iran, who might be assumed to have had a greater stake in Sunnism. There are accounts of Sunni clerics who refused to convert and were either executed or fled the Safavid domains. Some may also have outwardly converted while inwardly maintaining their Sunni beliefs. However, we also find numerous examples of Iranians who had been Sunni religious scholars converting and occupying government positions, even up to the post of Sadr (the chief administrator of religious endowments and other religious finances), during the time of Shah Isma'il. Part of the explanation of this may lie in the different spheres of activity between the incoming Arab scholars such as al-Muhaqqiq al-Karaki, who were mainly interested in imposing Shi'i religious jurisprudence on the country, and the converted Iranian scholars whose expertise and activities were in other areas, such as grammar, philosophy and astronomy, and who administered religious endowments and acted as judges in the Safavid administration. The latter were helped in making the transition in that many of them were sayyids (descendants of Muhammad) and were thus already accorded respect in the Shi'i worldview.

The comparative ease with which the population of Iran moved from being mostly Sunni to being mostly Shi'i was not due to any one of the above factors, but a combination of all of them probably largely explains what occurred. The centuries preceding the sixteenth century had produced a situation where the majority of the population, as a result of the above factors, had strongly positive feelings towards Imam 'Ali and to a lesser extent towards the other Shi'i Imams. They were thus primed to accept Shi'i Islam. However it should also be noted that this positive feeling towards 'Ali and the Shi'i Imams was very different to the legalist Twelver Shi'i Islam taught by clerics such as al-Muhaqqiq al-Karaki. It is perhaps fortunate for the future of Shi'i Islam in Iran that there were initially very few trained Twelver clerics to impose this rigid legalistic Shi'i Islam upon the people and so conversion meant at first only a confirmation of the positive feelings they had for the family of 'Ali. The changes that were made in the early Safavid period were not in the everyday life of ordinary people but at the public level, with such matters as the call to prayer (*adhan*) being altered to the Shi'i formula and the first three caliphs being cursed from the pulpit. It was only later that the more legalistic Shi'i Islam became systematically imposed upon the populace and it was then that one begins to see a more marked resistance, most notably among the Afghans who eventually rose in rebellion and overthrew the Safavid dynasty.

Developments during the Safavid and Qajar period

The Safavid period was the first time since the Buyids that popular Shi'i Islam could give free reign to a variety of expressions. It was during this period that manifestations of popular Shi'i religiosity, such as the ritual mourning processions for the Imam Husayn and the recitals of the stories of the martyrdom of the Imam Husayn, developed more fully. It was also during this period, as far as can be ascertained, that theatrical performances of the martyrdom of the Imam Husayn and other events first started. During the Safavid period, the devotion of ordinary people towards the Sufi saints, which had been a major factor in popular religiosity in previous centuries, was gradually transferred to the Shi'i Imams, who now became the spiritual intermediaries and intercessors of the masses. This change was manifested in the mourning rituals during the month of Muharram and the visitation (*ziyarah*, *ziyarat*) of shrines of the Imams and their descendants (*imamzadehs*), where special prayers of visitation (*ziyarat-namehs*) were recited (see pp. 190–1). Muhammad Baqir Majlisi, more than any other figure, was responsible for a major shift in Shi'i popular religiosity. Through his translations into Persian of devotional material, legal manuals and stories of the Imams, Majlisi moved Twelver Shi'i Islam in a much more emotive and nationalist direction with an emphasis on the miraculous and the supernatural.

The Safavid period also saw anti-Sunni sentiments rise among the Shi'is of Iran, egged on by the anti-Sunni rhetoric of scholars such as al-Karaki and Muhammad Baqir Majlisi. This antagonism towards Sunnis was fed by the depiction of the evils of the persecutors of the Imams in stories of the martyrdoms of the Imams as told in the recitals (*rawdah-khanis*) and the theatrical performances (*ta'ziyahs*). The shrines of prominent Sunnis were desecrated and customs such as cursing the first three caliphs and celebrating the death of the caliph 'Umar became widespread.

The developments under the Safavids were intensified during the Qajar period. For example, buildings (*takiyyehs*) were erected for the theatrical performance of the martyrdom of Husayn and the ritual mourning processions in Muharram were undertaken by organized groups (*dastehs*), either sponsored by wealthy citizens or organized by the guilds or quarters of a city. Not until the late eighteenth century and early nineteenth century did Shi'i practices, such as theatrical performances and self-flagellation that had been developed in Iran during the Safavid period, begin to spread to Iraq, and the late nineteenth century before they came to Lebanon. In India, especially in Mumbai (Bombay) in the nineteenth century, the Muharram observances had a carnival atmosphere and Sunnis and Hindus also participated. Towards the end of that century there was, however, an attempt by resident Iranian Shi'is to return the commemorations to a more sombre and funereal observance. For a time in the early twentieth century, the British banned the Muharram commemorations in Mumbai. By the second half of the twentieth century, the commemorations were mainly confined to Shi'is and were of a funereal nature.

In Awadh in north India, the British deposed the Shi'i ruler in 1856 and this led to an important change in the recitals of the stories of the martyrs (called *rawdah-khani* in Iran but *majlis* and *marsiyah-khanis* in India). Whereas previously these had been patronized by the king and attended mainly or only by the upper classes, they now became open to all classes; whereas previously the language of these recitals had been Persian (the language of the literate upper classes), it increasingly became Urdu (the language of the majority of the Muslims).

By Qajar times, the Shi'i clerics in both Iran and Iraq were largely independent of the state financially and so ordinary people often asked them to intercede for them when they came up against the state, usually over either taxes or criminal behaviour. With the firm establishment of the Usuli School in Iran, Iraq and Lebanon, the concept that every Shi'i needs to look to a *mujtahid* for guidance in their daily affairs took hold much more firmly. From being at the periphery of the life of the believer and only involved in such social transactions as marriage, death and inheritance, clerics were able to thrust themselves into the centre of the life of the believer, insisting that even in the ordinary actions of everyday life, it is necessary for a devout believer to turn to a *mujtahid* for advice and guidance. This in turn has led to the practice, among those *mujtahids* who wanted to become a *marja' al-taqlid*, of writing manuals covering most common aspects of everyday life (*risaleh-ye 'amaliyyeh*). These manuals only became the norm for aspirants to be *marja' al-taqlid* in the late nineteenth century and more particularly the early twentieth century. Most recent such works are based on Shaykh Kazim Yazdi's *al-Urwat al-Wuthqa*. Outside Iran, Iraq and Lebanon, the move towards the norms of the Usuli School was much slower and the concepts of *mujtahid* and *marj'a al-taqlid* took longer to take root. Indeed, it can be said that some areas of the Shi'i world, such as Pakistan, were functionally Akhbari (although most were unaware of that designation) until the 1979 Islamic Revolution in Iran.

One of the most important changes in the Shi'i world in the eighteenth and nineteenth century was the conversion of the tribes of south Iraq to Shi'i Islam. This occurred partly because these tribes changed from being mainly nomadic and began to settle in the areas around Najaf and Karbala where water was available for agriculture (canals had been built through the beneficence of wealthy Shi'is such as the Nawabs of Awadh) and partly as a result of the work of Shi'i emissaries and sayyids among the tribespeople. It is also probable that the Shi'i figure of Imam Husayn resonated with tribal values of courage, hero- ism and honour. The first to convert in the eighteenth century were the tribes that had been in south Iraq for a long time such as the Muntafiq. Later, tribes such as the Shammar that had been driven north into south Iraq by the advent of the Wahhabis in Arabia also converted. The result was that what in the twentieth century was to become the nation of Iraq changed from having a Sunni majority to having a Shi'i one (although reports indicate that the nomadic tribes had barely been Muslims at all before this change).

The personal religious outlook

One can think of the religious life of an ordinary Shi'i as having a bank account with God. If at the end of life, one has a substan- tial positive balance, one goes to paradise, if one has a substantial negative balance, one goes to hell. For those in between, some Shi'is consider that the intercession of the Imams will be suffi- cient to take them to heaven while others speak of an inter-world or purgatory (*barzakh*), where believers who have committed minor offences and are just short of what is needed for heaven are punished until fit for heaven.

To avoid negative charges to one's account, one must live one's life within the boundaries of the *shari'ah* that are considered permissible (*halal*) and not stray into areas that are forbidden (*haram*). All one's daily actions can be divided into five categories, which with the resulting change in one's account from performing that action or not performing it can be represented in the accompanying table.

Table 3 Classification of the actions of daily life

Action	Performing that Action	Not Performing that Action
Obligatory (*wajib*)	+	–
Desirable (*mustahabb*)	+	0
Neutral (*mubah*)	0	0
Undesirable (*makruh*)	0	+
Forbidden (*haram*)	–	+

+ = credit to account
– = debit to account
0 = no change in account

A credit to the account can come from obligatory actions such as the daily prayers and the yearly fast of Ramadan. But they can also come from supererogatory acts (acts that are beyond what is obligatory), which are classed as desirable. These include such acts as giving to charity but there are a number of specifically Shi'i ones, ranging from visiting an *imamzadeh* to giving *sufrehs* (meals given usually with an accompanying sermon or recital of the story of one of the Imams). The believer is constantly on the look-out for *thawabs* (pronounced in Persian *savabs*), good deeds which result in a positive charge to one's account. Failing to carry out an action that is obligatory or performing an action that is forbidden will result in a debit to one's account.

This means that a person is judged mainly by his or her actions; correct actions (orthopraxy) rather than correct beliefs (orthodoxy) determine whether one is considered to be a good Twelver Shi'i. This particularly applies in environments such as the bazaar, where everyone is watching everyone else. Most ordinary Shi'is need to consult a cleric frequently during the course of their lives as situations arise where it is not clear what the proper Islamic course of action should be. The local cleric may sometimes be derided and looked upon as a charlatan by some, but there is usually respect for the senior clerics, the *maraji' al-taqlid* (singular: *marja' al-taqlid*) who are now given the title *Ayatullah al-'Uzma*.

As described at the beginning of Chapter 7, Shi'i religious leaders should, in theory, only make rulings on matters of ritual and the actions of daily life, the peripheral elements of the religion (*furu' al-din*), and not on matters of belief, the principle elements of the religion (*usul al-din*). In practice, however, the senior religious figures are usually regarded as being more than just sources of knowledge about correct ritual and actions. They have what in sociology is called 'charismatic authority'; stories are told about miracles related to them. The word used for miracles here is *karamat*, to distinguish them from the miracles of the Prophets, which are called *mu'jizat*, but the effect is the same: to elevate the senior clerics to a spiritual status above that of ordinary human beings. With this higher status, they become intermediaries between God and the individual believer and indeed become dispensers of Divine Grace; ordinary people ask them for blessings and regard things they have touched as blessed. In this elevated role, one finds senior clerics making pronouncements on matters well beyond that of their formal role of pronouncing on correct ritual and actions; for example, they make rulings on what is correct belief and expect their pronouncements to be obeyed.

Individual piety

There are many acts of individual piety performed by Shi'is. Apart from formal rituals such as the daily ritual prayers, the yearly fast and the pilgrimage to Mecca (which should be performed at least once in a lifetime if the person has the means), there is also individual prayer (*du'a*) and intimate conversations with God (*munajat*). Prayers given by the Imams are often used. A particularly popular collection of prayers is that of the fourth Imam 'Ali Zayn al-'Abidin, called *al-Sahifah al-Sajjadiyyah*.

PRAYER OF IMAM ZAYN AL-'ABIDIN REGARDING GOD'S CONCEALMENT OF SINS

All praise be unto Thee, O God, for Thine act of concealment after Thou didst come to know and for Thy pardoning after becoming informed. For each one of us has fallen short and yet Thou has not spread this abroad; each of us has committed vile acts yet Thou hast not exposed us to dishonour; each of us have concealed evil deeds yet Thou didst not point us out. How many an act prohibited by Thee have we performed; and how many a command that Thou hast ordained for us have we neglected, and there is the evil that is ours, and the sins we have committed. Thou alone dost gaze upon them and Thou alone hast the power to make them known to the people. Thy protection of us has become a veil over their eyes and has stopped up their ears.

So make Thou Thy concealment of our defects and Thy hiding of our true nature an admonisher unto us, a restraint upon our evil nature and our committing of sins, and a cause for our striving for an all-absolving repentance and a praiseworthy way of life. Bring near the time for this and do not designate for us forgetfulness of Thee. Verily are we longing for Thee and repenting of our sins.

Bless Thou, O God, Thy favoured ones among Thy creation, Muhammad and his kindred, the pure and the elect from among Thy creatures. Render us attentive and obedient even as Thou hast commanded.

(*al-Sahifah al-Sajjadiyyah*, no 34)

Individual piety is usually directed towards the Imams and for women often towards Fatimah, the daughter of the Prophet Muhammad, and her daughter Zaynab, who was present at Karbala and played a heroic role in its aftermath. 'Abbas, the brother of Imam Husayn, is often prayed to for help when a particularly difficult task presents itself. These figures are regarded as role models and are prayed to for help in trouble and danger. The Twelfth (Hidden) Imam is called on as the focus of hope for triumph, justice and salvation in the future and invocations are addressed to God to speed his advent. The Imams are also regarded as intercessors for the faithful Shi'is on the Day of Judgement and so they are prayed to for help, and their shrines are visited if a person can. However, if the shrines of the Imams are distant, a substitute for this is a visit to a local *imamzadeh* (a shrine of a particularly holy descendent of the Imams). Another way of showing respect for the Imams is to show respect for their living descendants who are called Sayyids. Marriage into such a family is considered a great honour and Sayyids are often asked to bless a marriage or a newborn child.

Above all however, it is Imam Husayn who catches the imagination, stirs the emotion and is the focus of devotion of the Shi'i masses, both in their individual devotions and in their communal ones. The story of his martyrdom moves men and women to tears. The fact of his self-sacrifice is regarded as having redemptive power for those who mourn for him and call on him. He will intervene with God on the Day of Judgement for those who are his devotees.

Very much part of the popular religion but more marginal to Shi'i Islam are practices such as the use of talismans, charms and amulets, often created from arranging the names of God, the Prophet, the Twelve Imams or various symbols in particular forms, to bring good luck, ward off evil or bring about healing. These are part of the folk religion which extends out to areas that are clearly not part of Shi'i Islam, such as belief and practices concerning the Evil Eye.

Communal practices

Groups of devout Shi'is often get together informally for religious meetings. These groups are often based around an occupation, an ethnic background or, particularly in the case of women, on friendship. While mostly of a purely religious character, in the years leading up to the 1979 Iranian Revolution these groups were an important launching pad for revolutionary activity. Such groups are usually called *hay'ats* in Persian and various religious activities may take place or be planned at such meetings.

The most common practice is the *rawdah-khani* (pronounced in Persian *rowzeh-khani*), the recital of the story of the Imam Husayn and his martyrdom by a professional storyteller, usually with some moralizing at the end. This can happen in a mosque or public place but people will also often hold such recitals in their houses. The skill of the storyteller (*rawdah-khan*) is judged by the extent to which he can raise the emotions of the audience, resulting in weeping, wailing and chest-beating. If held in a home, the recital is usually accompanied by a meal (*sufreh*), especially if being hosted by a woman for other women.

Although the *rawdah-khani* can be at any time of the year, it is most frequently held during the period of 'Ashura (the first ten days of the Islamic month of Muharram). Other commemorations held during this period include ritual processions through the streets. The processions usually accompany a large, often stylized, replica of the tomb or shrine of Imam Husayn carried on shoulders or pulled on wheels. The procession will then also include lines of men chanting rhythmically, often while beating their chests. In some parts of the Shi'i world (Iran and Pakistan in particular), the rows of men often practise various forms of self-injury: self-flagellation with whips; adding razors to the whips to cut the back; or cutting one's forehead or scalp with swords and knives (practices known as *tatbir*, *qummeh-zani*, etc.).

In some parts of the Shi'i world, there are theatrical re-enactments (*ta'ziyahs*, *shabih*) of the martyrdom of Husayn and of certain stories associated with it. It has features similar to the Oberammergau Passion Play: it is often performed by the ordinary people of a village or district (although there are also professional troupes), it is a dramatic performance where the power of the narrative makes up for any defects in production and acting skills, and it depicts the martyrdom of a religious figure. But there are also important differences: Christian passion plays are a celebration of the life of Christ overcoming the humiliation of the crucifixion through the resurrection; the Shi'i play is a mourning rite for a martyred religious leader – there is no triumphant ending. The play depicting this martyrdom is usually performed on 10 Muharram, the anniversary of Husayn's death at Karbala in 680. But for the preceding nine days there are numerous other plays taken from the story of Husayn, the events at Karbala, the lives and martyrdoms of the other Imams, and sometimes other religious stories (all are usually linked in some way, often supernaturally, to the Karbala story). Performances may be staged at other times of the year. Although in the larger cities there are special buildings for these performances, elsewhere, the performance is usually in an open space with an improvized circular stage. The audience encircles the stage but much of the action, such as the scenes of battle, occurs around the stage, often with horses. All the actors are men (even for the women's parts) and attendance at the performance is free (it is usually financed by wealthy patrons but sometimes by ordinary people). This art form began in Iran during the Safavid period, came to its peak of development and popularity during the nineteenth century, but was discouraged and even suppressed by the Pahlavi dynasty during the twentieth century. This suppression has continued in the Islamic Republic. As an art form, it has attracted the attention of many Westerners from the nineteenth-century literary critic, Matthew Arnold, to the contemporary theatre director, Peter Brook.

There are also many local variations of the Muharram rituals. In some parts of Iran, a composite picture denoting various scenes from the Karbala episode is painted on to a large piece of cloth and the storyteller stands in front of this in the street and recites the story. There are also important variations from one country to another in the mourning rituals and in the significance of the rituals for the community. In most Shi'i communities, the Muharram rituals are an occasion for cementing the Shi'i identity, but in India the Muharram ritual processions have (in the past at least) been an occasion in which everyone participates, Sunnis, Shi'is and even Hindus, and there is more of a carnival than a mourning atmosphere. Such commemorations, with similar broad community involvement and carnival atmosphere, spread with the Indian diaspora to South Africa and the West Indies. There are also other more subtle cultural differences. The story of Karbala as told in Iran emphasizes the willingness of Husayn and his companions to accept martyrdom in the path of God and the heavenly rewards for those who weep for Husayn; among the tribes of south Iraq, however, the story dwells on the Arab tribal virtues of manliness, honour and courage, embodied in Husayn and his brother 'Abbas, as they fight on and slay their opponents.

All the Karbala rituals particularly occur in the first ten days of Muharram and culminate on 10 Muharram, the commemoration of Imam Husayn's death. There is usually then a further enactment forty days later, on 20 Safar (called *Arba'in*, forty days being the traditional time after the death of any Muslim when a memorial meeting is held). Most of the senior clerics frown on the excessive emotion and the self-harming aspects of the Muharram rituals and from time to time there have been *fatwas* against this from the *marja' al-taqlids*. This, however, seems to have had little last-ing effect and the practices continue, albeit sometimes in private settings. Clerics who are lower in status are usually much more favourable towards the Muharram proceedings since they often benefit from them. They sometimes double up as a *rawdah-khan* or else they are offered inducements by the sponsors to attend so as to lend status to the rituals. Since the 1979 Iranian Revolution, however, the high-ranking clerics have had much more authority to suppress the more extreme examples of self-harm that draw blood; these have been made illegal in Iran.

The names given to the various aspects of the Karbala commemorations vary throughout the Shi'i world. In Iran, the general name of *'aza-dari* is given to these commemorations and the street processions that are the most public expression of these commemorations are usually referred to by the term *sinih-zani* (chest-beating), although that only actually describes one aspect of these processions. Table 4 gives some of the terms used in different areas.

Table 4 Names associated with mourning rituals for the Imam Husayn in various Shi'i communities

Country	Ritual storytelling	Theatrical performance	Building	Ritual Processions
Iran	Rawdah (pronounced rowzeh)	Ta'ziyah or Shabih	Husayniyyah	Sineh–zani (see above)
Iraq	Qirayah	Shabih	Husayniyyah	Ta'ziyah, Mawkib
Bahrain	'Ashura	Not performed	Ma'tam	Ta'ziyah
Lebanon	Ta'ziyah or Dhikra	Shabih or Tamthil al-Husayn	Held in private houses	No particular name
India	Majlis	Not often performed	Imambara	Jalus

While visitation to the shrines of the Imams and their relatives (*imamzadehs*) is a personal activity, it also has an important social dimension. It serves to reinforce Shi'i identity and solidarity. The economies of cities such as Najaf, Karbala and Mashhad have depended heavily on the pilgrims for more than two centuries. The pilgrims spend money on food, transport and accommodation, give religious taxes to the senior clerics in the city and many make use of other facilities such as temporary wives (*mut'ah* and *sigheh*, see p. 191). In years when the pilgrim traffic has fallen off due to war, political tensions or epidemics, the economies of the shrine cities suffer greatly. The advent of modern transport in the twentieth century means that the pilgrims spent less time travelling and usually less time in the shrine cities and for some of the twentieth century the Iranian government imposed restrictions on the amount of currency each pilgrim could bring to the shrine cities in Iraq. This led to economic decline in Najaf and Karbala. The Iraqi government was somewhat indifferent to this in the mid- to late twentieth century, since it meant a decline in Iranian influence in these cities and, in any case, the increasing income from oil more than offset these losses. There has also been a great traffic in corpses, especially since Safavid times, sent from all over the Shi'i world to be buried in the vicinity of the holy shrines, especially Najaf (in the belief that on the Day of Resurrection the deceased will arise in the company of the Imams buried in these cities). This has resulted in the Wadi al-Salam cemetery in Najaf being probably the largest cemetery in the world. The transport and burial of corpses has thus been another factor in the economy of the shrine cities.

Shi'i communal practices have often been in tension with the official religion as advocated by the clerical class, who frown on the excessive emotionality.

The Shi'i ethos

There are major contrasting role models for Shi'is. The first is the pattern of most of the Imams, who submitted to the wrongs done to them. The essence of this Shi'i attitude is summed up in the word *mazlumiyyah* (Persian *mazlumiyyat*) which means the patient endurance of suffering caused by the tyrannical actions of those who have power over you. All the Imams are considered to have displayed this virtue for at least part of their lives and the popular religious practices particularly emphasize the wrongs that they suffered at the hands of the Umayyad and 'Abbasid governments. The other role model is that of Husayn, who is praised for refusing to submit to the tyranny of the Umayyads. The essence of this Shi'i attitude is the word *qiyam*, which, in this context, signifies arising to take a stand against tyranny.

This paradox gives great flexibility to Shi'i political and religious leaders. They can, if the opposition seems overwhelmingly superior or it is expedient to do so, enjoin upon the Shi'i masses patient endurance (*mazlumiyyah*). And yet when the opportunity seems right, the Shi'is can be whipped up to the frenzy of revolution by appeal to the spirit of uprising (*qiyam*) of Husayn. This is what happened in Iran in 1978–9, when ordinary Shi'is were prepared to go into the streets unarmed, in eager anticipation of martyrdom.

For most Shi'is up to recent times however, the attitude of *mazlumiyyah* has prevailed. The Shi'ah are a people who have been persecuted in most geographical locations for most of their history. Their main religious commemorations are those of the martyrdoms of the Imam. Their main popular art forms also commemorate these martyrdoms. It is not surprising that Shi'is often see the world as a threatening place and themselves as the helpless victims of dark forces ranged against them. In such an environment, conspiracy theories easily take hold and scapegoats are readily found. The clerical class, as the leaders of the community, have often directed the people as to the identity of the scapegoat. While Shi'i Islam was a minority, the Sunni majority were blamed for Shi'i misfortunes and for a while under the Safavids they remained in this role. Later, internal scapegoats were found, especially among those who challenged the authority of the clerical class. The Akhbaris, Shaykhis, Babis and then the Baha'is have successively been cast as 'the enemy within'. From time to time, the government, reformers and modernizers or the Jews have also been cast in this role. Britain and Russia were the main external enemy for most of the twentieth century. In the build-up to the 1979 Iranian Revolution, the shah was identified with Mu'awiyah, the enemy of the Imam Husayn, and his government with the Umayyad rulers. Since the Revolution, America and Israel have become the major external scapegoats, while the Baha'is have resumed their role as internal scapegoats.

Of course, at times there has been some truth in the accusations. During the Qajar period, and for most of the twentieth century, the British and the Russians, and later the Americans were accused on various occasions of interfering in Iran, with justification for some episodes. However they became, in the popular imagination, the nefarious agents who caused every adverse episode that occurred in the nation and even to individuals. It used to be said, only half-jokingly, that if the cook burned the dinner in the kitchen, the British must have had a hand in it. This ethos has had a negative effect on Iranian life and discourse. People, indeed society as a whole, do not hold themselves accountable when things go wrong. Instead they blame others and turn their anger towards perceived oppressors and enemies. Leaders find it easy to divert public anger away from their incompetence and corruption and towards imaginary constructed enemies, both internal and external.

Table 5 Calendar of Shi'i religious commemorations

Muharram	1 – 10 Martyrdom of the third Imam, Husayn at Karbala
	9*, 10* Tasu'a and 'Ashura, culmination of Karbala commemorations
	25^ Death of fourth Imam, Zayn al-'Abidin
Safar	7 Birth of seventh Imam, Musa al-Kazim
	20* Arba'in (fortieth day after death of Husayn)
	28* Death of the Prophet Muhammad and second Imam, Hasan
	29*^ Death of eighth Imam, 'Ali al-Rida
Rabi' I	8^ Death of eleventh Imam, Hasan al-'Askari
	9 Death of 'Umar the second caliph (a joyful occasion for Shi'is)
	17* Birth of Muhammad (Sunnis celebrate this on 12th) and of sixth Imam, Ja'far al-Sadiq
Rabi' II	8^ Birth of eleventh Imam, Hasan al-'Askari
Jamadi I	5^ Birth of Zaynab, sister of Imam Husayn
Jamadi II	3*^ Death of Fatimah
	20^ Birth of Fatimah
Rajab	1^ Birth of fifth Imam, Muhammad al-Baqir
	3 Death of tenth Imam, 'Ali al-Naqi
	10^ Birth of ninth Imam, Muhammad al-Taqi
	13* Birth of first Imam, 'Ali
	15 Death of Zaynab, sister of Imam Husayn
	25 Death of seventh Imam, Musa al-Kazim
	27* 'Id al-Mab'ath (commemoration of the start of the Prophet's mission)
Sha'ban	3^ Birth of third Imam, Husayn
	5^ Birth of fourth Imam, Zayn al-'Abidin
	8^ Occultation of twelfth Imam, al-Mahdi
	15* Birth of twelfth Imam, al-Mahdi
Ramadan	Whole month of fast – frequent religious gatherings
	15 Birth of second Imam, Hasan
	19 Stabbing of first Imam 'Ali
	21* Death of first Imam, 'Ali
	23 Laylat al-Qadr (also 19 and 21), commemorating the first revelation of the Qur'an

Shawwal	1* 'Id al-Fitr (commemorates end of fast)
	25* Death of sixth Imam, Ja'far al-Sadiq
Dhu al-Qad'ah	11 Birth of eighth Imam, 'Ali al-Rida
	29 Death of ninth Imam, Muhammad al-Taqi
Dhu al-Hijja	7 Death of fifth Imam, Muhammad al-Baqir
	10* 'Id al-Qurban (Feast of Sacrifice)
	15^ Birth of tenth Imam, 'Ali al-Naqi
	18* 'Id al-Ghadir (celebrates Muhammad's designation of 'Ali as his successor at Ghadir Khumm)

---

* These more important commemorations are public holidays in Iran.
^ These dates vary from one Shi'i community to another.

6

The role and position of women

The role and position of women in Shi'i communities is more a matter of cultural than religious determination. Shi'i communities, being traditional, patriarchal societies, have treated women in the way that most traditional societies have treated them, while justifying and legitimising this treatment on religious grounds. A man is seen as an individual person whose behaviour and personality traits are individual and who has many social roles that he can occupy. For the woman, however, there is only one standard archetype by which she is judged. She either fulfils the archetype of a silent, submissive, domestic creature, nurturing, gentle and compassionate, and is judged a 'good' woman; or she is condemned as 'bad'; a sensuous, seductive, mysterious, assertive, deceitful figure, corrupting and leading society astray. Because of the danger posed to society and to the family by a 'bad' woman, the daily activity of all women must be strictly controlled.

There are, also, some specific features of Shi'i Islam that are both positive and negative for women. The favourable features of Shi'i Islam for women relate mainly to the special position of Fatimah in Shi'i Islam. Her station in Shi'i Islam is elevated to rank alongside Muhammad and the Twelve Imams as the Fourteen Pure Ones (*chahardah ma'sumin*); individuals who are regarded as being sinless and infallible. Her presence among this group has

added an element of the 'sacred feminine' to Shi'i thought that
is not present in Sunni Islam. As one of the Fourteen, Fatimah
has a redemptive role on the Day of Judgement, and women in
particular call on her in this capacity. Her role in Shi'i Islam is not
unlike the figure of Mary in Catholic and Orthodox Christianity;
this comparison is confirmed by references to Fatimah as 'virgin'
(batul) and even as the 'mother of her father' (umm abiha) on
occasions. The presence of a woman among this highest spiritual
echelon of Shi'i Islam gives women some intrinsic theological
worth.

In addition, Fatimah's position has led to some points in religious jurisprudence that are more favourable to women than
in Sunni Islam. After the death of Muhammad, Fatimah was in
dispute with Abu Bakr over her right to inherit some spoils of war
and land from her father. This dispute means that in Shi'i Islam
there are more favourable inheritance conditions for women. It
is not unknown, in countries such as Lebanon, for a man who
only has daughters to convert to Shi'i Islam in order to give
them a better inheritance than they would receive under Sunni
law. The Shi'i divorce laws are also slightly more favourable to
women. It has been suggested that while Sunni law is based on
the assumption that Islam continued and only modified the existing customary tribal law, Shi'i law assumes that Islam represents
a fundamental break with tribal society and a new legal system
based on the family.

While Fatimah is seen as a role model for the traditional
woman, Zaynab, the daughter of Fatimah and the sister of the
Imam Husayn, is a role model for women who want to play a
more socially active role. After the martyrdom of Imam Husayn
at Karbala, she boldly stood before 'Ubaydullah, the Umayyad
governor of Kufah, defended her family and preserved the life
of her nephew, the Imam 'Ali Zayn al-'Abidin. These scenes
are retold and re-enacted regularly as part of the Muharram
commemorations and so are kept fresh in people's minds.

There are also advantages given to women in Islam that apply across both Sunni and Shi'i law. Islam gives women rights that women in some countries in the West did not enjoy until comparatively recently; for example, the right to own property in their own name. But any slight advantage given to women in Islamic law, and in specifically Shi'i law, is more than offset by the numerous social restrictions and disabilities imposed on them. Women are exhorted to dress and behave modestly, to cover their body and hair, to lower their gaze in the presence of unrelated males, and not to speak to anyone other than their husbands or close relatives, except in a few circumstances. There are numerous restrictions relating to menstruation, since menstrual blood is ritually polluting: menstruating women cannot perform the ritual prayer, fast, perform the pilgrimage rites, should not enter a mosque or touch a Qur'an, and should not have sexual intercourse with their husbands. In addition, a woman may not go out of the house without her husband's permission or travel without her husband or a close male relative. The testimony of a woman is worth half that of a man (and not accepted at all on certain matters), and this ratio also applies to such things as inheritance and blood money (payable by someone who kills another person). Even a woman learning to read and write was considered reprehensible in classical texts.

The main negative feature for women that is specific to Shi'i Islam is the practice of temporary marriage (see p. 191). In the poorer sections of society, women, who are prevented from being able to support themselves through the social restraints imposed on them, are forced into temporary marriages, often on disadvantageous terms. Although this is not significantly different from the experience of poor uneducated women in most societies, what is unusual is that this exploitation is given religious sanction.

The lived experience of Shi'i women has been governed by the extent that these Islamic and Shi'i legal stipulations are balanced by local customs and national laws. Many Shi'i women live in traditional communities, where they can only exercise the theoretical rights they have in Islamic law if they are independently wealthy and have the necessary mental attitude, or if they have the support of their male relatives. In more modern societies, national laws may negate some aspects of religious law. In Iran, for example, the Family Protection Law of 1967 led to substantial improvements in the rights of women in matters such as marriage, divorce and the custody of children. This law was, however, repealed in the aftermath of the 1979 Iranian Revolution, although some elements were later brought back. Despite the seemingly harsh restrictions and social segregation imposed on women by the 1979 Revolution, middle-class urban women in Iran today are able to obtain an education up to university level (indeed girls now outnumber boys at Iranian universities) and go out to work, although there have been attempts to limit both. Even in traditional communities, moreover, there have always been examples of women working alongside men in the fields, unveiled and with great social freedoms, especially in some tribal and village societies.

In the Shi'i communities that have arisen in the West, some Shi'i women have raised their voices against the patriarchal assumptions of the *shari'ah*. In Quebec in 2005, for example, both Sunni and Shi'i women argued against allowing *shari'ah* tribunals to settle matters of family law. Women converts in the West have been at the forefront of the evolution of a more liberal, modern interpretation of Shi'i Islam.

Women in Shi'i history

Despite the above restrictions, there have been some important women in Shi'i history. As well as Fatimah and Zaynab, and Khadijah, the Prophet Muhammad's first wife and mother of

Fatimah, there is Shahrbanu, the daughter of the last Sasanian monarch Yazdigird, whose marriage to the third Imam, Husayn, serves well the cause of Iranian nationalism but is likely to be no more than a pious fiction. There is also Fatimah Ma'sumah (died 816), the sister of the eighth Imam, whose shrine is the centre of the religious complex at Qom.

There have also been a number of exceptional women married to rulers in Shi'i history: Sayyidah Khatun (Shirin, died 1028), who held the reins of power in western Iran under the Buyid dynasty for some thirty years; Tajlu Khanum (died 1540), the wife of the first Safavid ruler Shah Ismail, who was both a counsellor to her husband and the power behind the throne during the early years of the reign of her son Tahmasp I; Pari Khan Khanum (died 1578), who played a prominent political role during the reign of her father Shah Tahmasp I and after his death in 1576 held the reins of power as *de facto* ruler for a period (1577–8); Khayr al-Nisa Bigum (died 1579), who was involved in all important decisions from the start of the reign of her husband Shah Muhammad Khudabandah in 1578, and ruled Iran for some seventeen months during her husband's illness in 1578–9, during which time she led the Safavid army to war against the Ottomans. Several of these women came from Gilan and Mazandaran, where there seems to have been a tradition of women taking an active role in social affairs. During the Qajar period, Mahd-e Ulya (died 1873) was able to exert great influence on state affairs during the reign of her husband Muhammad Shah and the early years of the reign of her son Nasir al-Din Shah.

There were also a number of powerful and influential women in the Nawab dynasty of Awadh in India. Bahu Begum and Sadr al-Nisa Begum, the wife and mother of Shuja' al-Dawlih (reigned 1754–76), had extensive staffs, of some tens of thousands of people, and were wealthy enough to patronize the arts, sponsor religious ritual performances and even subsidize the state treasury when the govenment had to pay a large sum to the British.

Court women often led factions, which were usually focused on one or another possible successor to the current ruler. There was also a world of courtesans and female entertainers, many of whom were extremely cultured and well-educated and some of whom gained sufficient wealth and property to be independent. They made a great contribution to Indian music, poetry and dance; some specialised in the recital of poems, *marsiya* (*marthiyah*), lamenting the martyrdom of Imam Husayn. Their role in Lucknow society can be compared to that of geishas in Japan; indeed, the world of women in Lakhnau became so influential that British and Muslim observers in the nineteenth century condemned the rulers of Awadh as effeminate and dominated by their women, something they used in justification of the British taking control of the area in 1856.

Among the Isma'ilis also there were a number of powerful women. The Fatimid dynasty, which ruled in North Africa, Syria, and Arabia in the tenth and eleventh centuries depended for its legitimacy on descent through a woman, Fatimah, the daughter of the Prophet, hence the name Fatimid. Women seem to have played a prominent role in the early phase of the Isma'ili mission (*da'wah*) in North Africa, probably due to the greater social role of women among the Berber tribes of North Africa. The women of that area continued to appear prominently in the annals of the Zirid dynasty that ruled there, at first on behalf of the Fatimids and later independently. During Fatimid times, the mothers of caliphs often played an important role in ensuring the succession of their sons, which enabled them to become powerful figures at court: Karimah ensured the succession of her son al-Mansur; Rasad ensured the succession of her son al-Mustansir and continued to play an important role in state affairs; Sitt al-Mulk (died 1023) was influential during the reign of her brother al-Hakim and, after his disappearance in 1021, ensured the succession of al-Zahir and ruled as regent until her death. Aunts of the caliphs also attained positions of power in the reigns of the last three Fatimid caliphs, who all were children when they acceded to the caliphate. These women, as well as the women-folk of high government officials, possessed great wealth in their own right, some of it inherited, some given to them and some earned through trade and other activities. With this wealth, they built and endowed mosques and other public buildings.

It appears that under the Fatimids, ordinary women were relatively free to go out into the streets, go to the market or the public baths, and mix freely with men. Towards the end of their dynasty, however, the Fatimids seem to have become more disposed to controlling the activities of their female subjects. The caliph al-Hakim, in particular, instituted a number of decrees against women, ordering that they not go out at night, that they not wear jewellery in public and eventually even that they not go to public baths and cemeteries.

In Yemen, where women appear to have held a more promi-nent place in society, two Isma'ili Shi'i queens ruled for almost a century. The first was Asma (known as al-Sayyidah al-Hurrah, the noble or independent woman, died 1087) who, in the elev-enth century, ruled at first jointly with her husband, 'Ali, the founder of the Sulayhid dynasty and, after his death in 1067, continued to play an important role. The second was her niece and daughter-in-law Arwa (1048–1138), who held both spiritual and temporal authority in Yemen on behalf of the Fatimid caliph, initially from 1067 in the name of her paralysed first husband, al-Mukarram, then in the name of her son, also called al-Mukarram, after his death in the name of her second husband Saba, and finally in her own right. Arwa's religious importance lies in the fact that when the schism in Isma'ili Shi'i Islam occurred in 1094, she backed al-Musta'li (see pp. 202–3). When the second split occurred in 1131, she backed al-Tayyib and received author-ity from Cairo to appoint a Da'i Mutlaq (missionary in charge of the movement). The majority of Yemen's Isma'ilis followed her in these choices because of the high regard in which she was held. Today's Tayyibi Isma'ilis (the Dawudi and Sulaymani Bohras of India and Yemen) trace the spiritual authority of their leaders back to Arwa's appointment of the first one. During this period, the lands under the rule of these two women prospered.

The Qarmati Isma'ili Shi'is of Bahrain and al-Ahsa (tenth century) are reported to have allowed women to go unveiled and to mix freely with men, although this may have been an attempt by the enemies of the Qarmatis to blacken their name by painting them as sexually licentious.

Women as ideological battleground

Perhaps no area of Shi'i society has been as fervently contested in contemporary times as the social role of women. Conservative Shi'i writers have attacked the image of the Western, 'liberated' woman that has penetrated Shi'i society. They regard women in the West as being manipulated by society to become sex objects and consumers of cosmetics and other products of the Western economy. This degradation of women has led, they maintain, to promiscuity, adultery, divorce and the breakdown of the family unit in the West. Thus they reject all movement towards importing Western ideas of women's emancipation.

Women have become one of the main symbols of the ideological battle between conservatives/traditionalists and liberals/ modernizers in Iran in the last few decades. This battle has been fought not just in the national parliament, the government and the communications media, but also on women's bodies and in the streets. In Iran, the symbol of the conflict is the *chador*, a black, all-enveloping, sheet of cloth that leaves only the face exposed; conservative women even pull part of it over the lower part of the face. While conservative women use the *chador*, younger women are now using smarter and more practical alternatives, such as headscarves, wimples, coats and tunics, and many are flouting the spirit, if not the letter, of Islamic law by pushing the boundaries as far as they can. But if the letter of the law is transgressed, agents of the Islamic government patrol the streets and come down heavily on these women. Moreover, just as in the 1970s, when it was debated whether women were wearing the *chador* as a symbol of their Islamicization or as a symbol of their dissatisfaction with the shah's regime, so too it can be debated today whether young women are pushing the boundaries of the dress code as a symbol of their secularization or as a symbol of their dissatisfaction with the political regime. In both cases, the answer is probably a mixture of the two.

7

Shi'i doctrines and practices

This chapter contains a brief account of the doctrines and practices that are specific to Shi'is and in particular to Twelver Shi'is. As far as doctrines are concerned, the principal cause of differences is Shi'i views about the Imams and the fact that, at the end of the tenth century, when the Sunni majority was rejecting the rationalism of the Mu'tazili school, the Twelver Shi'is adopted most of its tenets into their theology. One important consequence of this adoption of Mu'tazili thought is that Shi'is consider that all theological and doctrinal matters can be proved by rational argument, since God must necessarily act in a rational manner (some indication of this is given below). With regard to practices, historically what set the Twelver Shi'is apart from the evolving Sunni community was their rejection of the authority and the rulings of the first three caliphs, as well as their rejection of the majority of the companions of the Prophet as sources for the transmission of Traditions. This, together with specific episodes in Shi'i history, has led to differences in Shi'i practices (the Shi'i implementation of the *shari'ah*) from Sunni ones.

There are several verses in the Qur'an which forbid the blind following of the rulings of others (*taqlid*) in matters of religion (Qur'an 33:67–8; 2:170; 5:104–5; 17:36; 21:52–4;

43:22–4). However, this prohibition is interpreted by the clerics to refer only to the fundamental tenets or doctrines of religion (*usul al-din*) and so belief in these fundamental doctrines must be the result of each individual's independent investigation and not be the result of merely following their parents or religious leaders. With regard to the practices of the religion (*furu' al-din*, subsidiary elements of the religion), the position of the predominant Usuli School of Twelver Shi'i Islam is that anyone who is not qualified to be a *mujtahid* must follow the rulings of a *mujtahid*. Despite this theoretical distinction between *taqlid* of doctrines and *taqlid* of practices, one finds *mujtahids* giving rulings on matters of doctrine which their followers are expected to obey (see p. 152).

Distinctive doctrines

In addition to the fundamental tenets (*usul al-din*) of *Tawhid* (Divine unity), *Nubuwwa* (prophethood, especially that of Muhammad) and *Ma'ad* (the Resurrection at the End of Time), where Twelver Shi'is are in agreement with Sunnis, there are two distinctively Shi'i tenets: Divine Justice (*'Adl*) and the Imamate (*Imamah*). The doctrine of Divine Justice was derived from the Mu'tazili teaching that human beings have free will and are therefore responsible for their own actions and God subsequently judges these actions according to His justice. The doctrine was adopted in opposition to the Sunni belief in *qadar* (predestination). Shi'is also believe that although God has knowledge of everything that has happened and will happen and this is inscribed on *al-Lawh al-Mahfuz* (the Guarded Tablet), He may change what He chooses to reveal to human beings about the future. The alteration in the revealed Divine Will is called *bada'* and has been extensively debated in Shi'i history.

Undoubtedly, it was an important doctrine in early Shi'i Islam; al-Kulayni devotes a whole chapter to the subject in his authoritative collection of Traditions. *Bada'* was used in Shi'i history to explain the fact that Imam Ja'far first appointed his son Isma'il as his successor and then Musa al-Kazim. Later Shi'i scholars rejected this explanation and pointed to Traditions from the Prophet Muhammad that appeared to indicate that Musa had been the intended Imam all along. Most Shi'i theologians today define *bada'* so as to make it the equivalent of *naskh* (the abrogation of one Divinely-revealed ordinance by a subsequent one). The doctrine of *bada'* is also applied to events in the future and in particular to the signs for the coming of the the Hidden Twelfth Imam (see p. 187).

The doctrine of the Imamate

In early Islam, the word 'Imam' referred to the supreme leadership of the whole Islamic community and so there were rival Sunni, Shi'i, Khariji, Mu'tazili and other theories of the Imamate and the word was used as an equivalent to 'caliphate'. Later, however, the Sunni theory focused on the political leadership of the community and favoured the term 'caliphate', while Shi'is tended to use the word 'Imamate' for their vision of the politico-religious leadership of the Islamic community after the death of the Prophet Muhammad. Shi'is agree with Sunnis that the function of a prophet is to reveal God's law to humanity and to guide human beings towards God. Of these two functions, the Sunnis believe that both ended with the death of Muhammad, while the Shi'is believe that, whereas legislation ended, the function of guiding human beings and preserving and explaining the Qur'an and the Divine Law continued through the line of Imams.

The station of the Imams

The Imam is the successor of the Prophet and the vicar or vicegerent of God on Earth. Thus not only does he have ultimate spiritual authority but all political authority and sovereignty is his. Obedience to him is obligatory to all on Earth. Although anyone can say the declaration of belief (*shahada*) and be a Muslim, to have true faith (*iman*) and be a true believer (*mu'min*) requires submission to the Imam of the age. To die without recognizing the Imam of one's time is to die the death of the time before Muhammad (al-Jahiliyyah, the time of ignorance). The Sixth Imam, Ja'far al-Sadiq, is reported to have said:

> We are the ones whom God has made it obligatory to obey. The people will not prosper unless they recognize us and the people will not be excused if they are ignorant of us. He who has recognized us is a believer (*mu'min*) and he who has denied us is an unbeliever (*kafir*) and he who has neither recognized nor denied us is in error unless he returns to the right guidance which God has made obligatory for him. And if he dies in a state of error, God will do with him what He wishes.

Indeed, since the Imams are the Light and Bounty of God (see below), the earth would not continue to exist if there were no Imam present. The Fifth Imam Muhammad al-Baqir, is reported as having said:

> By God! God has not left the earth, since the death of Adam, without there being on it an Imam guiding (the people) to God. He is the Proof of God to His servants and the earth will not remain without the Proof of God to his servants.

Thus the Imamate is not an institution confined to Islam. Twelver Traditions give a list of a continuous succession of

Imams from the time of Adam to the Twelfth Shi'i Imam (each prophet is also an Imam). The Twelfth Imam is considered to be the living Imam of the present age whose life has been miraculously extended, who is currently in hiding and who will appear at some point in the future. The Imams are also considered to be intercessors for the Shi'is on the Day of Judgment. The Imams are assisted by God through the Holy Spirit.

The attributes of the Imams

The attributes of the Imams are considered to be proven from both the Traditions and by logic:

1. Immunity from Sin and Error ('*Ismah*). The sinlessness of Muhammad, Fatimah and the Twelve Imams (The Fourteen Pure or Immaculate Ones) is considered proven by the Traditions. Shi'i Traditions consider that the Qur'anic verse: 'God desires to remove all uncleanliness from you, O members of his family, and to purify you completely' (33:33) applies to Fatimah and the Imams alone and not to the other members of Muhammad's family, such as his wives, as Sunnis maintain.

   In Shi'i texts, this concept of infallibility and sinlessness is mainly related to a perfect observation of the *shari'ah*; in other words, the Imam is safeguarded by God from an action that is contrary to the *shari'ah*. The Imam is also infallible in the guidance he gives; the correct explanation of the Qur'an can only be obtained from the Imam; and the true Traditions (*hadith*) about the Prophet Muhammad are only those authorized and transmitted through the Imams (the companions of the prophet who transmitted the Sunni *hadith* are not considered trustworthy as they failed to support Imam 'Ali).

This matter is also proved from logic by Shi'i writers in that, since God has commanded obedience to the Imam, the Imam can only order what is right, or otherwise God would be commanding human beings to follow the pathway of error and this would be contrary to God's justice. If the Imam did not give infallible guidance, human beings could not be held accountable for their actions by God on the Day of Judgement.

2. Designation (*nass*). It is an important part of Shi'i doctrine that the Imam is appointed by God, who inspires in the heart of each Imam the name of his successor. It is this designation that gives the Imam his authority, regardless of whether he holds temporal power or not. He is the true religio-political ruler of the world, whether recognized or not.

There can only be one Imam at a time, but once his successor is appointed, the successor becomes the Silent Imam (*al-Imam al-Samit*) until the present Imam, the Speaking Imam (*al-Imam al-Natiq*) dies. Each Imam sets up a covenant with his followers regarding the next Imam. The sixth Imam al-Sadiq is reported to have said:

> Do you imagine that we place this Cause of ours (the Imamate) with whomsoever we wish? No! Not at all! By God! It is a covenant of the Apostle of God with 'Ali, the son of Abu Talib, and then one man after another until finally it comes to the Lord of this Cause (the Mahdi).

The concept of a covenant (*'ahd*) is thus an important one in Twelver Shi'i Islam. Each prophet sets up two covenants with his followers, one regarding the next prophet who will eventually come and one regarding his immediate successor, the Imam. Then each Imam sets up a covenant with his followers regarding the next Imam. The conferment of the

Imamate by designation is also considered a logical necessity, since the Imam must be immune from sin and error and only God can know who is immune and can therefore designate the Imam. This designation can similarly only be conveyed to humanity by one who is himself immune from error, the previous prophet or Imam.

3. Being the most excellent of people (*afdal al-nas*). This again is considered proven by both the Traditions that extol the Imams and by the logical necessity of his being immune from sin. Also it is considered that if there were anyone better than he, God would choose that person to be His Proof (*hujjah*) on earth and His Guide (*hadi*) to the people.

4. Knowledge (*'Ilm*). The Imam is considered to have perfect knowledge of the Qur'an and the *shari'ah*. The Traditional proof for this relates to the Quranic verse 'He it is who has sent down the Book ... and none know its explanation except God and those who are deeply-rooted in knowledge' (3:7). Imam al-Sadiq interprets this verse thus: 'We are the ones who are deeply-rooted in knowledge and we know its explanation.' This concept is again considered proven by logic, since God holds human beings responsible for obeying His injunctions and it would be contrary to His justice not to allow someone (the Imam) to be on Earth who has the perfect knowledge to be able to interpret these injunctions correctly.

There is some disagreement concerning the time and manner of the transfer of this knowledge from Imam to Imam. With respect to 'Ali, there are numerous Traditions attesting to how assiduous 'Ali was in collecting knowledge concerning the revelation and how he would not go to sleep each evening until he had ascertained what revelations had been vouchsafed to Muhammad that day and the circumstances of the revelation. However, with respect to some of the later Imams, and in particular the Ninth and Tenth Imams,

Muhammad al-Taqi and 'Ali al-Naqi, who became Imams while they were mere children, the emphasis is on a miraculous transfer of knowledge at the moment of death of the previous Imam.

5. Spiritual authority and guidance (*Walayah* or *Wilayah*). As noted previously (see p. 20), the words *mawla* and *wali* are difficult to translate and the word *walayah* comes from the same root. No single English word conveys all of its meanings, but among the words that can be used in this context include: authority, guardianship, patronage, protection, friendship, companionship, spiritual guidance and sanctity. In the first place, it denotes the station of the Imam as the friend of God and thus protected by God and sanctified by this relationship. It also denotes the relationship between the Imam and his followers, which combines the authority and rule of the Imam, his love and care for his community and his friendship for and spiritual guidance of the individual believer. For more mystically-oriented Shi'is, it also denotes the ability of the Imam to initiate his followers into the inner truth of religion and to guide them on the spiritual or mystic path. The relationship of *walayah* requires that the true Shi'i reciprocate this love and be obedient to the commands of the Imams, which, for Usuli Shi'is, have been made known since the Greater Occultation through the mediation of the clerical class. Shi'i Sufis tend to regard the shaykh of their order as the true revealer of the will of the Imam and thus the mediator of the Imam's *walayah*; hence the tension between the clerical class and the Sufi orders. Some scholars have asserted a difference between two pronunciations of this word: *wilayah* (referring more to the aspects of power and authority in the legal and political spheres) and *walayah* (referring more to the aspects of love and guidance), but most do not make this distinction.

This notion of *walayah* is very important, some would

say key, to understanding Shi'i Islam. It is the basis for the charismatic leadership of the Imams as divinely guided, infallible interpreters of the revelation given to the Prophet Muhammad (*walayah* as authority but also as loving guidance): it involves sacred power, sacred love and sacred guidance. But in reciprocating this *walayah*, the Shi'ah themselves become a charismatic community: metaphysically shards of light created from the light of Muhammad and 'Ali; and in the world, the *khass* (the spiritually distinguished, the anointed) as distinct from the *'amm* (the generality of the people).

The Imams in Qur'an commentary

There is a tradition of Shi'i commentary on the Qur'an which interprets much of the Qur'an as relating to 'Ali and his descendants, the Shi'i Imams. Although linked most closely to the Akhbari school, such interpretations of the Qur'an have widespread acceptance among Shi'is. A few of the many possible examples are:

1. 'You are a warner and to every people there is a guide' (Qur'an 13:7). Many sources, including Sunni ones such as al-Suyuti, acknowledge that when this verse was revealed, Muhammad said: 'I am the warner and you, O 'Ali, are the guide and through you will be guided those who are to be guided.'

2. 'Your guardian (*wali*) can only be God, His apostle and those who say their prayers, pay alms (*zakat*) and bow down before God' (Qur'an 5:55). As noted previously (p. 20), the word *wali* can mean either friend, helper or master. Many of the commentators, both Sunni and Shi'i, are agreed that this verse refers to 'Ali and was revealed after 'Ali had given his

ring away to someone in need who had entered the mosque while prayers were in progress. The verse itself can be translated: '... those who pay alms while bowing down before God', thus referring more closely to this episode.

3. 'Only the unjust would deny our signs' (Qur'an 29:49). The Imams are the Signs of God (*ayat Allah*) on earth. Many other references to 'sign' or 'signs' are also held to be references to the Imams (e.g. 7:9; 10:7; 10:101; 22:57; 38:29).

4. 'Guide us to the Straight Path' (1:6). The Imams are the 'Straight Path' (*al-sirat al-mustaqim*) referred to in this opening chapter of Qur'an (and also in 6:153; 15:41; 16:76; 20:135; 43:42).

5. 'The Way'. The Imams are the Way (*al-sabil*) referred to in several verses (25:827; 6:153; 29:69; 31:15).

6. 'Do you not see those who exchange the Bounty of God (*ni'mat Allah*) for disbelief' (14:28). The Imams are the Bounty of God and the people referred to in this verse are their opponents and especially the Umayyads (see also 16:83). The Imams are also 'the Favours of God' (*ala' Allah*, 7:69; 55:13).

7. 'He who disbelieves in idols and believes in God has grasped hold of the firmest handle (*al-'urwa al-wuthqa*) which will not break' (2:256). The 'firmest handle' is love for the house of the Prophet (the Imams).

8. 'Hold fast to the cord of God (*habl Allah*)' (3:102). The cord or rope of God can mean the Qur'an or the religion of Islam, but it is also interpreted as referring to the Imamate.

9. 'Therefore believe in God and His Apostle and the Light which we have sent down' (64:8). The light (*nur*) of God is within the Imams. Several other verses mentioning light are stated to refer to this light (e.g. 4:174; 6:122; 7:157; 9:32; 24:36; 57:28; 66:8).

Similarly, the Imams are: the Proof of God (*hujjat Allah*) to humanity (Qur'an 6:149); the Possessors of Knowledge (3:7;

13:43); the Possessors of Authority (4:59); the Truthful Ones (9:119); the Family of Ya Sin (37:130); and the People of the Remembrance (16:43–4).

The inheritance of the Imams

The station of the Imam is enhanced by certain books entrusted to them. These include a number of books that had been in the possession of the Prophet Muhammad: Al-Jafr (The Divination), Al-Sahifah (The Book); Al-Jami' (The Compilation); another is the Book of Fatimah (Mashaf Fatimah), a book revealed by Gabriel to Fatimah to console her on the death of her father, the Prophet. All of these items are, of course, now with the Twelfth Imam in occultation and will be with him when he appears.

Another book that is with the Imams is a copy of the Qur'an written by 'Ali and containing 'Ali's commentary and this is a matter of controversy. There is clear evidence in the most respected volumes of Shi'i Traditions (such as Kulayni's al-Kafi and Majlisi's Bihar al-Anwar) that the Twelvers originally believed that passages (and even whole surahs) that extolled 'Ali, referred to his successorship or were about the Imamate, were deleted or substituted in the Qur'an and that the true text of the Qur'an is with the Hidden Imam. Present-day Shi'i scholars state very firmly, however, that they fully accept the current text of the Qur'an and that these Traditions about deleted and substituted verses are not trustworthy. They say that the book that is with the Hidden Imam is the text of the Qur'an as we now have it, but with 'Ali's authoritative commentary. This matter is, however, frequently brought up in Sunni attacks on Shi'i Islam.

The Imam also has knowledge of one of the great mysteries in Islam, the Greatest Name of God. Indeed, it is through his knowledge of this that he has been given his powers. Imam 'Ali is reported to have said:

> Our Lord has given to us knowledge of the Greatest Name, through which were we to want to, we would rend asunder the heavens and the earth and paradise and hell; through it we ascend to heaven and descend to earth and we travel to the east and to the west until we reach the Throne (of God) and sit upon it before God and He gives us all things, even the heavens, the earth, the sun, moon and stars, the mountains, the trees, the beasts, the seas, heaven and hell (cf. Qur'an 22:18).

Going on from the above-mentioned Qur'an interpretations of the Imams as the Light of God, Muhammad, Fatimah and the Imams are conceived in their mystical dimension as being a light that God created before He created the world. This light then became the cause and instrument of all the rest of creation. The following Tradition is attributed to the Prophet: 'God created 'Ali and me from one light before the creation of Adam ... then He split (the light) into two halves, then He created (all) things from my light and 'Ali's light'.

Although the consensus of the Shi'is is that the full prophetic revelation (wahy) that came to Muhammad and the other Messengers of God (such as Moses and Jesus) did not come to the Imams, nevertheless some Shi'i scholars allow that a lesser form of wahy came to the Imams. This type of wahy is explained in a Tradition ascribed to Muhammad al-Baqir, the Fifth Imam: 'It is not the wahy of prophethood but, rather, like that which came to Mary daughter of 'Imran (Qur'an 3:45) and to the mother of Moses (Qur'an 28:7) and to the bee (Qur'an 16:68)'. In any case, if there is disagreement among the Shi'i scholars on the question of wahy, there is no disagreement on the fact that the Imams received inspiration (ilham) from God and hence were given the title al-muhaddath (one who is spoken to). The following is attributed to Muhammad al-Baqir, the Fifth Imam: "Ali used to act in accordance with the book of God [the Qur'an], and the Sunnah [customary practice] of His Messenger

[Muhammad] and if something came to him and it was new and without precedent in the book or the Sunnah, God would inspire him'.

The Twelfth Imam, his occultation and his advent

The doctrine of the Occultation (*ghaybah*) declares that the Twelfth Imam, Muhammad ibn Hasan, did not die but has been concealed by God from the eyes of humanity. His life has been miraculously prolonged until the day when he will, by God's permission, manifest himself again. The occultation has been in two stages, the Lesser Occultation lasting sixty-seven years, during which the Imam remained in contact with his followers through the four agents; and the Greater Occultation, which extends from 941 to the present day, during which he is still alive and in control of human affairs as the Lord of the Age (*Sahib al-Zaman*), but no longer communicates directly. However, it is popularly believed that the Hidden Imam still occasionally manifests himself to the pious, either when awake or more commonly in dreams and visions. It is also popularly believed that written messages left at the tombs of the Imams can reach him. This severance of communication with the Hidden Imam is not considered to contradict the dictum that the Earth is not left without an Imam, for, say the Shi'i writers, the sun still gives light and warmth to the Earth even when hidden behind a cloud.

The reappearance of the Hidden Imam is envisaged as occurring shortly before the final Day of Judgement. The Imam will appear as the Imam Mahdi, together with the return of Christ, the Imam Husayn and also the other Imams, prophets and saints. He will lead the forces of righteousness against the forces of evil, led by the one-eyed Dajjal and the Sufyani and including all those who opposed the Imams during their lifetimes, in one final apocalyptic battle in which the enemies of the Imams will be defeated. The Imam Mahdi will then establish his rule and fill the Earth with justice. He will rule for a number of years, variously said to be seven, nine or nineteen. Strictly speaking, the term 'return' (*raj'ah*) only applies to the return to life of people who have died, such as the Imam Husayn. It is more correct to refer to the *zuhur* (appearance) or *qiyam* (arising) of the Twelfth Imam, who did not die and is in occultation. 'Return' is envisaged by Shi'is as involving only the Imams, their supporters and their enemies. Those who were neutral, or unaffected by the struggle, will remain in their graves until the Day of Resurrection.

The idea that the Twelfth Imam will bring justice to the world is a central concept in Shi'i expectation and there are probably more Traditions about this than any other aspect of the appearance of the Twelfth Imam. However, it is important to note that the word 'justice' here, and in most other places where it appears in this book, does not equate with Western ideas of equity and fairness before the law. Rather, the interpretation of the word 'justice' by Twelver Shi'i scholars relates to a correct imposition of *shari'ah* law. Thus it is not so much that the Hidden Imam will act justly in the Western sense of that word when he establishes his rule, but that *shari'ah* law will be applied universally and correctly.

A messianic expectation of the appearance of the Twelfth Imam plays an important part in Twelver religiosity. Shi'is pray, especially in times of social hardship, for God to hasten his advent and relieve their suffering. There are many Traditions about the signs that will presage his appearance. In general, the world will be in a state of moral decadence, with corrupt political leaders. Even Islam itself will be in a degraded state with the clerical class being the most corrupt people on Earth.

There are many other Traditions giving specific details of what will occur with the coming of the Imam Mahdi; many of these contradict each other. There will be a caller calling out from heaven; the Arabs will throw off the reins of the authority of the foreigners and take possession of their land; there will be a great conflict in Syria until it is destroyed; death and fear will afflict the people of Baghdad and a fire will appear in the sky and a redness will cover them. In the last two centuries, many have claimed to discern these signs in the current state of affairs and have stirred up messianic expectation; most recently in Iran (in particular President Ahmadinejad) and Iraq (the Jund al-Sama' in Najaf in 2007 and the Ahmad al-Hasan movement in Basrah in 2008).

Regarding the Mahdi, he will announce himself in Mecca between the Corner (of the Ka'bah) and the Station (of Abraham) and will summon the people to pay allegiance to him, then he will go from Mecca to Kufah. He will be a young man of medium stature with a handsome face and beautiful hair that flows onto his shoulders; his beard and hair will be black. He will do what the Prophet did, demolishing whatever precedes him just as the Prophet demolished the structure of the Time of Ignorance (al-Jahiliyyah – the period before Islam); he will come with a new Cause – just as Muhammad, at the beginning of Islam, summoned the people to a new Cause – and with a new book and a new religious law (*sunnah*), which will be a severe test for the Arabs; between the Mahdi and the Arabs (the Quraysh), there will only be the sword; the Qa'im when he arises will experience as a result of the ignorance of the people worse than the Apostle of God experienced at the hands of the ignorant people of the Time of Ignorance. However, these signs are under the purview of the doctrine of *bada'* (alteration in the revealed Divine Will, see pp. 174–5) and Shi'is are commanded that if the Mahdi comes in a different way, they are not to deny him.

THE SIGNS OF THE ADVENT OF THE IMAM MAHDI

The following typical Tradition recorded in Kulayni's al-Kafi (al-Rawdah) *demonstrates why many Shi'is consider that the signs for the reappearance of the Hidden Imam Mahdi have been fulfilled and his reappearance is imminent:*

When you see that truth has died and people of truth have disappeared, and you see that injustice prevails through the land; and the Qur'an has become despised and things are introduced into it that are not in it and it is turned towards men's desires; and you see the people of error having mastery over the people of truth; and you see evil out in the open and the doers of evil are not prevented nor do they excuse themselves; and you see moral depravity openly manifest and men being content with men and women satisfied by women, and you see the believer silent, his word not being accepted; and you see the sinful lying and he is not refuted nor does his deceit redound upon him, and you see the lowly despising the great, and you see the ties of kinship severed, ... and you see men spending their wealth on things other than pious deeds and no one opposes or hinders them; ... and you see one person molesting his neighbour and no one prevents it; ... and you see alcoholic drinks being drunk openly; ... and you see women occupying places in the assemblies just as men do and usury is carried out openly and adultery is praised; ... and you see the forbidden thing made legal and the legal thing forbidden, and you see that religion becomes a matter of opinion and the Book and its laws fall into disuse; and you see the leaders drawing close to the unbelievers and away from good people; and you see the leaders corrupt in their rule; ... and you see places of entertainment appearing which are frequented and no one is prevented from entering them; and you see a worshipper only praying in order that the people may see him; and you see the experts in religious law devoting themselves to things other than religion, seeking the world and leadership, ... and you see the pulpit from which fear of God is enjoined but the speaker does not act in the manner he has enjoined others to act; ... then be aware [of the advent of the Mahdi] and seek salvation from God.

Distinctive practices of Shi'i Islam

As well as these tenets, there are a number of practices that are distinctive to Twelver Shi'is, some of which occasion criticism from other Muslims. These practices are based on the Shi'i interpretation of the Qur'an and on the Shi'i collections of Traditions. With regard to the text of the Qur'an, Twelver Shi'is in the modern era accept the same text of the Qur'an as Sunnis (but see p. 183). With regard to the Traditions as a whole, since the Shi'is believe that most of the companions of the Prophet Muhammad sinned in rejecting the authority of 'Ali, they do not accept the Sunni compilations of the Traditions of the Prophet, which were recorded on the authority of those companions. Instead they rely on compilations of Traditions recorded on the authority of the Twelve Imams. These include Traditions about the words and actions of the Prophet Muhammad and his interpretation of the Qur'an, but also, since the Imams are regarded as having been sinless and infallible, their words and actions are also recorded in the Shi'i compilations of Traditions.

In general, Shi'i practices in many areas of the *shari'ah* are very similar to Sunni ones. The differences between Sunnis and Shi'is in such matters as ritual prayer (*salat*), fasting (*sawm, siyam*) and the pilgrimage to Mecca (*hajj*), are minimal and are not much greater than the differences between the four schools of Sunni law. The following are some distinctive Shi'i practices:

1. *Khums*. This is a one-fifth tax that was authorized in the Qur'an (8:41) to be paid to the Prophet, and, for Shi'is, to the Imam, and spent on the Prophet, his family, orphans, the needy and travellers. Sunnis consider this tax to have lapsed with the death of the Prophet but Shi'is say that the law still stands. *Khums* is levied by Shi'is on net income

(after paying all expenses), net increase in land holdings, stored gold, silver and jewellery, mined products, items taken from the sea and war booty. Following the Greater Occultation, the payment of this tax was suspended, but later the clerical class asserted their right to be paid this money in their role as deputies of the Imam (see pp. 100–2) and the right to spend the money for charitable purposes and on themselves and their students. Today, this money is paid by the believers to the *ayatollah* that they follow (their *marja' al-taqlid*) in his capacity as the representative (*al-na'ib al-'amm*) of the Imam.

2. *Taqiyyah* (concealment of belief). Shi'is consider that the Quran (16:106) and the Traditions of the Imams justifies them concealing their true beliefs and outwardly appearing to be Sunnis during persecution, especially if there is any danger to their lives or property. This was, of course, important during much of Shi'i history, when they were a persecuted minority. Today, it contributes to the distrust that Sunnis feel towards Shi'is.

3. *Ziyarah* (Persian *ziyarat*, visitation). As well as performing the pilgrimage to Mecca, Shi'is also visit the shrines of the Imams, especially those of Imam 'Ali at Najaf and Imam Husayn at Karbala, but also the shrines of the seventh and ninth Imams at Kazimayn, of Imam Rida at Mashhad and of Fatimah Ma'sumah, the sister of the Imam Rida, at Qom. These shrines are, for many Shi'is, closer and therefore less expensive than the journey to Mecca. Rituals have developed for these visits, including the recital of a prayer of visitation (*ziyarat-nameh*). Those performing the visit used to be given the designation Karbala'i and Mashhadi in front of their name (for visitors to Karbala and Mashhad respectively), in parallel with the designation of al-Hajj or Hajji for pilgrims to Mecca. In addition to these main shrines, there are hundreds of minor shrines of relatives of the

Imams, called *imamzadehs*. Each of these also has a ritual and a *ziyarat-nameh*. Shi'is will often visit a nearby *imamzadehs* as a day out. One feature of *ziyarah* is that, when visiting the shrine of Imam 'Ali, for example, the pilgrim will sometimes address the Imam's tomb as though the Imam himself is present as a living person. This is a result of the Shi'i belief that the body of the Imam does not decay and is thus, in a sense, alive and will return to life to accompany the Hidden Imam Mahdi when he appears.

4. *Mut'ah* (temporary marriage, Persian *sigheh*). Marriage for a set term (even a matter of hours) and for a pre-determined financial arrangement (dowry) is allowed in Shi'i law (see also p. 166). Shi'is maintain that this practice was allowed in the Qur'an (4:24) and in the time of the Prophet and only later prohibited by the second caliph, 'Umar. In contemporary Iran, some clerics promote this practice as a way for young people to get to know prospective marriage partners by living together under *mut'ah* before committing to marriage. They state that this is a way for young people to let off their sexual energy while remaining within the *shari'ah* and thus avoiding the sexual licence rampant in the West. They maintain that this is an example of how well-suited Shi'i Islam is to the modern world. Despite the attempts of some clerics to praise and promote this form of marriage, it is looked down upon by most ordinary people and often such liaisons are kept secret from other family members. Iranian feminists object that, in practice, it is mostly used by wealthier men to take advantage of vulnerable poorer women (although this is, in fact, no worse than the experience of vulnerable poor women in other patriarchal societies). Sunnis deride the practice as merely legalized prostitution.

5. *Najasah* (ritual impurity) of non-Muslims. The idea that touching non-Muslims renders a Muslim ritually impure

(which means they cannot perform the ritual prayers until they go through a ritual of purification) can be inferred from the Qur'an (6:125; 9:28). Although Sunnis have occasionally acted on this verse, it never became part of the Sunni *shari'ah*. In Shi'i Islam, however, this became part of the *shari'ah* and was applied to the People of the Book (*ahl al-kitab*, that is, Jews, Christians and Zoroastrians) as well as those of other religions who are considered *mushrikun* (polytheists), especially if there is any wetness involved in the contact. As a consequence, during Safavid times regulations were imposed that compelled non-Muslims to identify themselves by wearing a patch of yellow cloth and distinctive headwear. More strict interpretations of the law of purity held that non-Muslims could not trade in the bazaar, because the crowded conditions made contact with Muslims inevitable, and could not go out of their house on days when it was raining, lest drops of water passed from them to a Muslim thus rendering the Muslim impure. In addition, a series of regulations was imposed on non-Muslims, often called the stipulations of 'Umar because they are attributed to the second caliph. For example, they could not ride horses and had to dismount if they met a Muslim who was walking, and they could not build their houses higher than Muslim homes. During the Qajar period, these regulations were enforced occasionally in various towns of Iran when a cleric was asserting his power. In contemporary times, moderate clerics have partly mitigated these rulings (especially for Muslims living in the West), allowing, for example, that people of the Book are not ritually impure, with some going as far as to say that all human beings are pure.

There are many other differences between Shi'i and Sunni practice. Minor differences include the words used in the call to prayer (*adhan*), the manner of ritual ablutions (*wudu'*), the way of saying ritual prayers (*salat* – Twelvers run together some of the prayers so that they are only said three times a day instead of five, as in Sunnism, and it is customary for the head to be laid in prostration on a cake of baked mud from Karbala). The inheritance laws are a little more favourable to women and divorce is made a little more difficult for men.

8

Alternative Shi'i communities

The main focus of this book has been on the history, doctrines and development of the Twelver sect of Shi'i Islam; this chapter is a brief review of the other Shi'i groupings. In the early history of Islam, many Shi'i sects arose. As each of the Imams died or was killed, his following divided into sects: some would say that the recently deceased Imam was the last Imam, who had not died but was in occultation and they were awaiting his return; some would gather around one or other of his sons as the next Imam; and some would go off to another member of the Hashimite family and follow him as Imam.

Thus a large number of Shi'i sects are described in the Islamic literature and indeed, whole books written describing them. Most of these sects, if they existed at all, had only a brief existence and then disappeared. Some, such as the Kaysaniyyah and the Khattabiyyah, died out but influenced other groupings that have survived to the present day (see pp. 56 and 60). Some Shi'i groupings, usually ones gathered around charismatic figures, advanced ideas that were considered to put the group outside the pale of Islam. These groupings, as explained in the Introduction, are referred to as the Gnostic Shi'is and their movement as Gnostic Shi'i Islam. In Shi'i history, they have been called by the pejorative title *ghulat* (extremists), although of course these groups did not consider themselves extremists. Indeed, it is likely that their ideas were widely discussed among the Shi'ah, especially in Kufah, where many of these sects arose. Only in retrospect, with the coalescence of ideas about what is acceptable Islamic belief and what is not, were they labelled as extremists for holding ideas that no longer fitted within the Islamic framework. Their concepts have been described elsewhere (see pp. 57–8) and these concepts undoubtedly had widespread support and influence. Although there was a separation between the Twelver Shi'is and the Gnostic Shi'i groups during the time of the Lesser Occultation (see pp. 64–5), groups holding Gnostic views and revering the Twelve Imams persisted across the Middle East and emerged in later periods, among Iranians as the Hurufis, among the Arabs of south Iraq and south-east Iran as the Musha'sha' movement and among Turkish peoples as the Safavid and other orders. Some of these Gnostic Shi'i groups have continued to the present day.

In a small book such as this, there is not space to describe all of these Shi'i sects. This chapter is a brief review of those Shi'i groupings that have survived to the present day. These groups may be divided into two sets: the first includes those who do not accept the Twelve Imams of the Twelver line – the Zaydis, Isma'ilis and Druze; the second comprises those who accept the Twelve Imams but are outside orthodox Twelver Shi'i Islam because of the influence of Gnostic beliefs – the 'Alawis, Alevis, Ahl-e Haqq, and Bektashis. These latter four, although described as four separate groups, have many doctrines and practices in common and there are many variations within each group. Their history and the evolution of their beliefs and practices have yet to be fully researched and explained. They may perhaps be better thought of as a spectrum of religious doctrines and practice, some elements of which may have had their origins in the early Gnostic Shi'i Islam of Kufa but subsequently evolved along different pathways due to geographical separation and linguistic differences.

The history of schism in Shi'i Islam is often conceptualized as branches coming off mainstream Twelver Shi'i Islam. This is, however, a retrospective imposition of today's reality – the predominance of Twelver Shi'i Islam over the other Shi'i groups – on the history of Shi'i Islam. In fact, it is very likely that when the division between Zaydi Islam and the Twelvers occurred in the early eighth century or when Isma'ili Shi'i Islam emerged in the late ninth century, it was the Zaydis and the Isma'ilis that were then the mainstream of Shi'i Islam and were the majority, while the Twelvers were a minority. Even earlier, in eighth-century Kufa, it may be that Gnostic Shi'i Islam was the mainstream and the proto-Twelvers were a minority. Even within the history of Twelver Shi'i Islam, the positioning of the Usuli School as the mainstream is more of a reflection of today's realities and not those of the seventeenth century, when the Akhbari School was the mainstream and the Usulis were a minority.

Zaydi

The Zaydis were probably the largest group of the Shi'ah in the early period of Islamic history until the rise of the Isma'ili caliphate in the tenth century. They are named for Zayd, a son of the fourth of the Twelver Shi'i Imams, 'Ali Zayn al-'Abidin. Zayd claimed to be the legitimate Imam, instead of his half-brother Imam Muhammad al-Baqir, on the basis that he would rise (like Imam Husayn) and fight for the leadership of the Islamic world. Thus a sect came into existence that considered that legitimacy belonged to any member of the family of the Prophet who would rise to seize power. Indeed, many who could be considered Zaydis seem to have deemed anyone from the extended Hashimite family (everyone descended from the Prophet's great-grandfather Hashim) to be potentially legitimate leaders. One of those who arose as a Zaydi Imam in this early period, for example, was 'Abdullah ibn Mu'awiyah, a descendant of 'Ali's brother. In terms of their political activity, they were more radical than the Imams of the Twelver line, who were politically quietist after Imam Husayn. Doctrinally however, they accommodated the emerging Sunni tradition more than the Twelver line of Imams, in that they did not consider the first three caliphs as illegitimate. However, the Zaydiyyah were never a unified movement and different elements had varying beliefs. Later, for example, in some groups, legitimacy for leadership was narrowed to the descendants of 'Ali and Fatimah and the legitimacy of the first three caliphs was denied. In terms of theology, the Zaydiyyah also adopted various positions at different times.

There were a number of Zaydi revolts in the name of Zaydi Imams, especially in Iraq, between 740, when Zayd launched his revolt, and 864. The Umayyad and 'Abbasid caliphates managed to fend off these uprisings. After this, Zaydism shifted to the periphery of the Islamic world. Along the south Caspian littoral (present-day Mazandaran and Gilan) during the ninth to tenth century, a number of small Zaydi states were established. The first Zaydi missionary was Yahya ibn 'Abdullah, who arrived in Daylam (modern Gilan) at the end of the eighth century; eventually al-Hasan al-'Utrush al-Nasir li'l-Haqq (a descendant of Imam Husayn) established a Zaydi state in this area at the beginning of the tenth century and gave rise to the Nasiriyyah branch of Zaydism. Meanwhile, al-Qasim ibn Ibrahim (a descendant of Imam Hasan) began to teach in Tabaristan (modern Mazandaran) in the middle of the ninth century and gave rise to the Qasimiyyah branch of Zaydism; eventually al-Hasan ibn Zayd (a descendant of Imam Hasan) established the first Zaydi state in Tabaristan, with its capital in Amul, in 864. The Zaydis in this part of the world were divided both politically and doctrinally between the Nasiriyyah, predominantly in Daylam, and the Qasimiyyah, predominantly in Tabaristan. Among the Qasimiyyah, Mu'tazili doctrines came to predominate in the eleventh century, while at about that time, the Nasiriyyah came under pressure from Isma'ili expansion from the west. Eventually, the last Zaydi Imam surrendered to the Safavids in 1526 and the Zaydis of Gilan and Mazandaran converted to Twelver Shi'i Islam.

There was also a Zaydi Imamate in Morocco from the eighth to the tenth century, under the Idrisid line of Imams. Idris I (died 791), a great-grandson of Imam Hasan, fled the Abbasid domains after an unsuccessful Zaydi rebellion in 786 and, with the help of Berber tribes, succeeded in setting up a Zaydi state in the western Maghrib (now called Morocco). He founded the city of Fes, which his son Idris II made his capital. The dynasty was opposed at first by some Berber tribes that had adopted the Khariji creed and later by the Fatimids. In 927, they were evicted from Fes and the last of the dynasty was executed in 985. However, their influence continued. They are often regarded as the founders of the modern state of Morocco and various dynasties claiming descent from the Prophet Muhammad have ruled the country (including the present rulers, who gained power in 1666), although they were no longer Zaydi Shi'is.

One of the Qasimiyyah of Tabaristan, al-Hadi ila'l-Haqq, moved to Sa'dah in Yemen in 897 and began teaching there, converting the populace to Zaydi Shi'i Islam. The Zaydis of Yemen also adopted Mu'tazili theology but a number of sectarian splits occurred in the eleventh century. Under the Imamate of Ahmad al-Mutawakkil 'ala'llah (died 1170), some degree of unity was restored. Zaydi scholars were brought from the Caspian but there was not full unity or disappearance of the divisions until the Imamate of Imam 'Abdullah al-Mansur bi'llah (died 1217). During the fourteenth century, there was a *rapprochement* with Sunnism, through the acknowledgement of the early caliphs and companions of the Prophet, and also with Sufism. This was however reversed in the sixteenth century, particularly with the Imamate of Imam al-Qasim al-Mansur (died 1620), who was inimical to Sufism because of the strongly pro-Sunni and pro-Ottoman stance of the Sufi orders at this time. He likened the Sufis to the Isma'ilis who were the other main enemy of the Zaydis in Yemen. In parallel with this was a movement led by Muhammad al-Wazir (died 1436) that sought to bring Zaydism closer to Sunnism by accepting Sunni Traditions.

Al-Mansur succeeded in expelling the Ottomans from north Yemen and although the Ottomans regained control of the coastal area in 1849, they were not able to control all the highlands. With the collapse of the Ottoman Empire in 1918, Imam Yahya proclaimed an independent state of North Yemen. In 1962, however, his grandson Muhammad al-Badr was deposed by Egyptian-trained army officers. There followed a six-year civil war, which the forces of al-Badr were on the point of winning when Saudi Arabia, which had been backing al-Badr, withdrew its support. Consequently, al-Badr's campaign collapsed and he fled to London. In 1978, Ali Abdullah Saleh, a Zaydi (but not of Hashimite descent and therefore not eligible to rule as a Zaydi Imam), became president of North Yemen. The union of North Yemen (Yemen Arab Republic) with South Yemen (People's Democratic Republic of Yemen) in 1990 left the Zaydis in a minority in the new state but Saleh was made president of the union. From 1992 onwards, however, there was fighting between the north and south until the defeat of the south in July 1994. In 2011, Saleh was overthrown and replaced by a new president, Abd Rabbuh Mansur Hadi, a Sunni from the south. In 2004, a Zaydi insurrection began under the leadership of a cleric, Hussein Badreddin al-Huthi (al-Houthi). He was killed in fighting in 2004 and the present leader is his brother Abdul-Malik. Their supporters continue to control Sa'dah and its province in the north-west of the country and parts of adjacent provinces. From there, they have pushed south and captured the capital Sana'ah. The Houthis say they are protecting their religious community, while the government (which includes Zaydi Shi'is) says that the Houthis want to impose Shi'i law on everyone and are supported by Iran. The actions of the Houthis have strengthened the hand of the Sunni forces, including Islamic State and al-Qa'idah, in the south and the most likely outcome now seems to be the partition of the country into a Zaydi-controlled north and a Sunni-controlled south. Zaydis are estimated to be about 11 million, 45% of the population in Yemen, and there are some 1.5 million Zaydis in Saudi Arabia.

Isma'ili

From the tenth century until the thirteenth century, the Isma'ilis were probably the largest group of Shi'is, and certainly the most powerful. The Isma'ilis believe that since Imam Ja'far al-Sadiq had appointed his eldest son Isma'il to be his successor as Imam and Isma'il died before Ja'far, the rightful successor to the Imamate was Isma'il's son Muhammad and his descendants (see p. 45). There was then a period of obscurity lasting for about a century until the 870s, when there began active Isma'ili propaganda, led by 'Abdullah ('Ubaydullah, died 934), who was based in Salamiyyah in Syria, and by Hamdan Qarmat in the Kufah area. At first the claim was that the Imamate stopped with Muhammad, the son of Isma'il, whose return as the Mahdi they awaited. The propaganda (da'wah) of this group was very success-ful and by 883 had spread to Iran, Iraq, Syria, al-Ahsa, Bahrain, Central Asia, Yemen and Sindh (where a small Isma'ili state was established during the last half of the tenth century). It is likely that many of the converts came from Twelver Shi'i Islam, whose

Imam had recently gone into occultation leaving them leaderless and in disarray.

In 899, however, 'Abdullah in Salamiyyah claimed that he was in fact a descendant of Isma'il (the son of Imam Ja'far al-Sadiq), that there had been a succession of Imams in hiding from the time of Isma'il and his son Muhammad, and that he, 'Abdullah, was now the rightful Imam. He took the title al-Mahdi. This proclamation split the movement, with Hamdam Qarmat rejecting 'Abdullah's claim and taking with him the Isma'ilis of Iraq, western Iran, al-Ahsa and Bahrain, while those in eastern Iran split between the two factions, and the community in Sindh and most of those in Yemen and Syria backed 'Abdullah al-Mahdi. The group around Hamdan Qarmat propagated an egalitarian social teaching that appears to have been very attractive. By 899, they had established a state in al-Ahsa and Bahrain and became known as the Qarmatis (Qaramitah, anglicized as Carmathians).

Fearing for his safety after the Qarmatis became active in Syria, 'Abdullah left for North Africa in 902 where a propagandist he had sent, Abu 'Abdillah, had had success among the Kutama Berbers. These Berbers formed a fighting force that in 910 established 'Abdullah's rule over the central part of North Africa (present-day Tunisia, western Libya and eastern Algeria) with his capital at first in Raqqada and later at Mahdia, both in present-day Tunisia. This established the Fatimid dynasty. 'Abdullah's descendants went on to conquer Egypt in 969, where they built a new capital, Cairo, and the al-Azhar university, which is now widely regarded as the foremost educational establishment of Sunni Islam. Syria, the rest of north Africa, and much of western Arabia, including Mecca and Medina, were also conquered.

Hamdan Qarmat mysteriously disappeared shortly after 'Abdullah's proclamation in 899 and the Qaramitah became divided into factions and gradually lost their hold on all but the

Isma'ilis of al–Ahsa and Bahrain. Here, however, their power was consolidated and they even campaigned against the Fatimids in the late tenth century. They earned the opprobrium of the Muslim world when they attacked Mecca and carried off the Black Stone of the Ka'bah in 930. The Qarmati state was finally overcome in 1077 and the Qarmati branch of the Isma'ilis disappeared from history, although it may have left some traces behind in the interest that certain Twelver Shi'i scholars from this region took in philosophy and mysticism.

Doctrinally, Isma'ili teaching concentrated on explanations of the mystical or inner (*batin*) meaning of the Qur'an by the Imam. History is cyclical and progresses through seven stages, each under the authority of a speaking (*natiq*) prophet, who brings a message and is accompanied by a silent (*samit*) interpreter of the inner meaning of the message, who is also called the *wasi* (inheritor), and a succession of seven Imams; the seventh Imam then becomes the *natiq* of the next cycle. The sixth *natiq* was Muhammad, his *samit* was 'Ali and the seventh Imam after 'Ali was Muhammad ibn Ismail, whom the Qaramitah believed will return as the Qa'im and Mahdi, while the Fatimid rulers claimed to be descendants of his, continuing the line of the Imamate. Until the coming of the Qa'im, the *batin* must be kept secret. Under the Fatimids, Isma'ili cosmology absorbed a great deal of Greek thought, such as the idea that God is unknowable and the first emanation from God is the Intellect (*'aql*) from which all other beings are derived.

The Fatimid caliphate began its decline in the middle of the eleventh century, with the loss in 1049 of much of its territory in the centre and west of north Africa, and the invasion of Syria and Palestine by Turkish forces and the Crusaders, although Isma'ili doctrine was at this time extending its influence in Yemen, India and central Asia. In 1094, a succession dispute split the Fatimid Isma'ilis into two factions, the Musta'li and Nizari.

The Musta'li supported the caliphs in Egypt. In 1130, this branch split again, with one group, the Hafizi, continuing to support the Fatimid caliphate but disappearing after the fall of that caliphate in 1171. The other branch, the Tayyibis, recognized as their Imam and caliph the infant Abul-Qasim Tayyib, who went into occultation in 1132; ever since, this branch has had no revealed Imam. Leadership of the Tayyibis was transferred to Yemen under a series of Da'i Mutlaqs (missionaries in charge of the movement, see pp. 170–1). After a period of residence in the Yemen, the Da'i Mutlaq moved to India in about 1567. They became known in India as Bohras. There was a further split in 1591 into the Sulaymani Bohras, who remained mostly in Yemen (their headquarters are at Najran in south Saudi Arabia on the border of Yemen and they are also found in the Haraz mountain area of Yemen) with a few followers in Baroda, Mumbai and Hyderabad in India (600,000 in all); and the Dawudi (Dawoodi) Bohras, who are mostly to be found in the Indian provinces of Gujarat and Maharashtra (their headquarters are in Mumbai), in south Arabia, the Persian Gulf, East Africa and Burma (one million in all). There have been a number of minor splits in Dawudi Isma'ilism, such as the Alavi Bohras (in 1625, headquartered in Vadodara, Gujarat). The Musta'ili Tayyibis have been chief among the Isma'ilis in maintaining the interest that the Fatimid Isma'ilis had in cosmology and philosophy.

The other main division of the Isma'ilis, the Nizaris, rejected the Fatimid caliphs after 1094. They were led by Hasan al-Sabbah (died 1124), who claimed to be the *hujjah* (literally 'proof', the representative) of the rightful Imam, Nizar, who was imprisoned in Egypt. Al-Sabbah was based in the fortress of Alamut in the Qazvin area; most of the Isma'ilis in Iraq and Iran, and eventually Syria, followed him. In the face of repeated attacks from the Saljuq Empire, the Nizaris established themselves in a chain of fortresses across Iran, Iraq and Syria. The Nizaris focused on the doctrine of the Imamate, developing particularly the idea of the special ability of the Imam to give authoritative, divinely-inspired, teaching (ta'lim). Hasan al-Sabah appointed Buzurg-Ummid to succeed him; he in turn was succeeded by his son Muhammad and grandson Hasan II, who came to have the title 'Ala Dhikrihi al-Salam. In 1164, Hasan II proclaimed that the Resurrection had occurred (albeit interpreted symbolically and spiritually), that the Islamic shari'ah was no longer in force and that the Hidden Imam had appointed him caliph. Over the next few years, it was explained that the term caliph meant that Hasan was God's representative on Earth, in other words the Imam, and indeed that he was the expected Qa'im, who comes at the end of a cycle and begins a new one; thus although he appeared to have been the son of Muhammad and grandson of Buzurg-Ummid, he was in fact the descendant of Nizar and the Fatimid caliphs. Hasan was assassinated less than two years later, in 1166. Nizari Imams subsequently reinstituted the Islamic shari'ah. Hasan II's descendants ruled as Imams at Alamut until 1256 when that fortress was destroyed by the Mongols. A short time later, in 1273, the last of the Syrian Nizari fortresses was captured by Baybars, the Egyptian Mamluk ruler. Iranian and Syrian Isma'ilism was severely weakened, although a residual community survived and a number of local Nizari leaders came to power in Daylam (Gilan) and Mazandaran in the fourteenth to sixteenth centuries.

From the thirteenth century to the eighteenth century, the Nizari Imams remained in concealment. The various Nizari communities looked to local leaders for guidance and wide divergences appeared. In many places Nizari Isma'ilism camouflaged itself as Sufism, with which it already had many commonalities. Nizari Isma'ilism flourished, in particular, in the Badakhshan area in north-east Afghanistan, reaching as far as Kashgar, and in Sindh, Maharashtra and Gujarat in India, where they are known as Khojas. The Khojas had many converts from Hinduism and blended features of Hinduism into its teaching, which was largely done through hymns called *ginans*. There were however a number of splits in Nizari Isma'ilism. In the fourteenth century, the line of Nizari Imams was split into two rival lines, the Muhammad-Shahi and the Qasim-Shahi, but the former ceased in the eighteenth century. In addition, the Khoja community in India suffered a number of sectarian splits, the most important of which was the Imam-Shahi sect which began in the sixteenth century. In the fifteenth century, the Qasim-Shahi Imams based themselves in the village of Anjudan near Mahallat in Iran and were able to begin to establish contacts with the other Nizari communities and unite them. Then in the eighteenth century, the Imams moved to Kirman and were governors there. In 1841, the Nizari Imam Hasan 'Ali Shah, who was governor of Kirman and had been given the title of Agha Khan by Fath-'Ali Shah, rebelled against Muhammad Shah. He was defeated and fled, eventually reaching Mumbai (Bombay), which has remained the headquarters of the Nizari Imams ever since.

The successors of Hasan 'Ali Shah have kept the title Agha Khan and become international figures, due in no small part to the wealth made available to them by the Nizari faithful. Many Isma'ilis are successful businessmen and merchants and have a reputation for trustworthiness and philanthropy. The present Agha Khan, Shah Karim, has been very concerned with the social and economic development of poorer Isma'ili communities. The Nizaris are the largest and most widespread community of Isma'ilis. They are most numerous in India but there are also important communities in East Africa, Pakistan, Iran, Syria, Afghanistan, Central Asia and reaching into China. In modern times, there has been extensive migration to Europe, North America and other parts of the world.

It is very difficult to estimate the total world population of Isma'ilis. Figures published since 1990 range from two million to twenty-five million. The area with the largest proportion of Nizari Isma'ilis in the population is the Badakhshan region and surrounding areas. This area spreads across south Tajikistan, north-east Afghanistan, including the Wakhan corridor, northern Pakistan and into western China. Although a large area, it is very sparsely populated. Maximum estimates of the Nizari population would be: most of the Badakhshan province of Afghanistan (700,000), one-third of the Pakistan province of Gilgit-Baltistan (700,000), the adjoining Khowar district (200,000), three-quarters of the Kuhistoni Badakhshon (Gorno-Badakhshan) province of Tajikistan (150,000) and adjoining areas in Xinjiang autonomous region of China (50,000). In the rest of Afghanistan and Pakistan, there may be as many as a million Isma'ilis (mainly in north-east Afghanistan and Sindh). In India, there are economically important but numerically small populations of Khojas, mainly in Maharashtra, Rajasthan, Gujerat and Andra Pradesh (Hyderabad), numbering two million at most. In the rest of the world, there are small pockets of Isma'ilis in Iran, Syria, Lebanon, East Africa, and in recent years, in Britain, Canada, United States, Australia and other countries in the West, which probably number no more than one million in all. Thus the total for Nizari Isma'ilis is no more than seven million. To this can be added some two million from the two branches of the Musta'ili Isma'ilis. This gives a maximum total of nine million Isma'ilis.

Druze

There was one further major schism among the Isma'ilis: the Daraziyyah or Druze. In about 1017, during the reign of the Fatimid caliph al-Hakim, some of the Isma'ilis began to attribute divinity to him. Although the movement is named after Muhammad al-Darazi, it was in fact an Iranian named Hamzah, and his successor Baha al-Din al-Muqtana, who developed the doctrine and who, along with al-Hakim, are the main authors of the Druze scripture, the *Rasa'il al-Hikmah* (the epistles of wisdom). Al-Hakim mysteriously disappeared in 1021 and is expected by the Druze to return and initiate a new era. Hamzah also disappeared and the movement was led by al-Muqtana, who withdrew from society in 1037 but continued to send out letters until 1043. At this time, all active missionary work ceased and the community fell into a mode of passively waiting for the return of al-Hakim and Hamzah that has continued to the present day. The movement disappeared in Egypt but became established among the Isma'ilis of western Syria. Although severely persecuted by the Fatimids and later by the various Sunni rulers of the area, it has survived until the present day.

There was much inter-family conflict among the Druze and a long-standing feud with the Christian Maronite community. In the seventeenth century, many Druze moved into the Hawran highlands south of Damascus, which became known as Jabal al-Daruz. A number of Druze shaykhs set up semi-autonomous fiefdoms and between 1921 and 1936, the French set up a Jabal al-Daruz state in Syria.

The Druze call themselves the Banu Ma'ruf (the sons of beneficence) or more commonly the Muwahhidun (the mono-theists), because they worship the One God, of whom al-Hakim is the incarnation or manifestation (*tajalli*) and only through al-Hakim can human beings purify themselves. Islam and its *shari'ah* are regarded as abrogated (and so they do not carry out the Muslim daily obligatory prayer, fast, or make the pilgrimage to Mecca). Thus the Druze do not regard themselves as Muslims and are not so regarded by most Muslims. They believe in re-incarnation or transmigration of souls and in the predetermina-tion of all matters by God.

The social structure of the Druze community has gradually evolved. Its present form consists of an elite called the *'uqqal* (singular *'aqil*, sages, about 20% of all Druze), who have been initiated into the secret truths of the religion. From among this group, the most learned and pious are called *ajawid* (the magnanimous) or shaykhs. Those not initiated are called *juhhal* (singular *jahil*, ignorant ones). The Druze have a strict moral code, emphasizing mutual help among the members of the community, sincerity and truthfulness, although dissimulation of their beliefs (*taqiyyah*) to others is permissible. The *'uqqal* keep to even stricter codes of behaviour. Women have a large measure of equality within marriage, which is monogamous, and they can become *'uqqal*. The Druze do not marry anyone outside the community and no one can convert into the community.

At present the Druze consist of a community of about a million, spread among south-west Syria (Hawran/Jabal al-Daruz region, 500,000), south Lebanon (the Chouf and Jabal al-Shaykh regions, 300,000), north Israel (120,000) and small communities in Jordan and the rest of the world.

'Alawi (Nusayri, Alawite)

The 'Alawis are a religious community that until 1920 was usually called the Nusayris, named after Muhammad ibn Nusayr al-Numayri (or Namiri, ninth century), a follower of the tenth Imam 'Ali al-Naqi and eleventh Imam Hasan al-'Askari. He regarded the Imams as divine and was backed by the powerful Shi'i Banu al-Furat family. Successive leaders of the movement developed other aspects of the doctrine in Kufah until al-Khasibi (died about 969) took the movement to north Syria, ruled by the Shi'i Hamdanid dynasty from their capital at Aleppo. In Iraq and Syria, the Nusayris were in dispute with another Shi'i Gnostic group, the Ihqaqis, followers of Ahmad ibn Ihqaq (died 899). This conflict continued until at least the thirteenth century but after that, the Ihqaqis disappeared from history. Under the leadership of Maymun Tabarani (died 1034), the Nusayris relocated to the Lattakia area where the movement was adopted by a local dynasty and the religion spread among the villages of the hills behind Lattakia, known as the Jabal al-Ansariyyah or Jabal al-Nusayriyyah. From there, the movement spread along the north Syrian coast. The region came under Crusader and Isma'ili rule until finally being conquered by Salah al-Din in 1188. Subsequently, the Nusayris were persecuted by the successive Sunni rulers of their lands. For a time in the nineteenth century, the Ottomans allowed them a certain degree of self-rule but then imposed central authority on them again.

After World War I, the French Mandate authorities proposed the setting up of an Alawite state centred on Lattakia as part of their plans for Syria. An 'Alawi region was given autonomy from 1920 but reincorporated into Syria in 1937 prior to independence in 1946. At this time a large number of 'Alawi fighters joined the Syrian army. In 1963, a group of army officers, including some 'Alawis, seized power and established the Ba'th party. Further coups put Hafez al-Assad, the leading 'Alawi army officer, into power in 1970 and he was declared president of the country the following year. There has been Sunni resistance to the 'Alawi seizure of power ever since, with a major uprising in 1982 in Hama and another beginning in 2011. In addition, in 1938 the Sanjak (administrative district) of Alexandretta (Iskenderun) became an independent state and a republic. After nine months, in 1939, the French gave the northern part of the west Syria coast, centred on Iskenderun and the town of Antakya (Antioch), to Turkey. This area contained many 'Alawis. They have continued to speak Arabic (although the younger people now speak Turkish) and are known as Arap Alevileri (Arab Alevis) to distinguish them from the much larger number of Turkish Alevis in Turkey. In 1974, the 'Alawis obtained a legal decision that they are a legitimate Muslim people from Imam Musa al-Sadr, the Twelver religious leader in Lebanon. The 'Alawis have in recent decades come much closer to orthodox Twelver Shi'i Islam, mainly through the influence of the Islamic

Republic of Iran. 'Alawi students study at Qom and at Twelver institutions set up in Damascus.

The doctrines of the 'Alawis incorporate elements of Islamic, Christian, Jewish, Greek and Persian thought. They believe that from the time when the Souls of Light, the 'Alawis, fell from heaven after rebelling against God and took on human form until the time of 'Ali, there were seven manifestations of God, which called upon them to return to God. Each manifestation consists of a *ma'na* (meaning or essence) accompanied by two lesser figures: the Name (*ism*) or Veil (*hijab*) and the Gate (*bab*). In the Islamic dispensation these three figures were 'Ali, Muhammad and Salman the Persian respectively. After 'Ali, each of the Imams of the Twelver line was successively the *ma'na* and Ibn Nusayr was the *bab* of the eleventh Imam and of the Hidden Twelfth Imam. It was Ibn Nusayr who was given the true secret teaching of the Imam. Human beings are condemned to metempsychosis (*tanasukh*), being reborn as other human beings or, if they have opposed the leader of the 'Alawis, as animals, until they recognize the *ma'na* and then are liberated and can take their rightful place as Souls of Light, eventually attaining the Divine Presence. Occasionally these Souls of Light come to Earth as prophets or 'Alawi shaykhs. The 'Alawis call themselves the Muwahhidun (monotheists) and are divided into an inner circle (*al-khassah*), who are fully initiated into the doctrines of the group, and the rest of the believers (*al-'ammah*).

One of the main practices of the 'Alawis is that of *ziyarah*, visiting the tombs of prophets and saints to benefit from the blessings (*barakah*) of those places. Among the most important of these is the shrine of Khidr at Samandağ, near Antakya. Specific rituals and laws surround the *ziyarah*. The 'Alawis celebrate the Persian New Year (Nevruz, Naw-Ruz), Christian festivals such as Christmas, and Shi'i festivals such as 'Id al-Ghadir. The 'Alawis are found among the Arabs of north-west Syria (three million;

12% of the population of Syria), south Turkey (700,000–1,000,000 in and around Antakya) and north Lebanon (120,000 in and around Tripoli).

Alevi

It is quite common to find the designation 'Alevi' being applied indiscriminately to a number of very different communities in Turkey. Often included in this designation are Arabic-speaking 'Alawis from around Antakya (see above), Azeri orthodox Twelver Shi'is whose presence in Turkey is the result of migration from Azerbeijan, Kurdish groups who are closer to the Ahl-e Haqq (see below) and the largest group, which is mainly ethnically Turkish but not a uniform group; it probably arose from the coming together of a number of religious strands. It is with these last two groups that this section of the chapter is concerned.

Insofar as these can be distinguished, the following are among the strands that have gone into making up Alevism. For the influx of Turkish peoples into Anatolia in the thirteenth century (fleeing ahead of the Mongol hordes), Gnostic Shi'i Islam appears to have been an attractive religious doctrine. As early as the thirteenth century, one finds Gnostic features among the Babai movement that rose in revolt against the Seljuks under the leadership of Baba Resulullah Ishak in about 1240. Another strand in the Alevi movement was the Qizilbash followers of the Safavid order, which became the Safavid dynasty of Iran. The Safavids had many followers in eastern Anatolia in the fifteenth century, who were severely persecuted and even massacred when the Ottomans began a campaign against Safavid Iran in the sixteenth century. Another strand in the formation of present-day Alevism were members of the Bektashi Sufi order (see below). In addition, Kurdish Alevis are linked to the Ahl-e Haqq of Iran and Iraq and it is probable that Isma'ili and 'Alawi influences also had a part in the development of Turkish Alevism. There is a strong influence from Sufism and almost certainly elements of native folk religion and central Asian shamanism as well. Accordingly, the beliefs of Alevis vary from one group to another. In general, Muhammad and 'Ali are regarded as a unity emanating the energy of God. The Twelve Imams are also venerated. The Alevis do not have mosques and, unless observing *taqiyyah*, do not practise the Islamic prayers or fast. Individual Alevis are expected to put themselves under the spiritual guidance of a *mürşhid*, *dede* or *rehber*. An Alevi is, however, not so much identified by beliefs as by participation in community rituals. The religion today focuses on communal religious worship, *âyin-i cem*, which includes Sufi features such as *dhikr* (repetitive chanting, literally remembrance [of God]) and *sama'* (dance, literally listening) and is held in a communal gathering place called a *cem evi*. The composition and recital of poetry in Turkish is also highly valued. In addition, there are various commemorations of Alevi saints and Shi'i Imams.

The Alevis and proto-Alevis have been persecuted in Anatolia from the time of the suppression of the Qizilbash and have practised *taqiyyah*. When Mustafa Kemal Atatürk founded the Republic of Turkey in 1923, his promise of secularization gave hope to the Alevis, but in the end this proved to be only a bureaucratization of Sunni control and the attempt by the state to impose religious homogeneity. When the one-party system ended in 1946, many Alevis were attracted to socialist parties because of their own low status in society. This coincided with the mass migration of people from the rural areas (where Alevis had lived) into the large cities. Following the 1980 military coup, which saw a reimposition of the Atatürk vision and the subsequent rise of politicized Sunnism, the Alevis attitude changed and, instead of *taqiyyah*, they now insisted on their own identity and political voice. This led to conflict, culminating in 1993, when radical Sunnis set fire to a hotel hosting an Alevi cultural event in Sivas, killing thirty-three Alevis. The situation caused many Alevis to migrate to Germany. The coming to power of the Islamic Justice and Development Party (AKP) in 2002 signalled a change from the previously secular Turkish state. For the Alevis, the manner in which the AKP has imposed a conservative Sunni interpretation of Islam with the excuse of maintaining national unity means that little has changed from the Atatürk period. The general term 'Alevi' in Turkey often includes individuals who are orthodox Twelver Shi'is and the Arab 'Alawis. If these are excluded, the Alevis constitute some 10–20 million people in Turkey. They are mostly ethnic Turks (mainly in the eastern half of central Anatolia) but 20% are ethnic Kurds, mainly in the provinces of Tunceli and Elazığ. Most large cities in Turkey have an Alevi community. There is also a large Alevi community in Germany (500,000).

The Bektashi order

The Bektashis can be regarded as a Sufi order that has strong elements of Gnostic Shi'i Islam. Its development was closely linked to that of Alevism, in particular with regard to the influence of movements such as the thirteenth-century Babai order and the fourteenth-century Hurufis (see pp. 144–5), such that in Turkey, it cannot be regarded as separate from Alevism. This brief survey is mainly therefore about the Bektashis in the Balkans.

Among the beliefs of the Bektashi order are that 'Ali is elevated to a divine trinity of God, Muhammad and 'Ali and the Twelve Imams are venerated. The Bektashi order spread throughout the Ottoman domains, establishing itself particularly strongly in Bosnia and Albania (especially south Albania). It also became the main religious movement among the Janissaries, the crack regiment of the Ottoman army. With the abolition and suppression of the Janissary corps in 1826, the Bektashi order was also persecuted. In Turkey, the suppression was renewed when Mustafa Atatürk banned all Sufi orders in 1925 and the order moved its headquarters to Tirana in Albania. In the Balkans, the order suffered a further period of suppression during the communist era. Since the end of communism, the order has been restored and some 20% of the population of Albania (approximately 600,000 people) have links with it. There are communities of Bektashis in Bulgaria, also called Alians, Kuzulbashis (Qizilbash) and Alevis. They live mainly in the north-east of the country, in the Razgrad, Sliven and Silistra provinces, and number some 50,000. In Macedonia, however, the order is not officially recognized and its main lodge or retreat (*tekke*) was taken over by the officially-recognized Sunni religious authorities in 2002. The Bektashis live mainly in the Kichevo and Tetovo areas in western Macedonia and number about 5,000. There is also a small Bektashi community in Kosovo, centred on Prizren and Gjakova (Ðakovica) in south-west Kosovo. Because of the marked veneration of the Imam 'Ali and the Twelver Shi'i Imams in the order, the Iranian government has made a major effort to spread its version of Twelver Shi'i Islam among Albanians in recent years.

Ahl-e Haqq or Yarsan

The designation Ahl-e Haqq or Yarsan does not refer to a single religious group with a clearly defined set of doctrines and practices. It is more a label given to a grouping of loosely-knit movements. The history of this movement is hard to evaluate since it has largely been secretive, and so there are few external references to the group. Its internal accounts are largely mythic and of limited use for reconstructing a history. The traditional view is that the movement was founded by Sultan Sohak (Ishaq, Sahak), who claimed descent from the Twelver Imam Musa al-Kazim, was born in Iraqi Kurdistan in the late fourteenth century and moved to the Avroman area in Iranian Kurdistan. But elements of the tradition possibly go back to a certain Baba Khushin and the poet Baba Tahir in eleventh-century Luristan. It may even be that the origins of the Ahl-e Haqq go back to the split between orthodox Twelver Shi'i Islam and Gnostic Shi'ism that occurred in the tenth century (see pp. 64–5). The spread of Ahl-e Haqq teachings among the Turkomans of Azerbaijan and northern Iraq dates to the fifteenth century and was part of the spread of the teaching of the early Safavid order and the poetry of Shah Ismail. Another important figure was Khan Atash, who lived in Azerbaijan in the eighteenth century.

While Imam 'Ali occupies a high station in the Ahl-e Haqq doctrines (and their detractors call them 'Aliyullahi, those who make 'Ali to be God), it is Sultan Sohak who is regarded as having revealed the *Haqiqat* (truth), the final stage of religious development. Now, the Ahl-e Haqq await the coming of the Lord of Time and the Final Judgement. Human beings go through cycles of reincarnation or metempsychosis until they are purified. The Ahl-e Haqq gather in ceremonies that resemble Sufi assemblies, with repetitive chanting (*dhikr*) leading to states of ecstasy. Again like Sufi orders, each person must have a spiritual guide (*pir*). The Ahl-e Haqq honour all the Imams of the Twelver line but they do not keep Islamic laws, such as prayer and fasting (their fast is for three days), do not consider the Qur'an a sacred book and consider 'Ali to be above Muhammad in their religious hierarchy. They consist of about a million people mainly among the Kurds of west Iran (especially in the area around Kirmanshah), but also among some Kurds and Arabs in north Iraq and in small pockets scattered throughout Iran, especially in a band of territory from Mazandaran and Tehran, through Qazvin, Zanjan and Azerbaijan, on into the Caucasus. The exact relationship between the Ahl-e Haqq and Kurdish Alevis in Turkey cannot be determined from current research.

9

Shi'i Islam in the contemporary world

There have been many major changes in Shi'i Islam and in Shi'i communities during the twentieth and into the twenty-first centuries. The twentieth century began with Shi'i clerics stepping into the political area in Iran, supporting the Constitutional Revolution, and ended with a wide-ranging politicization of Shi'i Islam in the Islamic Revolution in Iran in 1979, and several other uprisings and revolutions in countries such as Iraq, Lebanon and Bahrain, where Shi'is have become more visible and are asserting themselves, demanding power more in keeping with their proportion of the population. There have been two major results from this. First, the emergence of Shi'i communities, inspired by the Iranian Revolution, in parts of the Islamic world such as Africa and south-east Asia where no communities existed before. Some of this has been due to the spontaneous conversion of people inspired by Khomeini and the Revolution and some to active proselytization by missionaries sponsored by the Islamic Republic of Iran. The second result of the Iranian Revolution has been the emergence in the twenty-first century of a severe Sunni backlash in most parts of the Islamic world, resulting in a marked increase in Sunni-Shi'i conflict and violence. The situation in countries such as Syria, Iraq and the Yemen is changing quickly, such that anything written about the Shi'is in these countries becomes rapidly out-of-date, while the situation in other countries, such as Bahrain and Lebanon and even Iran, might change radically at any time. Despite this limitation, in this chapter, after two introductory sections looking at the world Shi'i population and the world Shi'i religious leadership, there is a survey of the main countries where Shi'is live. (For information about Shi'i groups other than Twelvers in these countries, see also the previous chapter.)

The world Shi'i population

It is impossible to be sure how many Shi'is there are in the world, since most countries do not ask detailed religious questions in their census returns. Even those that do sometimes do not differentiate between Shi'i and Sunni Muslims. In some countries, Shi'is may be hesitant about revealing their identity because of possible persecution. In some countries, such as Turkey, Syria and Yemen, there is the additional complication that most of the Shi'is are not Twelver Shi'is. With all of these reservations, and with the knowledge that all estimates must therefore be highly provisional, Table 6 offers an estimate of the Twelver Shi'i and other Shi'i populations in the world in 2014.

The religious leadership

At the beginning of the twentieth century, Najaf was the world centre of Shi'i scholarship and the leading *mujtahids* there played an important role in supporting the Constitutional Revolution in Iran. This group included Mulla Muhammad Fadil Sharabiyani (died 1904), Shaykh Muhammad Hasan Mamaqani (died 1905), Mirza Husayn ibn Khalil (Khalili) Tihrani (died 1908) and Mulla Muhammad Kazim known as Akhund Khurasani (died 1911). Khurasani was in many ways

Table 6 The Shi'i world – statistics

Country	Total Population (millions)	Twelver Shi'is (millions)	Twelver Shi'is as percentage of population	Percentage of total world Twelvers	Other Shi'is (millions)
Iran	78	69	90%	43%	1 (H, I)
Pakistan	189	28	15%	15%	1.5 (I)
India	1272	25	2%	15%	3 (I)
Iraq	35	21	63%	13%	1 (H)
Azerbaijan	9.5	7.5	80%	4%	0
Afghanistan	32	4	12%	2%	1 (I)
Turkey	76	3	4%	2%	16 (V, A, B)
Saudi Arabia	29	2	7%	1%	2 (Z, I)
Lebanon	4.5	2	40%	1%	0.3 (D, A)
Nigeria	178	2	1%	1%	0
Indonesia	254	2	<1%	1%	0
Tanzania	51	1	2%		0.1 (I)
Egypt	84	0.8	1%		1 (I)
Bahrain	1.3	0.6	45% (60%)		0
UAE	9	0.6	7% (15%)		0
Kuwait	3.2	0.5	16% (40%)		0
Tajikistan	8	0.3	3%		0.3 (I)
Syria	24	0.2	1%		3 (A, D, I)
Qatar	1.8	0.2	10%		0
Yemen	25	0.1	<1%		11 (Z, I)
Other Asian Countries		1.5			0.7 (I, D)
Other African countries		1			0.7 (I)
Europe		1			2 (B, L, I, D, A)
Americas		0.7			0.4 (B, I, L, D, A)
Australasia		0.3			0.1 (I, L, D)

In this table, estimates are given for 2014. In the Gulf states, a large proportion of the population are non–citizen immigrant workers. Therefore percentages are also given in parentheses of Shi'i citizens as a proportion of all citizens. A more detailed analysis of these figures can be found in the relevant sections of this chapter. Information on 'Other Shi'is' can be found in Chapter 8.

B (Bektashi), D (Druze), H (Ahl–e Haqq), I (Isma'ili), L (Alevi), A (Alawi), Z (Zaydi).

Table 6 (contd.)

		Twelver Shi'is as percentage	Other Shi'is as percentage	All Shi'is as percentage
World Twelver Shi'i population	175,000,000			
World Other Shi'is population	44,000,000			
World All Shi'is population	219,000,000	80%	20%	
Total world Muslim population	1,600,000,000	11%	2.8%	13.8%
Total world population	7,250,000,000	2.4%	0.6%	3%

See Bibliography for further details of the sources used for the statistics in this table.

the most important of this group, famed for his teaching methods and the author of an important text, the *Kifayat al-Usul*. Twice he mobilized the Shi'is in Iraq to go to Iran in support of the Constitutional Revolution but circumstances intervened to prevent the march (on the second occasion, it was his death that halted the march). However, it appears that towards the end of Khurasani's life, many clerics became worried about the amount of secularization occurring in Iran as a result of the Constitutional Revolution and, especially after Shaykh Fadlullah Nuri's execution by the Constitutionalists in Tehran in 1909, the sentiment in Najaf turned against Khurasani and Constitutionalism.

World War I caused a major change in circumstances. By this time, following the death of the other clerics mentioned above, Sayyid Kazim Yazdi (died 1919), the author of *al-Urwat al-Wuthqa*, a work on jurisprudence, had become the leading

Shi'i cleric. He was in many ways the opposite of his colleagues; he had been against the Constitutional Revolution and had led the opposition to Khurasani. With his death, there was another major change in orientation of the Shi'i leadership since the main focus of his successor as leading *marja'*, Mirza Muhammad Taqi Shirazi (died 1920), a resident of Karbala, was his implacable opposition to the British occupation and mandate government in Iraq. He even issued a decree calling for a *jihad* against them. The next *marja' al-taqlid*, Shaykh Fathullah Isfahani, known as Shaykh al-Shari'ah (died 1920), survived his predecessor by only four months.

An event of great importance in Shi'i history was the transfer of Shaykh 'Abdul-Karim Ha'iri-Yazdi (died 1937) from Sultanabad (Arak), where he had been teaching, to Qom in 1920. He set up a teaching centre there and attracted many Iranian students. He was one of a number of clerics who were recognized as being *marja' al-taqlids* after Shaykh al-Shari'ah. Apart from him, there was a group of *marja' al-taqlids* resident in Najaf: Shaykh 'Ali Kashif al-Ghita (died 1926), Shaykh Muhammad Husayn Na'ini (died 1936) and Shaykh Diya al-Din 'Iraqi (died 1942). As they died, one after the other, Sayyid Abul-Hasan Isfahani (died 1946) became recognized as the sole *marja'*. His successor, Sayyid Aqa Husayn Tabataba'i Qummi, a resident of Karbala, survived him by only three months, dying in February 1947. At this time, Ayatollah Burujirdi (died 1961), who had come to Qom from Burujird and begun teaching there two years earlier, was recognized as sole *marja'*. From the 1930s to the 1950s, Najaf declined in numbers (from 8,000 to 2,000 students) and importance as a centre for Shi'i studies, while Qom correspondingly rose (from 1,000 to 5,000 students). By the end of Burujirdi's fourteen years of leadership, most Iranians and Turks were going to Qom, although Arabs and some Indians continued to go to Najaf.

Burujirdi played a very quietist role politically but towards the end of his life was moved to speak out against the Baha'is in 1955 and against the land reform proposals of the shah in 1960. After Burujirdi, the Shi'i world again entered a period when there were several competing *marja's* and this situation has continued to the present day. Initially these *marja's* were Ayatollahs Shari'atmadari (died 1986), Mar'ashi-Najafi (died 1990) and Gulpaygani (died 1993) at Qom; Ayatollah Muhammad Hadi Milani at Mashhad (died 1975); Ayatollah Ahmad Khwansari (died 1985) in Tehran; and Ayatollahs Abu-al-Qasim Khu'i (died 1992), 'Abdul-Hadi Shirazi (died 1961) and Muhsin al-Hakim (died 1970) in Najaf. Al-Hakim received the broadest support but was unable to consolidate his position sufficiently, especially among the clerics of Qom, to become regarded as the sole *marja'*.

The events of the 1979 Islamic Revolution in Iran catapulted Khomeini to prominence but he was never able to gain the position of sole *marja'*, even within Iran. His popularity, and the attention given to him by the media have however, resulted in a major change in the ethos and discourse of Shi'i Islam. While the function of the *marja'* is still seen as providing answers to the practical problems of the everyday life of individual Shi'is (and most *marja' al-taqlids* have now set up websites from which one can ask questions of the *marja'* and receive electronic *fatwas*), most *marja's* have been forced to make pronouncements on a wide range of social and political issues, well outside the range of the usual discourse of *mujtahids* prior to Khomeini.

While in theory each Shi'i individual is free to choose a *marja'*, in practice, most Shi'is follow a senior cleric in their place of residence, and these senior clerics in turn follow the senior clerics in the major centres of Shi'i scholarship where they trained. The choosing of a person as a *marja'* develops by consensus among the senior figures at the major centres of Shi'i scholarship, Najaf, Karbala, Qom and Mashhad. There is no nomination or voting procedure; individuals emerge through a process of acclamation and consensus.

There have been a number of important developments in the institution of the *marja'* in recent decades. It has become possible for people to divide the function of being *marja'* between two different *marja'*s; this occurred particularly with Khomeini, where people followed him in political matters while they followed another *marja'* in ritual and other personal matters. This has led to an increasing trend towards individuals choosing the *fatwas* of different *marja'*s according to their liking. Although in Usuli theory it was not considered permissible to follow a dead *marja'*, it has become increasingly the case that people continue to follow a major *marja'* such as Khomeini or al-Khu'i even after their death.

At the major centres of Shi'i scholarship, the main Grand Ayatollahs appear to be Sayyid Ali Sistani (born 1930), Bashir al-Najafi (born 1942, originally from Pakistan), Mohammad Ishaq Fayyad (born 1930, originally from Afghanistan), and Sayyid Muhammed Sa'id al-Hakim (born 1936) in Najaf; Nasir Makarim Shirazi (born 1927), Hossein Vahid Khurasani (born 1921), Sayyid Mahmud Shahrudi (born 1948), 'Abdullah Jawadi Amuli (born 1933), Lutfullah Safi Gulpaygani (born 1919), Sayyid Kazim Ha'iri (born 1938), Sayyid Musa Shubayri Zanjani (born 1927), Sayyid Sadiq Shirazi (born 1942), Muhaqqiq Kabuli (born 1928, from Afghanistan), Bayat Zanjani (born 1942), Sayyid Muhammad Sadiq Rawhani (born 1926) and Yusif Sani'i (born 1937) in Qom (the last two have been formally stripped of their title as a result of their opposition to the government of Iran but their followers reject this); Muhammad Taqi al-Mudarrisi (born 1945) in Karbala; and of course Sayyid Ali Khamene'i (born 1939) in Tehran. As with Khomeini, although many follow Khamene'i in political matters, there are comparatively few who consider him learned enough to follow in religious matters. Previously, it used to be considered that a Grand Ayatollah had to be resident in one of the main centres of Shi'i learning: Qom, Najaf and to a lesser extent Mashhad and Karbala. Now there are individuals claiming this title and living far afield; for example Muhammad Husayn Najafi (born 1932) in Sargodha (Pakistani Punjab); Muhammad Asif Muhsini (born 1936) in Afghanistan; Sayyid Rida Husayni Nassab (born 1960) in Toronto, Canada; Abdul-Latif Birri (born 1948) in Dearborn, near Detroit, United States; as well as others in Iran, such as Sayyid 'Ali Muhammad Dast-Ghayb (born 1935) in Shiraz.

In all it would appear that Sayyid Ali Sistani has the largest number of followers in the Shi'i world and should be accredited as the leading *marja' al-taqlid*. It is galling to the leadership in Tehran, and Khamene'i in particular, that he rejects the concept of *Velayat-e Faqih*, as interpreted by the Iranian leadership. He has avoided engagement in politics as much as possible and only made pronouncements when events in Iraq have demanded some response. In this, Sistani has followed the precedent of his teacher al-Khu'i and most of the major Shi'i clerics who preceded Khomeini. Sistani is however elderly and it is difficult to see what will happen after him. A number of clerics favourable to the *Velayat-e Faqih* are lining up to take Sistani's position of pre-eminence, several of them evidently being groomed and financed by the Islamic Republic of Iran.

One of the features of recent Twelver Shi'i history is what may be called 'title inflation' (the process whereby, over time, a title increases in the numbers of those holding it and consequently decreases in value). Since there is no formal institutional way of conferring titles, the number of holders of the title given to the highest ranking Shi'i clerics has gradually inflated over the years and a new grander title has had to be found which can then be assigned to those who truly are the highest ranking clerics. When the title 'Hujjat al-Islam' was given to Mirza-ye Shirazi, the highest ranking *mujtahid* of the Shi'i world in the late nineteenth century, it was a great honour and intended to indicate his overall superiority to the other *mujtahids* of his era. Today, the title has lost most of its value; tens of thousands of Shi'i clerics now hold the title Hujjat al-Islam. It is being given to clerics who have passed only the initial stages of training in the religious colleges, even before they obtain their final certificates. Similarly, from about the 1930s onwards, a new title was devised for the very highest ranking clerics, that of 'Ayatollah' (the sign of God). At the time it was a bold move, since it is one of the titles of the Hidden Imam and to give it to another human being was an indication of the very great honour being given to the recipient and was presumably intended to stop 'title inflation'. Now however, the title has lost value and there are thousands of Ayatollahs. Every cleric who has achieved their final certificate of completion of training now calls himself an Ayatollah. So, in the last decades of the twentieth century, a new designation emerged: 'Ayatullah al-'Uzma' (the most mighty sign of God, usually translated as Grand Ayatollah) for the highest-ranking Shi'i clerics. At first there were only about half a dozen in the world. However, we are currently seeing this title inflate as well. It is difficult to keep up with the numbers now claiming the title of Grand Ayatollah but it is well over fifty. Khomeini's assumption of the title 'Imam' can be considered to be the ultimate in title inflation and has yet to experience a loss in value. Although this title is usually explained away by saying that it only means 'leader', in the fevered atmosphere of the Islamic Revolution in Iran, there is little doubt that for many people at the emotional level, it meant the Imam, in the full Shi'i sense of that word. It should be noted that the application of the titles of Ayatollah and Grand Ayatollah to scholars from before the twentieth century in printed and online lists and biographical literature is retrospective; there is no indication that these individuals were called by these titles in their own time. At the other end of the spectrum, because the words '*akhund*' and '*mulla*' have over the years deflated in value and are often used somewhat pejoratively now, there has been an increasing use of the word *ruhani* (*rawhani*, literally: spiritual) or *'alim* to designate members of the clerical class.

Over the years there have been several efforts to bridge the divide between Sunnis and Shi'is. One of the most successful was the Centre for Islamic Ecumenical Studies (Dar al-Taqrib al-Madhahib al-Islamiyyah) established at al-Azhar University in Cairo (widely regarded as the most important centre of Sunni learning in the world) in 1948. The activities of this centre culminated in a *fatwa* signed by Shaykh Mahmud Shaltut, the Shaykh al-Azhar, on 6 July 1959, declaring Twelver Shi'i Islam as a school that it is legitimate for Muslims to follow alongside the four Sunni schools of law.

Following the 1979 Islamic Revolution in Iran, Khomeini made considerable efforts to bring Sunnis and Shi'is closer together (in opposition to the 'Great Satan' in the West, that is the United States of America). One result of these reconciliation efforts was the Amman Declaration of November 2004. This declared that eight schools (*madhhabs*) were legitimate schools of Islam and no Muslim could declare anyone following these schools to be an infidel or apostate. These eight schools consisted of the four Sunni schools of law, Twelver and Zaydi Shi'i Islam and the Ibadi and Zahiri schools. Signatories to the agreement also agreed not to declare practitioners of the Ash'ari creed, Sufism and Salafism as apostates or infidels. The Declaration was signed eventually by more than five hundred senior Islamic clerics and senior government officials representing Muslims in more than fifty countries.

Since the start of the twenty-first century however, any Sunni-Shi'i *rapprochement* that may have been achieved has been more than reversed with the increasing tensions and violence in many parts of the Islamic world. The overthrow of centuries of Sunni dominance in Iraq and the installation of a Shi'i government there, Shi'i uprisings in Bahrain and Yemen, as well as a more assertive political position taken by Lebanon's Shi'is, have led to an attempt to reverse this Shi'i tide by suppressing Bahrain's Shi'is, overthrowing Syria's 'Alawi Shi'i-led government that supports the Lebanese Shi'is and rolling back the advance of the Zaydi Shi'i Houthi rebels in Yemen. As a consequence, there are now proxy wars being fought by the two main protagonists, Shi'i Iran and Sunni Saudi Arabia, in Iraq, Syria and to some extent in Yemen, while there is increasing Sunni-Shi'i violence in Pakistan, Lebanon and Bahrain. That in turn has led to anti-Shi'i rhetoric and action both by Sunni governments and by non-governmental Salafi and Wahhabi movements in many countries across Africa and Asia and much anti-Wahhabi and some anti-Sunni rhetoric and action in Iran.

Iran

The role of Shi'i clerics in the Constitutional Revolution of 1906 is in need of reappraisal. In the literature about this Revolution, much emphasis has been placed on the support given to the revolution by some of the senior clerics in Najaf (Akhund Khurasani, Mirza Husayn Khalili and Mulla 'Abdullah Mazandarani) and Tehran (Sayyid 'Abdullah Bihbihani and Sayyid Muhammad Tabataba'i). They argued that the Constitution is mandated by Islam and should be supported by all Muslims. While there is no doubt that the support of these figures gave legitimacy to and rallied support for the Constitutionalists, it should not be forgotten that senior figures, such as Sayyid Muhammad Kazim Yazdi in Najaf and Shaykh Fadlullah Nuri in Tehran, opposed the Constitution and supported the reactionary Muhammad 'Ali Shah. Nuri for example, although he briefly supported the Constitution in 1906, when he thought it would increase the power of the clerical class, later held that the establishment of the Constitution was adopting a reform advocated in the Baha'i holy book, which would weaken the *shari'ah* and increase European penetration of Iran. He felt that the laws of the nation should be dictated by the *shari'ah* and not by parliamentary assembly. Similarly in the towns of Iran, some clerics supported the revolution and others opposed it.

The influence of Nuri and other anti-Constitution clerics caused serious flaws to be embedded in the Constitution that was signed into law. Instead of the equality of all Iranian citizens before the law that had been the initial aim of the Revolution, the Constitution embodied legal disabilities for members of the minority religions and completely denied the Baha'is a legal existence. The fact that a large religious minority had been excluded from the Constitution, and thus effectively excluded from Iranian society, was a poisonous precedent for the next hundred years. Over the succeeding decades, it meant that conspiracy theories could be concocted and published without fear of contradiction, linking the Baha'is as 'enemies within' to external powers such as Britain and Russia, and later America and Israel. It led to anyone who proposed political or social reform or a campaign against corruption being accused of being a Baha'i and thus being silenced. It made it easier for the government to create other 'enemies within' of its opponents and violently suppress them rather than engaging them in open debate. Instead of the emergence of a public sphere of discourse in which all could engage openly and honestly, the sphere of national public debate tilted towards one that was imbued with fear, the main protagonists often being demagogues and much of the time the agenda a series of exaggerated conspiracy theories. The division in Iran created by clerics such as Nuri also played a major role in weakening the Constitutional Revolution and plunging the country into chaos in the second decade of the twentieth century.

This chaos ended with the *coup d'etat* that brought Reza Khan (1878–1944) to power in 1921. When he proposed the establishment of a republic in 1924–5, the senior clerics in Iran, seeing that Atatürk's establishment of a republic in Turkey had been followed by many measures against the religious establishment, opposed the idea. Reza Khan complied, caused parliament to declare him king and then proceeded to take measures against clerical power anyway. These included regulating religious education (1929–34), enacting a civil code of law (1924–40), restricting the functioning of religious courts (1931), setting up civil courts (1932–36), transferring functions such as the registering of legal documents and property to the civil courts (1932), and prohibiting the wearing of the veil (1936). So powerful was Reza Shah that few clerics dared oppose him. One who did was Sayyid Hasan Muddaris, who opposed the shah's secularisation programme in the Iranian Parliament. He was imprisoned in 1929 and killed in 1937.

Reza Shah's forced abdication (after an invasion by Allied forces in 1941) and the succession of Muhammad Reza Shah led to a relaxation of strict controls over the clerics and they soon began to reassert their power in society. The British and the Americans, who had spear-headed the invasion of Iran, encouraged this resurgence of the clerical class because they considered it a bulwark against communism, which was becoming very influential. Some of the anti-religious measures of Reza Shah, such as the ban on the veil, were reversed. The clerics formed associations and movements and began to publish books and magazines. Several of these associations were dedicated specifically to countering the Baha'i Faith, such as the Anjuman-e Tablighat-e Islami (The Islamic Propagation Society), which published books and articles. Much more insidious in its activities was the Anti-Baha'i Society; it sent agents to disrupt Baha'i meetings and infiltrate the Baha'i community. Started in 1953 by Shaykh Mahmud Halabi (died 1998), this society later became known as the Hujjatiyyah and has been an important forum for conservative clerics since the 1979 Iranian Revolution.

Another Islamic movement that came to prominence at this time was the Fida'iyan-e Islam, formed in 1945 and led by Navvab Safavi. It had a secular leadership and a populist agenda of conservative Islam. It had great support in the bazaar and among the poorer classes, but was behind a number of assassinations between 1946 and 1951. It linked up with the right-wing National Front party of Muhammad Mosaddeq (died 1967) and the populist religious leader Ayatollah Abul-Qasim Kashani (died 1962), who in his call for greater religious control of the state was a predecessor of Khomeini. This alliance brought Mosaddeq to power as prime minister in 1951; he began a programme of ridding Iran of foreign influence, most notably by nationalizing the oil industry. He also forced the departure of the shah, who opposed him. The alliance soon fell apart, however, with Kashani and other clerics fearing the increasing influence of the communist Tudeh party on the National Front. When the shah staged his return in 1953, in an American-led coup, Ayatollah Kashani, Ayatollah Burujirdi and all the leading clerics of the country welcomed him back, having mobilized the crowds who overthrew Mosaddeq. The Fida'iyan-e Islam were ruthlessly crushed and their leader Navvab Safavi executed in January 1956.

In exchange for this clerical support, the shah allowed the clerics a free hand against the Baha'is. During Ramadan 1955, with Ayatollah Burujirdi's encouragement, a cleric named Muhammad Taqi Falsafi was allowed to broadcast vituperative sermons against the Baha'is on the national radio. This stirred up the mob and beatings, killings, looting and raping went on for several weeks throughout the country, usually incited by the clerics in each locality. The shah appeared, at first, to countenance these disturbances, probably as a useful smokescreen to hide the fact that he was in the midst of signing the Baghdad Pact (CENTO), that formally allied him with the much distrusted British and Americans. It may even have been that the shah had negotiated a secret deal whereby the clerics agreed not to agitate against such issues in return for being allowed a free hand against the Baha'is. Eventually, however, international pressure forced the shah's government to restore order.

The good relations between the shah and the clerics lasted until 1960 when Ayatollah Burujirdi felt impelled to speak out in favour of landowners against the Shah's attempt at land reform (these landowners provided a significant proportion of Burujirdi's income). Over the next few years a series of issues set the clerics against the shah: the question of women's rights and enfranchisement; the regime's foreign policy and, in particular, the close links with Israel; the growing Western cultural penetration of the country; and the increasingly totalitarian and corrupt nature of the regime. This culminated in 1963, after the death of Burujirdi, in a joint campaign by the leading clerics against the shah's reforms, resulting in violent demonstrations. It was in the course of this campaign that Khomeini first came to national attention. He was arrested, tried and sentenced to death. Only the joint proclamation by the Grand Ayatollahs of Iran elevating him to the rank of Grand Ayatollah saved him. Khomeini was exiled in 1964 and moved to Najaf in 1965, from where he began a relentless campaign against the shah.

The firm measures taken by Muhammad Reza Shah in 1963 and the activities of his secret police (SAVAK) gave some fifteen years of apparent calm. But under the surface, there were many developments. The clerics were debating how best to organize themselves so as to respond to the challenges of modernity and to the pressures of the shah's regime. The writings of some, such as Ayatollah Mahmud Talaqani (died 1979) and Ayatollah Shaykh Murtada Mutahhari (assassinated 1979) put forward a modern presentation of Islam that was very popular with students, who increasingly saw Islam as a way of protesting against the shah's regime. Muslim intellectuals such as 'Ali Shari'ati (died 1977) were advocating a more socially and politically engaged formulation of Shi'i Islam that was against the neo-colonialism of the

West but also critical of the apolitical and obscurantist stance of most clerics. There were many other intellectuals writing along similar lines, such as Abul-Hasan Bani-Sadr (born 1933) and Engineer Mahdi Bazargan (died 1995). In all, these writers paved the way for the 1979 Iranian Revolution by reassuring students and the middle classes that Islam was not irretrievably obscurantist and stuck in the past and thus creating the alliance between these liberal progressive elements and the more conservative elements among the clerics and the Bazaar that was to be such an important factor in the Revolution.

At the same time, the shah was trying to bypass the traditional clerical class by creating an alternative religious structure. The university theology faculties, as well as the government-run college, the Madrasah Sipahsalar in Tehran, produced clerics who were appointed as the *imam-jum'ahs* (Friday prayer leaders) of many of the most important mosques. In place of obligatory military service, young men could enter a government religious corps and be sent to villages to give government-approved religious training in competition with the village mullas. This was financed by the government's control of religious endowments. Moreover, legislation increasingly moved areas of public life out of the hands of clerical judges and into the secular courts. However, the shah's attempt to persuade the people that this alternative structure presented a more modern and rational Islam ultimately failed and people continued to turn to and finance the traditional clerical structures.

The 1970s saw increasing unrest caused by inflation, unemployment and the corruption of the shah's regime. Ironically, the repressive measures taken by the shah helped the religious establishment. With the suppression of all political debate, religion became the only vehicle for expressing opposition to the shah and people's discontent was increasingly expressed in the guise of traditional religious activities. Informal religious groups (*hay'ats*, see p. 155) became places where activists could gather and plan political action. Also, apart from the mosque, where a member of the clerical class would preach (using code words such as Mu'awiyah and Umayyad for the Shah and the government), there were other locations where lay preachers would expound a political platform based on their interpretation of Shi'i Islam. One of the most well-known was the Husayniyyah Irshad in Tehran where 'Ali Shari'ati preached. There were disturbances in the universities especially at Tehran and also at Qom in 1970–2. In 1973, the Husayniyyah Irshad was closed down and Shari'ati arrested. In June 1975, on the anniversary of Khomeini's arrest in 1963, there was a demonstration by religious students at the Madrasah Faydiyyah, the leading religious college in Qom, leading to its closure.

In the meantime, Khomeini kept up a stream of writings and talks, clandestinely distributed in pamphlet form and on audio-cassettes. Until 1970, Khomeini, while critical of the Shah's government, had only called for its reform. But in that year, in a series of lectures given to his students in Najaf and later published in a book, *Hokumat-e Islami* (Islamic Government), Khomeini stated that the only acceptable form of Islamic government was one headed by an expert in Islamic law (*velayat-e faqih*, see pp. 127–9).

During 1977, mainly as a result of international pressure and President Carter's human rights policy, with its attendant threat of withdrawal of American support from regimes that violated human rights, there was an easing of censorship controls. This resulted in an immediate large increase in the circulation of protest literature and heightened unrest. A series of episodes in 1977 where the police dealt brutally with ordinary people led to increasing anger. In January 1978, police fired on a crowd of demonstrators in Qom, killing up to seventy demonstrators. This set off a pattern where a crowd would gather for the fortieth-day memorial meeting for those who had been killed (a memorial on the fortieth day is an Islamic custom). The police would fire on the crowd, killing some and leading to another fortieth-day gathering. Slowly, during 1978, these fortieth-day gatherings grew in numbers and became nationwide. After a number of demonstrations to mark the end of Ramadan on 3 September 1978, the government tried to ban demonstrations. Troops fired on a large demonstration in Tehran on 8 September and killed several hundred people. After this, martial law was declared but the demonstrations grew and there was a merging of the religious and the secular political demonstrators.

In October 1978, at the shah's insistence, Iraq expelled Khomeini. He went to Paris, where he was better able to communicate with his followers in Iran and better able to present his case to the world media, which then broadcast this to Iran. At this stage, many workers went on strike, including the important oil workers. The shah tried to negotiate with Khomeni, who had now emerged as the clear leader of the revolution but he refused to negotiate. Events came to a climax during the Muslim month of Muharram, when Shi'is commemorate the martyrdom of Imam Husayn. On 10 Muharram (11 December 1978) a crowd estimated to be of one million took to the streets of Tehran and began to take over government offices. Although in a few places the troops and police fired on the crowds, many went over to the crowd's side. The Shah made a desperate move, appointing Dr Shapour Bakhtiar (died 1991), a former aide of Mossadeq, as prime minister, but this failed to stem the tide that was flowing against him and he left the country on 16 January 1979. Two weeks later on 1 February, Khomeini returned in triumph and was led through the streets of Tehran by a vast crowd. On 12 February, Bakhtiar fled abroad and Khomeini was left in complete control of the country. The *Velayat-e Faqih* had begun.

The first priority was to hold a referendum on the future government of Iran. Although liberal elements in the Revolution wanted the people to have a free choice between several types of government in the referendum, the momentum was with Khomeini and the final wording of the document gave only a choice between monarchy and an Islamic Republic. The referendum was held on 31 March 1979 and there was an overwhelming mandate for an Islamic government. There was a further struggle regarding the wording of the Constitution. The liberal elements wanted a document similar to the 1906 constitution but with the monarchy removed. However the radical elements prevailed and the final document contained provision for a supreme clerical guide, the *faqih* or *rahbar* (leader) who, together with a twelve-member Council, would supervise the election and dismissal of the president and the members of the National Assembly and could veto any legislation of the National Assembly deemed to be contrary to Islam. The Constitution was approved by a referendum in December 1979. It was, of course, a foregone conclusion that Khomeini would occupy the position of supreme clerical guide.

Interestingly however, Khomeini, despite his enormous and unchallenged power, was unable to put in place the governmental structure that he had envisaged in his book *Hokumat-e Islami* (1970, see pp. 127–9 and p. 232) where he had first outlined his idea of *Velayat-e Faqih*. He had envisaged governing in the mould of Imam 'Ali; people would come to him with questions about governance, he would give answers according to the *shari'ah* and these would then be executed. He saw no place for parliaments, parties, elections or the complex, bureaucratic, Western-oriented state apparatus of the Pahlavi era. In the end, the practicalities of power forced Khomeini to accept all these. He had to give way over the idea of party politics and having a parliament, without which he realized he could not gain the acceptance of the Iranian people for his Revolution.

After the referendum approved his Islamic Republic, he set about trying to reverse many of the concessions he had been forced to make and effectively decreed a one-party political system. This is also probably why he established, in parallel with the constitutionally established government, a revolutionary governmental structure which continues to exist. There is the traditional constitutional structure, with a prime minister and later president at its head, government ministers, the judiciary, the police and army. And then there is a parallel revolutionary structure appointed by and answerable only to Khomeini and his successor Khamene'i. At first, this structure comprised a Revolutionary Committee, set up by Khomeini in October 1978, even before his return. This has now been replaced by the Guardian Council. There are also Revolutionary Courts, Revolutionary Guards and the *basij* (a paramilitary voluntary militia) who carry out the orders of this revolutionary structure; orders that usually come directly from the supreme leader. This alternative revolutionary structure is dominated by activist clerics and often overrules the decisions of the traditional government structures and interferes with democratic processes by determining who can stand for election in the traditional structure. Clerical guides are also put into the ministries and local government to determine whether the decisions being made are compatible with revolutionary ideology. Another area where Khomeini had to give up on his original idea was his declaration that clerics should not occupy government positions but only advise. Within two years, that policy was also overturned when a cleric, Muhammad Javad Bahunar (assassinated 1981), became prime minister.

A number of events over the next few years consolidated the power of the more radical elements among the clerics: the formation of the Islamic Republican Party gave them an organized base, the structure of the Constitution gave them the power to interfere in the election processes, and the occupation of the American Embassy on 4 November 1979 placed Iran in an isolated position on the international stage. Although the liberal Bani Sadr won the presidential election held on

25 January 1980, his attempts at introducing liberal measures were blocked by Sayyid Muhammad Bihishti (assassinated 1981), the head of the Islamic Revolutionary Party, which had managed to obtain a majority in the parliamentary elections, partly by blocking rival candidates on the grounds of rejecting their Islamic credentials.

Khomeini faced opposition from a number of senior clerics who disliked what he was doing. Most prominent among them was the Grand Ayatollah Shari'atmadari. In April 1982, it was announced that a plot to overthrow the Islamic republic had been uncovered and Shari'atmadari was accused of being one of the main instigators. Later, in an unprecedented development in Shi'i history, Shari'atmadari was declared to have been formally stripped of his position as *marja' al-taqlid*. The normal criteria of religious learning for being a *marja'* had been overtaken by revolutionary politicized criteria.

One result of the 1979 Iranian Revolution is the institution-alization of the Shi'i religious structure in Iran. Previously, the ethos within the clerical structure was very informal. People advanced in their careers based on family networks, personal charisma and to some extent their learning. Individual clerics acquired titles such as Hujjat al-Islam and Ayatollah by public acclaim. A *mujtahid* could set himself up as a *mujtahid* but would only actually become one if people referred to him with their issues and questions. Increasingly, since the Revolution, these matters have become formalized and being a *mujtahid* and having titles such as Hujjat al-Islam and Ayatollah have come under institutional control.

Khomeini's period of office as the supreme leader in Iran, from 1979 until his death in 1989, was marked by events such as the taking of hostages at the American Embassy in Tehran (1979–81) to which he gave his support; his *fatwa* against Salman Rushdie (1989); the Iran–Iraq war (1980–8) which was lengthened as a result of Khomeini's refusal to end it once the Iraqi forces had been driven back; and his orders for the execution of thousands of political and religious prisoners (especially in 1988), against many of whom there was little evidence of wrong-doing. Throughout this period he maintained a hostile rhetoric against the West, while enacting measures restricting the freedom of women and against the Baha'is in Iran. Khomeni had picked Grand Ayatollah Husayn 'Ali Muntaziri (died 2009) as his successor but when he began to criticize the direction that the government was taking, and in particular when he expressed his dismay at the executions in 1988, Khomeini moved against him, removed him from his position as successor and even stripped him of his title of Grand Ayatollah in 1989.

When Khomeini died, in June 1989, the Assembly of Experts was convened to decide on succession. None of the existing Grand Ayatollahs nor a council of clerics were deemed suitable. Eventually Khamene'i (born 1939), whom Khomeini had favoured, was selected but a hurried amendment had to be made to the Constitution to allow a cleric who was not a Grand Ayatollah to be named as the Supreme Leader. With that provision in place, Khamene'i was declared the new Supreme Leader. In 1994, he was declared a Grand Ayatollah and *marja' al-taqlid*, despite opposition from the other Grand Ayatollahs who did not think him qualified. Among those who expressed continuing opposition to Khamene'i and the style of leadership of the Islamic Republic, was Ayatollah Muntaziri. Eventually in 1997, Khamene'i ordered that Muntaziri be placed under house arrest, where he remained until 2003.

Khamene'i's time as Supreme Leader has been marked by a continuation of Khomeini's rigidly conservative interpretation of Islam and his anti-Western and anti-Israel stance in terms of foreign affairs, a suppression of political debate and continued pressure on religious minorities, especially the Baha'is, blocking every attempt at reform made by President Muhammad Khatami between 1997 and 2005, his support of Ahmadinejad's candidature for the presidency in 2005 (mainly because the other main candidate was Khamene'i's chief rival Hashemi-Rafsanjani) and the arrest and imprisonment of numerous journalists and human rights activists. Khamene'i endorsed Ahmadinejad again in the 2009 presidential election, which was followed by a period of social unrest in protest against the election result (the 'Green Movement'). In 2010–11, Khamene'i was in open conflict with Ahmadinejad. Following the 2009 elections, there were several demands that the Assembly of Experts examine Khamene'i's fitness to be the Supreme Leader. However, Khamane'i's support has remained solid among the Assembly of Experts and the leaders of the Revolutionary Guards.

The disillusionment with the government of the Islamic Republic among the general public has to some extent translated into a disillusionment with Islam. Although 85% of Iranians say they consider themselves religious, only 45% attend the mosque regularly (among the lowest percentages in the Middle East). An online survey, which is not reflective of the whole population but may well be indicative of the sentiments of young educated people, showed 53% considered themselves as having no religion.

Since its inception, one strand of the foreign policy of the Islamic Republic has been to try to spread Shi'i Islam. One way of doing this has been to bring students from all over the world to Iran to study Shi'i Islam and to return as clerics, or at least learned individuals, to their own communities. Most foreign students go to the International Centre for Islamic Studies in Qom; some 18,000 students are said to be there at any one time. The largest contingent are Afghans. Students get free food, lodgings and tuition, as well as a monthly allowance. Associated with and adjacent to this centre is the Imam 'Ali Madrasah, which specializes in catering for students from South Asia. There is a great deal of emphasis on propagating the doctrine of

Velayat-e Faqih among these foreign students so that it becomes better established throughout the Shiʻi world.

The second strand of Iran's foreign policy has been pan-Islamism, the uniting of the Islamic world against the West. Enthusiastically pursued by Khomeini, it appeared to gain ground as Iran's energetic stance against Israel won it the admiration of many Sunnis, but with increased Sunni-Shiʻi conflict in Iraq, Syria, Yemen, Bahrain and the Lebanon, this strand of Iran's foreign policy has completely unravelled.

In the last few decades Iran's Islamicists have, on the one hand, included the traditionalists (such as Khomeini, Khameneʼi and Mesbah-Yazdi), who maintain a conservative position on all aspects of social life, along with the neo-traditionalists (such as Motahhari and Shariʻati), who maintain the same position but use modern and scientific rhetoric to present it; and on the other hand, the modernists (such as ʻAbdul-Karim Sorush and Muhsin Kadivar), who are actively trying to adapt the traditional position to modern realities. The debate was lively in Iran for some time but in the end, the modernists were defeated and most were either imprisoned or forced to leave Iran.

The population of Iran is estimated to be 78 million. About 90%, or 69 million, are Twelver Shiʻi. Almost all of the Persian-speaking population, city-dwellers, villagers, and the tribes of the south and south-west are Twelver Shiʻi. Several of the most important non-Iranian ethnic groups, such as the Azerbaijan Turks and the Arabs of the south-west, are also predominantly Twelver Shiʻi. Three important ethnic elements (about seven million people) have remained Sunni: the Baluchis of the south-east, the Turkomans of the north-east, and the Kurds of the west. The latter also include about a million Ahl-e Haqq. The only important groups that are not Muslims are the Bahaʼis (numbering 300,000), and, according to the 2011 census, Christians (120,000), Zoroastrians (25,000) and Jews (9,000).

Iraq

When the British occupied Iraq during World War I, the Shi'ah were the main group that opposed their occupation and for a time Shi'i tribes were mobilized to fight alongside the Ottoman army. When it became clear that the British were staying, under a League of Nations Mandate, the Shi'ah under Mirza Muhammad Taqi Shirazi, Shaykh Muhammad Husayn Na'ini and Shaykh Abul-Hasan Isfahani rose against them. The opposition of the Shi'i *mujtahids* to the British began with an attempted revolt in 1920 and reached its climax in 1922–3 when Na'ini and Isfahani issued *fatwas* forbidding participation in the national elections.

At a conference of Shi'i clerics in 1922, a demand was made for Shi'is to be given half of all government and cabinet posts. There were then some disturbances and the politically active *mujtahid* of Kazimayn, Muhammad Mahdi al-Khalisi (died 1925) and his son Muhammad (died 1963), were expelled from the country. In protest, the leading clerics of Karbala and Najaf, including Na'ini and Isfahani, left Iraq for Iran in the summer of 1923. They went to the recently re-established centre of studies at Qom as guests of Shaykh 'Abdul-Karim Ha'iri-Yazdi. They had expected that their departure would provoke southern Iraq into revolt and induce the Iraqi government to request their return on their terms. In the event, nothing much happened in Iraq and the Iraqi *mujtahids* did not receive the support they expected in Iran. The Iraqi government was only too happy to have these *mujtahids* out of the country during the elections, allowing their return in April 1924, after the elections had ended, but under the humiliating condition that they refrain from engaging in political action.

Their departure did nothing except strengthen the position of Ha'iri-Yazdi and Qom *vis-a-vis* Najaf as an educational centre for Shi'i clerics. This episode points out an important difference between the Shi'i bazaaris and merchants in Iran, who have usually been in close alliance with the senior clerics and supported them both financially and politically, and their counterparts in Iraq who have not had such a close relationship and have often taken a line that follows their own interests rather than the opinions of the clerics.

The 1923–4 fiasco seriously dented the power and influence of the Najaf *mujtahids*. It caused a split between the Iranian *mujtahids* such as Na'ini and Isfahani and the Arab *mujtahids* such as Shaykh 'Ali Kashif al-Ghita. Arab Shi'is and the tribal shaykhs increasingly began to follow Arab *mujtahids* such as the successive heads of the Kashif al-Ghita, al-Sadr and al-Hakim families, even though formally the Iranian *mujtahids* were considered superior within the Shi'i religious hierarchy. Shi'i unity was further breached as the government won over the Shi'i tribal shaykhs by giving them financial and social concessions. Furthermore, the fiasco had the effect of making the government determined to undermine the influence of the mainly Iranian senior Shi'i clerics by emphasizing Pan-Arabism and enacting laws that consolidated Iraqi nationality, thus creating difficulties for the thousands of Iranians resident in the shrine cities. Over the next few decades, there were episodes of Shi'i unrest, caused in 1927 and 1933 by the publication of two anti-Shi'i books and in 1934–5 by the resentment of the Shi'i tribes of the south at certain government actions. Leadership of the community fell increasingly to politicians rather than clerics and indeed there was a movement towards eliminating religion from the arena of politics. There were successful Shi'i politicians over these decades but they represented secular parties rather than their religious community.

This secularisation of the public arena increased after the revolt of 1958 which overthrew the king and brought the socialists and communists into power. Most Shi'is, because of their poorer social and economic position, supported the communists and socialists (despite the rulings of the *mujtahids* warning against communism) and when the Ba'th socialist party came to power in the coup of 1963, Shi'is constituted 53% of the party. But gradually the Sunni element in the party predominated and by the time of al-Bakr's takeover of power in 1968, the Shi'i representation in the party had fallen to 6%. During this period, the Iraqi government pursued a policy of reducing Iranian influence in the shrine cities. As a result, the status of Iranian nationals in Iraq changed and many either took Iraqi nationality or returned to Iran. At the beginning of the twentieth century, Karbala and Kazimayn had a very strong Iranian influence, while Najaf was much more an Arab city. By the 1950s, Karbala and Kazimayn, which gradually became a suburb of Baghdad, were also Arab. Another phenomenon of the 1930s–1950s was the migration of Shi'is from the south of the country to Baghdad, helping to transform it into a city with a Shi'i majority. While an increasing proportion of government posts went to Shi'is, the numbers did not match the propor- tion of Shi'is in the population, which the census had shown to be greater than half. In 1968, with the coming to power of al-Bakr and the extinguishing of hope for social improvement for the Shi'is through political change by means of the existing political party system, a religious political party, the Da'wah Party, was created with the support of most of the leading Shi'i clerics of Iraq.

When Khomeini first arrived in Iraq in 1965, after being expelled from Iran, it is said Ayatollah Sayyid Muhsin al-Hakim, Iraq's foremost Shi'i religious leader at the time, disapproved of Khomeini's political stance but after meetings between the two, al-Hakim reversed his opinion. Ayatollah Sayyid Abul-Qasim Khu'i, who succeeded al-Hakim, opposed Khomeini's political activity and the concept of *Velayat-e Faqih*. A similar stance has been taken by Khu'i's successor, Ayatollah Sayyid 'Ali Sistani. At first Saddam Hussain tolerated Khomeini as a means of exerting pressure on the Shah of Iran. Later, he came to terms with the

Shah and in 1978 expelled Khomeini (he was the *de facto* leader of Iraq for some years before he became the formal leader in 1979).

In 1980, taking advantage of the chaos in Iran, Saddam Hussein invaded the oil-rich province of Khuzistan, which is inhabited by Arabic-speaking Iranians. The war dragged on until 1988, inflicting great damage on Iraq's economy. Shortly after the start of the Iran-Iraq war, Ayatollah Muhammad Baqir al-Sadr (one of the leading Shi'i clerics of Iraq) and his activist sister, Bint al-Huda, were imprisoned and then executed in 1980. Several hundred Shi'is suspected of being associated with the Da'wah party were executed and several thousand Shi'is, whose families had in some instances lived in Iraq for generations, were pronounced to be Iranian and expelled across the border.

What surprised many, however, was the inability of Iran to get the Shi'ah of south Iraq to give it much useful support during the Iran-Iraq War, despite the actions that Saddam Hussain had taken towards the leading Shi'i clerics. This was partly because of the distance between the senior Shi'i clerics and the Shi'i bazaaris and tribal leaders. It was also partly because the official Iraqi government propaganda cast the Iran-Iran war in terms of the struggle between the Arabs and the Iranians for supremacy that had occurred in the early days of Islam, trying to make the Shi'is of south Iraq identify more closely with their Arab identity in the face of the Iranian foe, rather than their Shi'i one and using certain symbolic key-words, such as Qadisiyyah (the battle at which the Arab Islamic armies defeated the Iranian Empire in 637). The Iranian propaganda sought to win the support of south Iraq's Shi'is by using symbolic key-words such as Karbala that emphasized their Shi'i commonalities. The Iraqi government effort was backed up by the diversion of resources to the Shi'i south and helped by the apolitical stance taken by the most senior Iraqi Shi'i cleric at this time, Ayatollah Khu'i.

After the first Gulf War in 1991, a Shi'i rebellion in the south was ruthlessly crushed and the shrines of Husayn and 'Abbas, which were the rebels' headquarters, were extensively damaged. Over the next decade, the Shi'i centres of learning at Najaf and Karbala suffered greatly as the government starved them of funds and did not allow foreign students to come to them. Shi'i mourning rituals for Imam Husayn were banned and clerics feared to venture out wearing clerical garb.

The second Gulf War of 2003 had an entirely different effect upon the Shi'ah. The overthrow of Saddam Hussein and the American pledge to establish democracy led the Shi'is to hope that the new state would at long last reflect their demographic superiority. In the event, Iraq descended into factional chaos with many Sunni former members of the Iraq army joining the Sunni insurrection in the west, the Kurds creating a semi-autonomous area in the north, while Shi'i militias, such as the Mahdi Army, led by Muqtada al-Sadr, were formed in Baghdad and the south. Shi'is dominated the various interim governments and the eventual national government established in 2005. Nouri al-Maliki, a Shi'i, became prime minister in 2006 and won a second election in 2010. Sunni Arabs, feeling increasingly marginalized by the government, have mounted various political protests, while terrorism and sectarian violence have continued. The most notable of the attacks on Shi'is were the terrorist attacks on pilgrims observing the day of 'Ashura in Karbala and Kazimayn on 2 March 2004 and the destruction of the al-'Askari shrine in Samarra in two attacks in 2006 and 2007. After a surge by American-led forces, supported by Sunni tribes, had defeated Sunni insurgents in 2007–8, Sunnis were disappointed by the failure of al-Maliki's government to protect them or give them justice, so they supported a new Sunni group, calling itself the Islamic State, which began a more systematic and organized campaign against al-Maliki's government in 2014, declaring the re-establishment of the Sunni caliphate and taking control of most of the Arab Sunni areas. Al-Maliki was blamed for the situation that had arisen and forced to resign in 2014.

There are no census returns to guide us, but it is estimated that Shi'is form the majority of Iraq's population (of 34 million) and that the proportion is from 60% to 65%; that is to say between 19 and 22 million. Shi'i dominance is boosted by the fact that the rest of the country, although Sunni, is divided between mutually-antagonistic Arabs (20%) and Kurds (15%). The Shi'is predominate in the southern half of the country, as far north as Baghdad, which was a mixed Sunni–Shi'i city, but is now predominantly Shi'i. There are also small pockets of Shi'is further north but most are Ahl-e Haqq and other Gnostic Shi'i groups and include Shi'i Turkomans (numbering between 500,000 and 1 million) and the Shabak people (numbering about 60,000), who are said to be descended from Qizilbash, who fled Anatolia during Ottoman persecution in the sixteenth century. There are about 100,000 Shaykhis in Basrah and perhaps 250,000 in Iraq altogether and about 100,000 Akhbaris in Basrah, Suq al-Shuyukh and other places in south Iraq.

Lebanon

According to legends among the Shi'is of Lebanon, Shi'i Islam came to the Lebanon when Abu Dharr, a loyal follower of the Imam 'Ali, lived for a time in the Jabal 'Amil after 'Ali's assassination. It is unlikely, however, that there were many Shi'is in Lebanon in the early Islamic period since the area was under the firm control of the Umayyad caliphate. In the ninth century however, Shi'i propagandists began to work in the area and significant conversions occurred once the Fatimids gained control. It is possible that the present Twelver community in the Lebanon came about as a result of these Isma'ili Shi'is changing to Twelver Shi'i Islam in the thirteenth century to escape the wrath of the Sunni Ayyubids who conquered the area.

MAP OF SYRIA AND LEBANON

Showing regions and towns mentioned in this book and
areas where the different groups of Shi'is live.

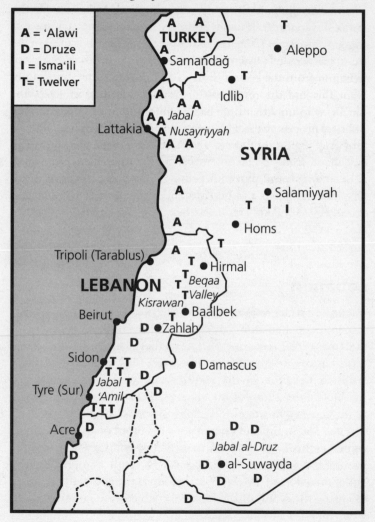

A = 'Alawi
D = Druze
I = Isma'ili
T = Twelver

At the beginning of the twentieth century, the Shi'ah were the poorest, least-educated, and least powerful of the main Lebanese confessional communities. At the end of World War I, the French were given the League of Nations Mandate over the Greater Syria area. They considered various proposals regarding its future and finally settled on a proposal, favoured by the Christians of the area, to separate what is now the state of Lebanon from the rest of Syria. The Sunnis in the area did not want this and the result of this dispute was that, in 1926, the Shi'ah, who until that time had been forgotten or ignored in the political process, were suddenly formed into a community separate from the Sunnis, since the Christians realized that the Shi'ah would probably prefer to be in a multi-confessional Lebanon than a Sunni-dominated Syria. As part of this process, the French Mandate authorities allowed Shi'is to administer themselves according to the Shi'i (Ja'fari) school of law.

In 1932, a census showed the Shi'ah to be 20% of the population (the third largest group, after the Christians and Sunni Muslims) and on this basis, a National Pact was made that the president of the country should be a Christian, the prime minister a Sunni and the speaker of the parliament a Shi'i; the parliamentary seats were divided Christians 54, Sunnis 20, Shi'ah 19, and Druze 6. The state of Lebanon came into being in 1944 on this basis. Subsequent efforts to have another census have been blocked, since the higher birthrate among Shi'is would show that they have become the largest religious community.

The religious head of the Lebanese Shi'i community for much of the first half of the twentieth century was Hajj Sayyid 'Abdul-Husayn Sharaf ud-Din, who had studied at Najaf. He returned to the Lebanon in 1904 and settled in Tyre (Sur). In 1911–12, he visited Egypt and had public debates with Shaykh Salim al-Bishri, the Grand Imam of al-Azhar. He died in 1957 and in his place Musa al-Sadr moved from Najaf to Tyre. He proved a dynamic leader who raised the profile of the Shi'i community and managed to get government funding for the development of south Lebanon. He founded the Shi'i Supreme National Islamic Council in 1967, and the Amal political party to represent Shi'i interests. Then in August 1978, Imam Musa al-Sadr (as he was by then called by the Lebanese Shi'ah) mysteriously disappeared on a trip to Libya. Following Gaddafi's downfall in 2011, the truth has yet to be completely clarified, but it seems that al-Sadr was killed on Gaddafi's orders.

The disappearance of al-Sadr caused considerable confusion among Lebanese Shi'is, especially since it was closely followed by the Islamic Revolution in Iran, the Iran-Iraq war and the Israeli occupation of south Lebanon in 1982. For a time the structure established by al-Sadr continued, with Nabih Birri (born 1938) as leader of the Amal party and Shaykh Muhammad Mahdi Shams ud-Din (died 2001) as chairman of the Shi'i Supreme National Islamic Council, pressing for Shi'i rights on the Lebanese political stage. They were antagonistic to the Palestinian refugees in south Lebanon (both because of their imperious control of the area and because they attracted Israeli retaliatory strikes) and at first they even welcomed the Israeli incursion in 1982. Amal's main power base was south Lebanon and south Beirut. It never managed to gain as much support among the Shi'ah of the Beqaa (Biqa') valley.

In 1982, a group of clerics, angered at Amal's acceptance of the Israeli incursion and inspired by the more extreme political views being expressed in Tehran, founded Hezbollah (Hizbullah), a religio-political-military movement, with considerable support from Iran. Patterned on the *Velayat-e Faqih* model of Khomeini, Hezbollah was led by militant clerics, advocating the creation of an Islamic state. It joined the Lebanese civil war on the side of the Sunnis and the Palestinians and against the Christian and Druze forces. It is widely held responsible for the 1983 US Embassy bombing that led to US withdrawal from direct involvement in the civil war. Using a combination of religious rhetoric, political manoeuvring, social development programmes and the backing of an effective militia, Hezbollah had by 1989 become a major actor on the Lebanese scene, with seats in parliament and even its own radio and satellite television stations. Although the 1989 Taif agreement ending the civil war was supposed to lead to the disbanding of militias, Hezbollah remained armed, pleading that it needed to defend the south against Israel. In 1992, Hasan Nasrullah (born 1960) became its head. Since that time, Hezbollah has been implicated in a number of bombings and attacks on Israelis, Israeli embassies and Jewish institutions around the world. Israel's withdrawal from south Lebanon in 2000 was widely regarded in Lebanon as a Hezbollah victory, brought about by its harassment of the Israeli forces. Hezbollah's launching of rockets into north Israel resulted in an Israeli military action in 2006. Hezbollah was widely regarded in the Arab world as having won this clash but a stalemate would be closer to the truth. Nevertheless, Israel's aura of invincibility had been broken and Hezbollah basked in glory. By occupying some Christian areas in Beirut, Hezbollah escalated the crisis in Lebanon in 2008 until a National Unity Government was formed.

The Shi'ah of Lebanon remain divided politically between Hezbollah and Amal, who have had two seats each in recent government cabinets. The Shi'i seats in parliament are also evenly split. The leader of Amal, Nabih Birri, was elected speaker of the national parliament in 1992. There is also a religious division between, on the one hand, supporters of Hezbollah, who under Hasan Nasrullah follow Khamane'i and the Iranian government's interpretation of Shi'i Islam, and, on the other hand, supporters of clerics such as Muhammad Husayn Fadlullah (died 2010), an independent-minded modernist cleric who opposed the concept of *Velayat-e Faqih* and set himself up as a *marja' al-taqlid*, and Sayyid 'Ali al-Amin, the senior cleric in Tyre (Sur) and the Jabil 'Amil, who opposes Hezbollah.

The Syrian civil war has resulted in proxy battles between Sunnis and Shi'is in Lebanon and both sides have sent fighters to Syria. This has caused a loss of the prestige that Hezbollah had gained in the Sunni world for its stand against Israel. Hezbollah is said currently to have up to 65,000 fighters and a large stock of long-range and anti-tank missiles and anti-aircraft defences sent from Iran and Syria. Most of Israel is now thought to be within the range of its missiles.

The total population of Lebanon is about 4.5 million. No census has been undertaken since 1932 because of the sensitivity of the balance between the various religious communities, so it is not known exactly what the proportions of the different religious communities are now. Most experts agree, however, that the Shi'is, who are often called Mutawali (plural: Matawilah) in Lebanon, are the largest community, numbering some 1.5 million (35%), Maronite Christians make up 21%, Sunnis 18%, Druze 6%, and other Christian groups 20%. Twelvers form the majority of the population in most of the towns and villages in the Jabal 'Amil, the south of Lebanon as far north as the Litani river, with Tyre (Sur), as the main city on the coast. Further north, Sidon has a mixed Shi'i-Sunni population; the towns and villages in its hinterland also have a lower proportion of Shi'is. The other main Shi'i area is the northern Beqaa (Biqa') valley, which stretches from Baalbek to Hirmal, both of which are important Shi'i towns. Further south in the Beqaa valley there are a small number of Shi'i villages in the area around Zahlah. Beirut has become an important centre for Shi'i Islam, with the migration of large numbers of Shi'is to its southern suburbs in particular, partly as a result of the conflict with Israel in the south. Between 15 and 30% of the city is now Shi'i. There is a small Shi'i population in the Kisrawan area, in the districts centred on Jubayl and Qartaba, including the resort villages of Afqa and Laqluq on Mount Lebanon.

Syria

It is unlikely that there were many Shi'is in Syria during the first 150 years of Islam, since Syria was the main base, and Damascus the capital, of the Umayyad caliphate. In the ninth century however, Shi'i propagandists began to work in the area and Salamiyyah was the base of the Isma'ili Imams during the ninth century. The tenth and eleventh centuries saw various Shi'i groups proselytizing in Syria, in particular the Fatimids from their headquarters in Cairo, the Nusayris in the north and the Druze in the central coastal area. After the collapse of the Fatimid Empire in the twelfth century, Isma'ili forts continued to hold out until the thirteenth century. Most of the Shi'is in Syria are 'Alawis, living in the north coastal areas around Lattakia. There is also a large Druze presence in the Jabal al-Duruz area south of Damascus and Isma'ilis have reoccupied the town of Salamiyyah and the area south of the town.

The Twelver presence in Syria dates from the eleventh to twelfth centuries, when Aleppo was under Shi'i control and became a major centre of Twelver scholarship. Although the Twelvers were eliminated from the city, they have maintained a presence in some villages in northern Syria. The majority live in villages in the region of Idlib to the south-west of Aleppo and in the region of Azaz to the north-west of Aleppo. There are also a few Twelver Shi'i villages in the area of Homs and Hama. A small Twelver Shi'i colony exists around the grave of Sayyidah Zaynab (Sitt Zaynab), now incorporated into the southern suburbs of Damascus. With the advent of the 'Alawi-supported government of the al-Assad family, there are now Twelver *madrasahs* and the publication of Twelver Shi'i and Shaykhi books in Damascus. It is as yet unclear what long-term effect the 2011 uprising and the rise of self-styled Islamic State will have on the 'Alawis and the other Shi'is in Syria. The United Nation's estimated population of Syria for 2014 was 24 million, of which 74% are Sunnis and

10% are Christians; 'Alawis are 3 million (12% of the population), Druze 500,000, Twelvers 200,000, and Isma'ilis 200,000.

Saudi Arabia

The Shi'i history of Bahrain and the Arabian province of al-
Ahsa (Lahsa), in particular the oases of al-Ahsa and al-Qatif,
adjacent to Bahrain, are closely interlinked. Indeed the whole
area of al-Ahsa and the archipelago that now constitutes the state
of Bahrain was known as Bahrayn in medieval times. Both al-
Ahsa and Bahrain have a large Twelver Shi'i population. This
probably existed from an early period but it is likely there were
conversions from Isma'ili Shi'i Islam in the eleventh century to
escape Sunni wrath at the time when the Qarmati Isma'ili state in
this area was subjugated by the Seljuks. Shaykh Ahmad al-Ahsa'i,
the founder of the Shaykhi movement (see pp. 117–19), was
from this area and there are Shaykhi communities here. They
were perhaps a majority of the Shi'is of al-Ahsa and al-Qatif at
the beginning of the twentieth century and they still constitute
about a quarter of the Shi'is of al-Ahsa. Their numbers are hard
to determine because many conceal their Shaykhi allegiance out
of fear of the Usulis, who are now the majority.

In the eighteenth century, the conservative Sunni Wahhabi
movement began in Najd, the part of Arabia adjacent to al-Ahsa.
This movement is vehemently anti-Shi'i and it destroyed Shi'i
and Sufi shrines wherever it could find them, including the shrine
of Fatimah and four of the Shi'i Imams in al-Baqi' cemetery in
Mecca in 1926. In 1792, it overran al-Ahsa and held it until
defeated by the Ottomans in 1818. In 1913, the region was again
captured by Wahhabi forces and incorporated into the Saudi
kingdom. There was a great deal of repression of the Shi'is and a
Shi'i revolt in 1929–30. The repression of the Shi'is eased a little
in 1930 following the Saudi family's suppression and disbandment

of the Ikhwan, the fanatical Wahhabi warriors that had brought them to power. In 1936, oil was discovered in al-Ahsa and many Shi'ah joined the workforce of the oil company. Although there had been calls for an improvement in the rights of the Shi'ah, and unrest in the 1950s, the 1979 Islamic Revolution in Iran led to an upsurge in these demands. This in turn caused panic in the Saudi government and among the Wahhabi clerics, resulting in sermons and *fatwas* by these clerics, who have stated that Shi'is are heretics and non-Muslims, that their religion is a Jewish conspiracy and that they are the agents of a foreign power, Iran. There have been increased government restrictions on the Shi'ah since the 1980s. Rioting in 1979 and 1980 was firmly put down, with helicopter gunships being used against the demonstrators. Periodic clashes between Iranian Shi'i pilgrims and Saudi police during the Hajj (which in 1987 resulted in 400 deaths) have also caused increased Sunni-Shi'i tensions within the country.

Shi'is have suffered socio-economic and educational discrimination and arbitrary arrests. They have been systematically excluded from all senior positions in the government, judiciary, police and the military. Moderate Shi'i activists have rallied around Hasan al-Saffar and have been pressing for an end to human rights abuses in the kingdom. In 1993, there was an agreement between the Saudi government and moderate Shi'i leaders to remove some of the restrictions on Shi'is in return for a cessation of the Shi'i anti-government campaign. A minority of radical Shi'is (Saudi Hezbollah) have, however, aligned themselves closely to Iran and a number of bombings have been attributed to them (for example, the bombing of the Khobar Towers in Dhahran in 1996). The advent of a Shi'i-led government in Iraq encouraged the Shi'is to press for more rights and, between 2003 and 2005, there were a number of advances along these lines. The Saudi royal family walked a fine line between appeasing Shi'i aspirations and calming Wahhabi unease at these developments. However, increasing Sunni-Shi'i conflict in the rest of the Islamic world from 2006 onwards, and particularly as a result of the Syrian civil war, has reversed this progress.

Estimates of the number of Shi'is in Saudi Arabia range from 10 to 15% of the population. This estimate includes, however, some 500,000 Isma'ilis mainly in the Najran area near the Yemeni border and some 1,500,000 Zaydis who are to be found in cities of southern and western Saudi Arabia (some are native to the area and some are Yemeni immigrants). The Twelver Shi'is in the present kingdom of Saudi Arabia mainly live in the al-Qatif and al-Ahsa governates of the Eastern Province of the country, the heaviest concentration being in al-Qatif, which is 97% Shi'i. Taking into account the total population of the Eastern Province (four million in the 2010 census), the fact that this province encompasses a large area beyond the Shi'i heartland and the fact that the Saudi government has encouraged Sunnis to settle there, the Twelver Shi'i proportion of the population of that province is probably no more than 40%. There are also Shi'is in Medina: the Nakhawilah, who live in the district of al-'Awali in Medina, some tribal people in Wadi al Fara' to the south-west of Medina, and families of Shi'i *sayyids*. Together with a small community of Shi'is in Mecca, they probably number no more than 35,000. The total Twelver population of Saudi Arabia is probably no more than two million (7% of the population). With the Zaydis and Isma'ilis, the total Shi'i population comes to four million (14% of the population).

Bahrain

In the modern period, the island of Bahrain has been under the control of Portugal (1521–1602) and Iran (1602–1717) before the Sunni al-Khalifah clan from Qatar conquered the island in 1782. They were confirmed as rulers in a treaty in 1820 with Britain, the main military power in the Gulf. They encouraged Sunni Arabs to settle in the island to reduce the Shi'i preponderance. Although most of the Shi'i world turned to Usuli Shi'i Islam in the early nineteenth century, this area, which had produced a number of important Akhbari scholars, such as Shaykh Yusuf Bahrani (died 1772), continued to have a large Akhbari community. Although the island had a large Shaykhi population a century ago, this seems to have more or less disappeared.

Shi'is have felt resentful of the Sunni ruling class and their own economic and political marginalization. During most of the twentieth century, the main opposition to the government was of a political and secular nature. Only with the Islamic Revolution of 1979 in Iran did a significant Shi'i Islamist opposition arise, led by an organization called al-Wifaq. The Bahraini government has accused this opposition of being Iranian-backed and has arrested many of its leaders. Most Bahraini Shi'is have a strong Arab identity and no desire for an Iranian takeover of Bahrain (an Iranian claim of sovereignty over the island is resurrected from time to time). Furthermore, a large proportion of Bahrain's Shi'is are Akhbaris and this differentiates them even more from Iran's Shi'is. But the more pressure the government has put on the Shi'ah, the more they turn to Iran for relief and the more they drift from an Akhbari identity that tends to be quietist and apolitical, towards an Usuli identity that tends to be more activist and political. In the period from 1994–8, there were street demonstrations, which were crushed. Following the 2011 uprisings in the Arab world, the majority of those who demonstrated for political change, and occupied an important roundabout in Manama city were Shi'is. The government reacted by calling in foreign troops from Saudi Arabia and the United Arab Emirates and crushing the demonstrations. Since then, there have been many allegations of arbitrary arrests, torture, and of expulsions of Shi'is from work and education. An Independent Commission of Enquiry into the unrest raised hopes when its report was accepted by King Hamad in 2011 but its recommendations have largely been sidelined. One result of the government's repression has been that a number of more radical Shi'i groups have separated themselves from al-Wifaq. The current religious head of Bahraini Shi'is is Shaykh 'Isa Qasim (born 1937); 'Abdullah al-Ghurayfi is also important and Shaykh 'Ali Salman is the Secretary-General of al-Wifaq.

Estimates that put the Shi'i population of Bahrain at 60–70% refer to Bahraini citizens rather than the total population. Taking the citizen population first, most of the Shi'is call themselves Bahrani (plural Baharnah) to designate that they were the original inhabitants of the island; they constitute about 250,000 people. A minority of the Shi'i citizens (100,000) are later Iranian immigrants (from Safavid times onwards) who have been on the island for generations, often speak Persian and are called the 'Ajam. It is likely that the proportion of Shi'is among the citizen population has dropped from 70% to 60% as a result of the Bahrain government's decision to naturalize more than 100,000 Sunni Arab and non-Arab immigrants to reduce the Shi'i preponderance among its citizens. However, Bahrain's population of about 1,300,000 is made up of about 50% citizens and 50% immigrant non-citizens. Muslims make up 99% of Bahraini national citizens but when the immigrant population is added, the proportion falls to 70%. The Shi'is make up about 60% (350,000) of Bahraini citizens, but when taken together with Shi'is from among the immigrant non-citizen population, the proportion of Shi'is in the total population drops to 45% (600,000).

Kuwait

The government of Kuwait is generally regarded as being among the most tolerant in the region. There have been some delays in granting permission to build Shi'i mosques but Shi'is are allowed to hold public rituals. Kuwait is the headquarters of the Ihqaqi sub-sect of Shaykhis.

Kuwait has a population of just over three million, but about two-thirds are non-citizen immigrants. Of the one million citizens, about 40% (400,000) are called 'Ajam, meaning that they are descendants of Iranians who migrated to this area many generations ago. Most are Shi'is. In addition, there are a small number of Arab Kuwaiti Shi'is and many Shi'i immigrants from India, Pakistan, Iraq, Bahrain and al-Ahsa (Saudi Arabia). The total Shi'i population is about 500,000 (16% of the total population).

Other Gulf states and Yemen

In the United Arab Emirates (UAE), there is a large number of traders and businessmen of Iranian descent, especially in Dubai and Sharjah. Shi'is number about 15% of UAE nationals or citizens. However UAE nationals are only 15% of the total population, the rest being immigrants. Together with Shi'i immigrants (from India, Pakistan, other Arab countries and East Africa), Shi'is form some 8% (700,000) of the total population of nine million.

People of Iranian descent form 6–10% of the 250,000 citizens of Qatar. Together with immigrant Shi'is from India, Pakistan and elsewhere, it is likely that Shi'is are at least 10% (180,000) of the total population of 1.8 million.

In Oman, Twelver Shi'i Islam is practised by the al-Lawati tribe, which numbers some 80,000, resident in Muscat and along the adjacent Batinah coast. There is a small number of people of Iranian descent, the 'Ajam, some Shi'i Arabs from Bahrain, Saudi Arabia and Iraq, generally called Bahrani, and some Shi'is among the Indian and Pakistani immigrants. Shi'is thus form about 3% (90,000) of the total population of the country.

The situation in Yemen with regard to Zaydis is described on pp. 198–200 and with regard to Isma'ilis on p. 203. There are a small number of Twelver Shi'is in Yemen, mostly recent converts after the Iranian Revolution of 1979.

Turkey

The picture regarding Shi'i Islam in Turkey is confused. Estimates of the proportion of Shi's in the population range from 10–30%. The largest group of Shi'is in Turkey is the Alevis. There are also many 'Alawis (Nusayris), who are also called Alevis but sometimes distinguished from the first group by the designation Arap Aleviler (Arab Alevis). Both these groups revere the Twelve Shi'i Imams (and are dealt with in Chapter 8) but those who follow the same religion as the majority in Iran are only a minority of Turkey's Shi'is and are usually distinguished from other Shi'is by the designation Câferî (Ja'fari). Many are Azeri Turks. This means they speak the same variant of Turkish as the Turks of Iranian Azerbaijan and the Republic of Azerbaijan. They are to be found in north-eastern Anatolia, particularly in Iğdır and Kars provinces (2.5 million) and in Istanbul (about 500,000). They are not officially recognized by the state but are able to build and operate their own mosques and appoint their own Imams. The leader of the community is Selahattin Özgündüz. In 2010, Recep Tayyip Erdoğan became the first Turkish prime minister to attend the Karbala commemorations held by the Shi'is in the Halkalı district of Istanbul.

Azerbaijan

The area now forming the Republic of Azerbaijan was part of the Safavid Empire and thus was converted to Twelver Shi'i

Islam at that time. It was incorporated into the Russian Empire in 1813, following two wars between Russia and Iran. When the Russian Empire collapsed during the Bolshevik Revolution, there was a brief period of independence before Azerbaijan was forcibly incorporated into the USSR. During the Soviet period, as elsewhere in the USSR, religion was suppressed, especially in the time of Stalin, and only allowed under the tight control of the government-appointed Islamic Spiritual Directorate for Transcaucasia, which dealt with both Sunnis and Shi'is. Many mosques were closed and until 1989, there was no formal training of Muslim clerics. Since independence from the USSR in 1991, the government has held to the line that the Republic is a secular state and has been wary of any manifestations of religious extremism whether among the Sunnis in the north or among the Shi'ah. Iran has tried to export its conservative and politicized version of Shi'i Islam to this country but only in the small town of Nardaran, near Baku, has this form of Islam taken root; for example, the women wear *chadors*. The Iranian effort has been blocked by the state, which has tried to create and promote an 'Azeri Shi'i Islam' and has banned the Islamic Party of Azerbaijan, which was promoted by Iran.

About 80% (7.5 million) of the population say that they are Twelver Shi'i Muslims; however for many this represents an identity rather than a religion since polls indicate that more than 50% of the population say that religion plays little or no role in their life and that they do not attend any religious meetings.

India

An All-India Shi'a Conference was convened in 1907 in Lakhnau and by 1910 had become representative of all of the Indian Shi'ah. Although some Shi'i *madrasahs* were established in the last decades of the nineteenth century, the founding of a

Shi'i College in 1917 in Lakhnau greatly increased the training not only of preachers of the Friday sermon in the mosque but also of the ritual storytellers of the Karbala narrative. However these evidences of the emergence of an increasingly distinct Shi'i identity also led to increasing inter-communal friction during the early twentieth century, culminating in clashes with Sunnis in Lakhnau in 1906–8 and in the 1930s. In the lead-up to Indian independence, the preachers and storytellers became the community's leaders as it increasingly established a separate identity from the Sunni community. This was partly encouraged by the Hindus, in order to split the Muslim minority and, indeed, the Shi'ah tended to support the Congress Party rather than the Muslim League. Following inter-communal violence, the state authorities banned the ritual processions marking the events of Karbala in Lakhnau in 1977 and only allowed a limited number from 1998 onwards.

In post-independence India, the rights of all religious minorities are recognized and the Day of 'Ashura is recognized as a public (gazetted) holiday. But Muslims, both Sunnis and Shi'is, feel discriminated against and local outbreaks of violence have occurred, especially in areas where Hindu nationalist politicians have whipped up hatred against Muslims, for example in 2002 during the Babri Mosque episode. In 2005, the All-India Shia Personal Law Board separated from the All-India Muslim Personal Law Board as a non-governmental organization to campaign for the rights of Shi'is.

In Kashmir, it was above all the 1979 Iranian Revolution that caused the Shi'ah who previously practised *taqiyyah* to assume a more public identity and become more assertive. There are a number of Shi'i organizations, such as the Jammu and Kashmir Shi'ah Association, the Anjuman-e Shari'ah Shi'ayan and the Itihhad al-Muslimin. In Kashmir, Shi'is are found in Srinagar, Baramulla, Budgam and particularly in the district of Kargil (90% of the population of the town and 60% of the population of the district). It is likely that there are about one million Shi'is here (10% of the population).

It is difficult to know how many Shi'is there are in India as a whole. Many practise *taqiyyah,* and in areas where Shi'is form a small minority of Muslims, they are often counted as Sunnis. There are three principal Shi'i areas in India: the Deccan plateau in central India (where there were a number of Shi'i dynasties in the sixteenth and seventeenth centuries), the region of Awadh in Uttar Pradesh (where the Shi'i Nawabs ruled in the eighteenth and nineteenth centuries), and Kashmir (where the Chak dynasty ruled in the sixteenth century). There are also about 40,000 Khojas in Gujarat and Maharashtra, who converted from Isma'ili Shi'i Islam to Twelver Shi'i Islam. There are large Shi'i communities in the cities of these areas and beyond: Lakhnau (15% Shi'is, 400,000), Hyderabad, Mumbai and New Delhi. In common with Sunnis, Shi'is tend to speak and write in Urdu and often speak other local languages and Hindi. There are Shi'i claims that Shi'is number around 40–50 million (4–5%) of India's population, but this figure seems excessive. More neutral observers put the figure at around 25 million, which represents 14% of India's Muslims and 2% of the total population.

Pakistan

The history of Shi'i Islam in Pakistan is complex. None of the peoples living in what is now the state of Pakistan became Twelver Shi'is in early Islamic history. The earliest Shi'i community in the area of Pakistan was probably the Isma'ili community in Sindh, which existed in the ninth century. It is likely that Twelver Shi'i Islam spread among some of the tribal peoples as a result either of travelling Shi'i-oriented Sufis, especially of the Nurbakhshi order, coming from Kashmir in the fifteenth century or Shi'i emissaries sent out by Safavid Iran in the sixteenth and seventeenth centuries.

This may have been how Shi'i Islam spread among the Turis or Torais and the Samilzai division of the Bangash, both being Pashtun sub-tribes in the Kurram valley adjoining Afghanistan.

In the province of Gilgit-Baltistan, the Shi'is make up about 90% (300,000) of the population of the Baltistan Division in the east of the province and are mainly orthodox Twelvers; the Balti people in the districts of Skardu, Ghanche and Nagar. Nurbakhshi preachers were instrumental in the conversion of Baltis in Baltistan and some of the Shi'is in the Ghanche District still adhere to the Sufi Nurbakhshi order and would be regarded as heterodox by most orthodox Twelver Shi'is. In the Gilgit Division of the province, to the north and west, the Shi'is are mainly Isma'ilis: the Wakhis and Burusho (Hunza) people in the districts of Hunza, Gilgit and Ghizer. The south of the province is predominantly Sunni. The Isma'ili area extends into the north of the adjoining Khyber-Pashtunwala province: the Khowar (Chitrali) people, who are some 30% Isma'ili.

The central part of Pakistani Punjab has a high number of Shi'is, especially in the Sargodha and Khushab districts. The Jhang district in the Punjab has been dominated by Shi'i land-lords. Two of the most militant Sunni movements that have terrorized Shi'is, the Sipah-e-Sahabah (which since its banning has re-emerged under the name Ahle Sunnat wal Jamaat) and the Lashkar-e-Jhangvi, arose among Sunni peasants of the Shi'i landlords, who had been driven off the land by mechanization and came to form the urban poor in the area. There are some small towns and villages in this district where the majority of the population is Shi'i. The province of Sindh was an import-ant Isma'ili centre in medieval times and there are still Isma'ilis and Twelvers among its people. The Talpurs, a Sindhi Baloch tribe, who became Twelver Shi'is under Iranian influence, ruled Sindh from 1783–1843, when the British took over. An area along the Indus river in the centre of this province (from the city of Sukkur in the north to Nawabshah in the south) has a

Shi'i majority (both Twelver and Isma'ili), with many from the Baluch and Sindhi tribes. With the division of India in 1948 and the conflict over Kashmir, many Shi'is migrated to Pakistan alongside Sunni Muslims (these migrants were called Muhajirs). They came from Kashmir into north Pakistan, and from other parts of India to settle in Lahore, Karachi and other large cities. But, given their suspicions that Pakistan was going to become a Sunni state, it is likely that the proportion of Shi'is that migrated was lower than Sunnis. There are also about one million Shi'i Hazaras in Pakistan, mostly in the Quetta area, who first fled Hazarajat in Afghanistan in the nineteenth century in the wake of persecutions by Abdul-Rahman Khan, the emir of Kabul; there have been further waves of Hazara migration since then.

Following the 1979 Islamic Revolution in Iran and more particularly since 2000, Pakistan has become a proxy battleground for Iranian-Saudi conflict. Since both the Saudis and the Iranians promulgate a more radically conservative and politicized version of their beliefs than that which previously existed in Pakistan, this inevitably led to an increase in Sunni-Shi'i conflict. Funds from the Saudis built Sunni mosques and *madrasahs* and Iranian funds built Shi'i ones. A separate Shi'i political party, the Tehrik-e Jafaria, was established, while the more militant Sipah-i Muhammad was eventually declared a terrorist organization and held responsible for the assassination of a number of militant Sunni leaders. Although violence has been inflicted by both sides, the number of Shi'is who have been killed is much greater than Sunnis. Thousands of Shi'is have died in conflict all over Pakistan, especially in Quetta and Karachi, in the last few decades and many more have been injured and become refugees. Shi'is accuse the government of turning a blind eye or even being complicit in the attacks or, at best, of being ineffectual in its response.

The Twelver Shi'is of Pakistan, the Kashmiris and Baltis in the far north-east, Punjabi villagers, Hazaras in Quetta, tribes in the Kurram Valley and Muhajir immigrants from India in Karachi and other cities have little in common with each other in terms of language and culture. In addition, caste distinctions, a relic of the Hindu past, can still be observed among many of the Shi'is of Pakistan. There is thus little national coordination among the Shi'ah. There are no census returns giving information about religion but most authorities agree that Shi'is make up 10–20% of the population of Pakistan (19–38 million, mostly Twelvers with some Isma'ilis), about 4% being Hindus and Christians and the rest Sunni Muslims.

Afghanistan

Shi'is have been an oppressed minority in Afghanistan for much of their history. Not until the 1940s was a Shi'i mosque built in Kabul and the Shi'ah emerged to some extent from *taqiyyah*. Their condition since the fall of the Taliban has, however, improved considerably. The 2004 Constitution made it legal for Shi'i jurisprudence to be applied in matters of family law. Twelver Shi'is are divided ethnically and geographically into the following groups:

1. Hazara (Hazarah). The Hazaras are probably descended from Mongol troops who settled and married Persian women. There are about three million of them; most are Twelver Shi'is, with some Isma'ili Shi'is and a few Sunnis. They form the third-largest ethnic group in Afghanistan. They occupy an area in the centre of the country to the west of Kabul, which is called Hazarajat and centred on Bamian. However, large numbers are also found in some of the large cities of Afghanistan; for example, Mazar-e Sharif in the north of the country is about 60% Hazara. It is reported that the Hazaras became Shi'is under Safavid influence in the sixteenth and

seventeenth centuries. They came to prominence in Afghan history through their resistance to Abdul-Rahman Khan in the late nineteenth century. After subduing the Hazaras, Abdul-Rahman faced three uprisings between 1888 and 1893, each of which was ruthlessly crushed with much loss of Hazara lives.

The Hazaras have traditionally held a low position in Afghan society, working as servants and manual workers in towns and as peasants in the rural areas. Their conditions improved during the twentieth century, except during the period of Taliban power (1996–2001), when they were heavily persecuted as heretics. After 2001, however, the Hazaras were well positioned on account of their community solidarity and ethic of hard work to advance socially. Many are educated and have moved into the middle class. Some (including some women) now occupy high political and government posts and, in the 2009 elections, Hazaras won 59 out of 249 seats, well in excess of their proportion of the population.

2. Qizilbash. These are thought to be descended from troops left behind after Nadir Shah's invasion from Iran in the eighteenth century. They speak Persian and live mainly in the Chindawal quarter of the city of Kabul and a small number of other towns. They have held important positions in the government. They are estimated to number about 200,000.

3. Farsiwans (Parsiwans, Tajiks). Herat used to be part of the Iranian province of Khurasan. The inhabitants were then mainly Iranians. Most of the city of Herat is still populated by the descendants of these people who speak Persian with a Khurasani dialect rather than the Dari dialect of the Tajiks of eastern Afghanistan. They are also Twelver Shi'is, as distinct from the Sunnism of most other Tajiks. Nevertheless, they are often referred to as Tajiks, but it is probably better to

refer to them as Farsiwans to distinguish them from the Tajiks of eastern Afghanistan. There are about 500,000 of them in Herat and some of the other towns and villages of western Afghanistan.

In addition to Twelvers, there are Isma'ili Shi'is in Afghanistan. Under the leadership of Sayyid Mansur Nadiri, those from among the Hazara in the Kayan district form a separate group, who reject the leadership of the Agha Khan. A larger number of Nizari Isma'ilis, who follow the Agha Khan, are to be found among the Pamiri people in the Badakhshan region in the far north-east of Pakistan, where they form the majority of the population in some areas. They speak an Iranian language and include the Wakhi people who live in the Wakhan corridor that separates Pakistan from Tajikistan.

The increasing Sunni-Shi'i tensions in the rest of the Islamic world is reflected in Afghanistan, but there is less tension here than in most other countries of the Islamic world where the two communities co-exist. Indeed, Afghanistan has an Islamic Brotherhood Council on which Sunni and Shi'i clerics work for religious harmony. Currently Grand Ayatollah Shaykh Muhammad Asif Muhsini is the spiritual leader of most Afghan Shi'is. With support from Iran, he runs a television station and has built a centre of Shi'i learning in Kabul, the Hawzih-ye Khatam al-Nabiyyin. Other important leaders are Ayatollahs Kaboli and Salihi. Twelver Shi'is represent about 12% of Afghanistan's population or about four million people.

Central Asia

The Twelver Shi'i population of the Central Asian countries of Turkmenistan, Uzbekistan, Kazakhstan, Kyrgyzstan and Tajikistan may be divided into two main groups: the Azeri

(Turkish-speaking) and the Tajik or Irani (Persian-speaking). The Azeri are migrants from Azerbaijan, across the Caspian Sea. The Tajik or Irani are either the descendants of the Iranian peoples who predominated in Central Asia before the invasion of Turkic tribes from about the eleventh century onwards or later immigrants.

In Turkmenistan, since the fall of communism, the state has been inimical to all manifestations of Shi'i Islam. There are a substantial number of Twelver Azeris but both their ethnic and religious identity is suppressed by the state. Shi'i mosques have been closed and Shi'i clerics persecuted. There are also some Iranian Shi'is in Ashgabat (Aşgabat) and elsewhere. It is difficult to make an estimate of the numbers of Shi'is because of the repression but it is possible that there are around 200,000 Twelver Shi'is in the country (3% of the population).

In addition to some 50,000 Azeris, Uzbekistan has a large number of Iranis, perhaps 200,000 in Samarkand, where two officially registered Shi'i mosques operate, and 100,000 in Bukhara, where there is one registered Shi'i mosque. In total, Shi'is make up about 1% of the population. The government remains inimical to Shi'i Islam (as indeed to all religious minorities) and does not allow new Shi'i mosques to be registered (there are said to be eight unregistered mosques in Samarkand), nor does it allow the establishment of a Shi'i *madrasah* or recognize the qualifications of Shi'i clerics trained abroad. All Islamic premises and institutions are under a Sunni-controlled government department, the Muslim Spiritual Administration. There are about 75,000 Azeris in Kazakhstan, and 15,000 in Kyrgyzstan, where there is a Shi'i mosque in Bishkek.

The Shi'i population of Tajikistan has until recently been mostly Nizari Isma'ilis of the Pamiri people. Although they predominate in the Kuhistoni Badakhshon (Gorno-Badakhshan) region in the south-east of the country, with its capital Khorugh, it is a remote and sparsely populated area and so they only constitute about 3% (250,000) of the total population of the country. They have opened an Isma'ili Centre in the capital Dushanbe. Tajikistan is the only country in the world other than Iran where the majority speak Persian, however the people are mainly Sunni Muslims. As with other Soviet countries, religion was suppressed during the communist era. In the country's civil war (1992–7), the Iranian government is thought to have at first given limited assistance to Islamist groups (especially the Islamic Revival Party of Tajikistan), although it later gained credit by helping to negotiate a peace. After this, Iran made a great effort to promote Iranian culture, with considerable success, and also undertook development projects in the country. Tajik students were sent to Iran for education, several hundred going to *madrasahs*. Problems arose however, when these students converted to Shi'i Islam and returned home as Shi'i proselytizers. The Sunni religious leaders in the country protested at this development. The government of Tajikistan, which has always pursued a secular policy and is very wary of Islamic extremism, has reacted by, to a limited extent, pulling back from its engagement with Iran, in particular bringing home students studying in Iran and reducing cultural visits. One of the country's leading political and religious personalities, Haji Akbar Turajonzoda, lived in exile in Iran in the 1990s and, although he has denied being a Shi'i, his mosque in Vakhdat was censured for commemorating 'Ashura in 2012. There are reports that there has been a favourable response to Iran's efforts at propagating Twelver Shi'i Islam in the southern regions around Kulyab (Kulob) in Khatlon province. Exaggerated claims are made in Iran but it is not possible to estimate how many Twelver Shi'is there are in Tajikistan as a result of this Iranian initiative. It may be that Twelver Shi'is constitute as much as 5% (400,000) of the population but is more likely to be around 3% (250,000). Taking this latter figure together with the Isma'ilis, Shi'is may make up 6% of the total population of Tajikistan.

Malaysia

The presence of Twelver Shi'is in Malaysia, which has mainly occurred following the 1979 Islamic Revolution in Iran (although there were small numbers of Shi'i Iranian, Arab and Indian merchants before then), has stirred up considerable opposition among the country's Sunni religious and political leadership. In 1996, the Fatwa Committee of the National Council for Islamic Religious Affairs in Malaysia repealed a 1984 ruling that allowed Twelver and Zaydi Shi'i Islam recognition and issued a *fatwa* stating that only Sunnism is true Islam and prohibiting the spread of Shi'i Islam. Universities have also held anti-Shi'i conferences. There have been anti-Shi'i government statements and decrees, despite the fact that the Malaysian government and senior clerics accepted the 2004 Amman Declaration that gives recognition to Twelver Shi'i Islam as a legitimate school of Islamic jurisprudence. Indeed, in July 2013, a total prohibition on the practice of Shi'i Islam by or its spread among the country's Muslims made Malaysia the first country in modern times to, in effect, outlaw Shi'i Islam. Shi'i homes have been raided and Shi'is imprisoned and denied the freedom to worship and to participate in public life. The official government estimate is that there are only about 1,500 Twelver Shi'is in the country, although reports of a quarter of a million Shi'is have appeared. There are also about 400 Tayibi (Dawudi) Isma'ili Bohras and a smaller number of Nizari (Agha Khani) Khojas who came to Malaysia as part of the migration of Indians to the country in the nineteenth and early twentieth centuries.

Indonesia

There are significant Shi'i communities in Indonesia. Legend in the Shi'i community dates its foundation to the arrival in Aceh of a son of Imam Ja'far al-Sadiq in the eighth century, but it was the arrival of Arab and Indian Shi'i traders from the thirteenth century onwards that created the basis of the present community. Aceh, in northern Sumatra, which was the first area to be Islamicized, was also the seat of the first large Shi'i community. The main Shi'i centres are in the coastal regions of West Sumatra and Aceh, where they practise the Muharram rituals. Since the 1979 Islamic Revolution in Iran, there has been a strong Shi'i propaganda movement in Indonesia and reports of many conversions. In particular the island of Madura and the neighbouring city of Surabaya and towns of Bangil and Pasuruan in East Java now appear to have large communities of Shi'is. This increase in the number of Shi'is resulted in a reaction and the Muslim Ulema Council of Sampang declared the Shi'is to be heretics. Shi'is were attacked in Sampang, Bangil, Pasuruan and Nangkernang village (East Java) in 2011–12. An Anti-Shia National Alliance has also been set up, which held its first convention in April 2014. There are also reported to be Shi'i communities established in the cities of Jakarta, Bandung (West Java), and Makassar (South Sulawesi). The total number of Shi'is in Indonesia has been estimated to be between one and three million.

Africa

The oldest Shi'i communities in sub-Saharan Africa are the communities of Arabs and Indian Khojas and Bohras who migrated to East Africa in the nineteenth century (probably the 1840s). They settled in Zanzibar initially and spread from there to Tanzania, Kenya and Uganda, with some going as far afield as Zaire, Mauritius and Madagascar as traders and businessmen. In Uganda, they suffered a major loss when Idi Amin expelled the Asian population in 1972. The Khojas are mainly Nizari Isma'ilis but disagreements in the community in 1905 led to the secession of a significant minority who became Twelvers, but who culturally remain Khojas. These Twelver communities are organized under the Federation of Khoja Shia Ithna-Ashari (Twelver) Jamaats of Africa, which was formed in 1945 and in 1975 expanded to become the World Federation of Khoja Shia Ithna-Asheri Muslim Communities, now headquartered in Stanmore, London. They number fewer than 30,000 in Africa (mainly in Tanzania with some in Kenya, Madagascar and Reunion Island). Many have migrated to Europe, where there are some 15,000 Twelver Khojas, mainly in England, and to North America. There are also some Shi'is of Arab origin, found mainly in Zanzibar, Mombasa and Lamu Island. In 1964, the Twelver Khojas in East Africa decided to begin to teach their religion to black Africans and the Bilal Muslim Mission was set up. By 1983, they had some 40,000 converts, mainly in Tanzania and Kenya, and by 2002 perhaps 100,000, many converting from Sunni Islam. Another mission is the World Islamic Propagation and Humanitarian Services mission, based in Dar-es-Salam. There are unsubstantiated claims that, with support from Iran and elsewhere, the number of black African Shi'is has increased greatly. In Tanzania, there are said to be more than a million Shi'is (10% of that country's Muslims) and the Imam Sadiq Madrasah has been established with Shaykh Hamid Jalal Hamid as its head. In Kenya, there are said to be 400,000 and in Uganda 100,000 (the leader of the community in Uganda, Shaykh Dactoor Abdu Kadir Muwaya, was shot dead on 25 December 2014). There are about 20,000 Nizari Isma'ilis Khojas in Kenya and 40,000 in Tanzania, while the Bohras (Dawudi Isma'ilis) number about 20,000 and are mainly resident in the coastal areas of Kenya and Tanzania.

Egypt has a long Shi'i history and was the centre of the Isma'ili Fatimid caliphate in the tenth to twelfth centuries. However, after the fall of the Fatimids, Isma'ili Shi'i Islam faded, although there are unconfirmed reports that some remain among the rural population of the Upper Nile in south Egypt, but keep a low profile. Only with the 1979 Islamic Revolution in Iran did Shi'i Islam in Egypt re-emerge, and it is likely that most of those calling themselves Shi'is in north Egypt today converted as a result of being inspired by Khomeini. Some have undergone training as Shi'i clerics at Qom. The rise of Twelver Shi'i Islam has led to a backlash, with mobs being incited against Shi'is and one notable incident in which four Shi'is were killed, including a local leader, and forty families evicted from a village. As with all religious communities that are persecuted, it is difficult to obtain any reliable estimates of numbers of adherents. Estimates a few years ago were of a few thousand; estimates now range from 700,000 to three million, but it is difficult to know whether this represents a growth in numbers, increased accuracy, or is a perceptual inflation caused by the exposure of the Shi'is in the news.

Shi'i Islam was unknown in Nigeria before the 1979 Iranian Revolution. Then, inspired by Khomeini, Ibrahim Zakzaky of Zaria (born 1953) began to preach his own syncretism of Sunni and Shi'i Islam and set up the Islamic Movement in Nigeria, with help from Iran. This movement has become increasingly orthodox Twelver Shi'i, under the guidance of Twelver clerics from other countries. Large Muharram ritual processions are held every year in cities such as Zaria. There have been clashes between Sunnis and Shi'is and between Shi'is and the police, and some deaths. In October 2010, a ship arriving in Lagos from Iran was found to have an unauthorized shipment of arms presumably destined for Nigeria's Shi'is. The Iranian foreign minister was dispatched to Nigeria and explained that it had all been a mistake and the arms were actually intended for the Gambia. It is estimated that there may now be two million Shi'is in Nigeria, mainly in Kano and Sokoto states in northern Nigeria.

When Lebanese traders settled along the West African coast, most were Christians but a substantial number of Lebanese

Twelver Shi'is settled in Sierra Leone from 1903. Several of these families have grown rich over the years, partly through diamond smuggling. A large proportion of Sierra Leone's private business sector is in their hands. The leader of Amal in the Lebanon, Nabih Birri, was born in Sierra Leone. Following the 1979 Iranian Revolution, the community became politicized and active in spreading Shi'i Islam. However, the total number of Shi'is in Sierra Leone does not exceed 40,000.

In Senegal, the arrival of the Lebanese cleric Shaykh Abdul-Mun'am al-Zayn, in 1969, marked the first appearance of Shi'i Islam in the country. He established an Islamic Centre in Dakar in 1978. Since the 1979 Iranian Revolution, the Iranian government has been active in providing aid to the country. In return, the Senegalese government allowed Lebanese Shi'i clerics to spread Shi'i Islam in the country. A large number of religious schools were set up throughout Senegal and the best graduates from these go to a religious college in Dakar, Hawzah al-Rasul al-Akram, and have been sent to Qom to complete their religious studies. In February 2011, however, Senegal cut diplomatic ties with Iran after the episode of the Nigerian arms shipment (see above), convinced that Iran was arming anti-government rebels through the Gambia. The Gambia, embarrassed by Iranian claims that the arms found in Lagos were intended for it (which would be in breach of United Nations sanctions against Iran) also cut diplomatic ties with Iran.

In South Africa, Twelver Shi'is were a small minority among the Indian migrants to the country in the nineteenth and early twentieth centuries. The 1979 Islamic Revolution in Iran created interest in Shi'i Islam in the country and in 1990, Sayyid Aftab Haider, a Pakistani cleric trained at Qom, came to Cape Town and established the Ahlul Bait Foundation in South Africa. There are also Khoja and Bohra Isma'ilis among South Africans of Indian descent.

Europe

Twelver Shi'i communities in the United Kingdom are mostly immigrants and are divided according to their origins. Thus there are communities of Iranian, Iraqi, Pakistani and East African Khoja Shi'is, each having their own community associations and mosques. Contact among them is poor because of language barriers, although the younger generation are overcoming this. There are centres for Shi'i learning in London and Birmingham. It is difficult to quantify the number of Shi'is in the country and one cannot assume that those identified in the national census as Iranians (80,000 in 2011), for example, are all Shi'is, since large numbers of Iranians came to Britain to escape the Islamic government in Iran and many of them have turned their backs on Shi'i Islam. However, it is reasonable to assume that there are about 300,000 Twelver Shi'is in the country (about 10% of the Muslim population).

In Germany, the majority of Shi'is are Alevis, who began to arrive in large numbers from Turkey in the 1980s. They have settled in the large industrial German cities of the Rhein-Ruhr area as well as Stuttgart, Hamburg and Berlin. The most prominent Alevi organization is the Alevitische Gemeinde Deutschland (in Turkish 'Almanya Alevi Birlikleri Federasyonu', AABF). An estimated 500,000 Alevis live in Germany, of whom two-thirds have German nationality. Twelver Shi'is (mainly Iranians and Turks) number about 250,000 (6% of the Muslims in Germany). There are also some 70,000 'Alawis. Thus the Shi'ah as a whole form about 20% of Germany's estimated 4.3 million Muslims.

The numbers of Twelver Shi'i immigrants in other European countries are much smaller, probably the next largest community being in France, with about 100,000 members. The Iranian government has been active in proselytizing across Europe, mainly among Muslims, and there are reports, for example, of conversions of Sunni Moroccans in Belgium. The situation regarding Bektashis in Albania and other Balkan countries is described in Chapter 8.

The Americas

The largest group of Shi'is in the United States used to be the Lebanese Shi'is, many of whom settled in the Dearborn suburb of Detroit in the 1920s to work in the automotive industry. The Islamic Center of America in Detroit is the oldest Shi'i institution in North America and has, since its rebuilding in 2005, the largest mosque in North America. Throughout the twentieth century, migrants came to North America from all parts of the Shi'i world, especially India. This accelerated towards the end of the twentieth century. Twelver Khojas from East Africa migrated to Canada after the revolution in Zanzibar in 1964 and after being expelled from Uganda in 1972. The 1979 Iranian Revolution brought a large wave of migrants. Estimates of Iranian migrants to the United States vary from 300,000 to one million (going especially to California, New York, Texas and Maryland) and to Canada from 70,000 to 120,000 (going especially to Toronto, Vancouver and Montreal). However, having fled the Islamic Revolution, most of these people regard themselves as irreligious, while some have converted to Christianity, the Baha'i Faith, Zoroastrianism and Buddhism. Polling of Iranians in the Los Angeles area indicates about half of these immigrants were non-observant Muslims even before they left Iran and of those who had been observant Muslims in Iran, about half ceased to be after they arrived in the USA. Subsequent regional upheavals have led to migrations of Iraqis, Bahrainis and more Lebanese.

There are major cultural divisions among the Shi'ah of North America depending on their ethnic origin. An attempt to bring the religious leaders of the various communities together as the Council of Shi'a Muslim Scholars in North America has only partially succeeded in bridging these divisions. The Universal Muslim Association of America has been more successful as a Shi'i umbrella group. There is also something of a split between younger members of the community born in North America, who together with converts favour more liberal and mystical interpretations of Islam and look to figures such as Mahmoud Ayoub and Abdulaziz Sachedina for leadership, and older, immigrant members of the community, who espouse a more conservative, traditionalist brand of Shi'i Islam and look to traditionally-trained clerics. Of the three million Muslims in the United States about 300,000 (10%) are Twelver Shi'is. In Canada, of the one million Muslims, about 120,000 (12%) are Twelver Shi'is.

There are Isma'ili communities in some large cities in Canada, such as Toronto, Montreal and Vancouver (Burnaby), and smaller communities in a few cities in the United States. There may be some 50,000 Isma'ilis in Canada and a somewhat smaller number in the United States.

Although there are only a very small number of Shi'is in the West Indies and Guyana, descended from Indian indentured labourers brought by the British to the area in the middle of the nineteenth century, they have had a great effect on the local culture. Muharram processions are a general celebration by the whole population, having largely lost their funereal character. In Guyana and Suriname, they were called Tadjah (from *taziyah*) but were banned by the British colonial authorities in the 1930s. In Jamaica, Trinidad and Tobago, they are called Hosay (from Husayn) and continue to the present day.

In South America, there are Shi'is among the descendants of Lebanese and Syrians migrants, mainly in southern Brazil (10,000) and northern Argentina (40,000). Some Druze and 'Alawis were also among this migration, which occurred in the late nineteenth and early twentieth century. In addition, Iranian government money has funded missionary activity (including the despatch of clerics such as Shaykh Talib Husayn al-Khazraji to

Sao Paulo), the building of mosques and centres in a few cities such as Buenos Aires, Sao Paulo and Curitiba, the translation and publication of books and the setting up of a *halal* food business that exports meat to much of the Islamic world. It is difficult to assess how many converts have resulted from all of this activity. If reports originating in Iran are to be believed, there are a million converts in Brazil, but given the census of all Muslims in the whole of Brazil was 35,000 in 2010, it would appear that these efforts have not been successful and these facilities are serving mainly the existing Shi'is of Arab descent, who have however been significantly radicalized. The situation is more difficult to assess in Argentina, as the government census does not include questions about religion, but it is likely that the same applies. Anti-Jewish bombings in Argentina in 1992 and 1994 were linked to Hezbollah and Iran.

Conclusion

The Shi'i world is at present in a state of flux. The political scene is rapidly changing. It is not yet clear whether or not the experiment with rule by religious leaders that was started in 1979 in Iran will succeed in spreading to other countries. The initial revolutionary fervour has cooled somewhat and attempts to export the revolution have had only limited success. Indeed the revolutionary structure faces formidable challenges within Iran itself. In Iraq, the Shi'i-dominated government also faces severe tests.

The future for many Shi'i communities is uncertain. Will the present Shi'i government in Iraq manage to maintain the unity of the country or will Iraq divide into a Shi'i south, a Kurdish north and a Sunni west? Will President Bashar al-Assad hold on to power in Syria? If he does not, will there be a Sunni massacre of 'Alawi Shi'is in retaliation for the brutalities of the al-Assad regime? Will Syria be divided, with the emergence of a small

'Alawi state centred on Lattakia and possibly a Druze state in south Syria (as the French proposed in the 1920s and 1930s, see p. 209 and p. 207)? Will the Houthis overrun Yemen? Will Yemen be divided into a Sunni south and a Zaydi north? Will Lebanon's Twelver Shi'is gain the increased power within Lebanon's political structure that they seek? Will the Shi'is in countries such as Pakistan, Bahrain and Saudi Arabia continue to be oppressed or will their situation improve? Will Iran's missionary efforts to spread Shi'i Islam (mostly by converting Sunnis) succeed or will the backlash it has created leave Shi'i Islam worse off in some areas? Will the present level of Sunni–Shi'i tensions continue to worsen? Will the self-styled Islamic State continue to extend its control and influence and, since it has vowed to obliterate Shi'i Islam in the Islamic world, will this lead to massacres of Shi'is?

As well as these external political questions, internal questions remain to be resolved. Will Khomeini's concept of rule by an expert in religious law (*velayat-e faqih*) become universally accepted among Shi'is or will it be pushed back? Will the present signs of discontent among Iran's population increase to the point of overturning the Islamic Republic? Will the institutionalization of the Shi'i religious hierarchy and the modernization of the educational methods in religious colleges that has occurred in Iran spread to the other Shi'i communities?

The last forty years have seen enormous changes in Shi'i Islam and the pace of change shows no signs of slowing. Shi'i Islam itself has grown and spread to new areas. Shi'i religious leaders have increased greatly in influence and established political control over a large area. And yet, there are indications that these developments have possibly not benefited Shi'i Islam in all ways. In some areas, the Shi'is are suffering from a Sunni backlash against these Shi'i advances. But also, paradoxically, Shi'i Islam may have been weakened to some extent by these developments, at least in Iran. Because of the brutal methods used by the Iranian regime to suppress opposition and the corruption that is evident, the religious leadership has lost a great deal of its moral authority; whereas the ordinary people of Iran used to look to their religious leaders as their champions against an oppressive state, now the religious leaders are the oppressive state.

In most parts of the world and for most of their history, the Shi'is have been a persecuted minority with little political power. This communal experience of persecution complements the ethos of Shi'i Islam, which is dominated by the martyrdom of its holiest figures and the commemorations of these martyrdoms. Over the centuries, in view of their lack of political power, Shi'i communities have largely been led by their religious leaders, who have gradually gained increasing influence and control over them. In Iran, and now Iraq, the Shi'is have gained control of their own destiny, but Shi'is in other countries are still struggling for recognition and a proportionate stake in society.

Glossary

akhbar see hadith

akhund this designation was initially a title of respect for members of the clerical class (as when for example the title of Akhund was given to Shaykh Muhammad Kazim Khurasani in the early twentieth century), but now it is used as a description of any cleric and is even a little pejorative, depending on the context of its use.

'alim see *'ulama*

'Ashura commemoration of the martyrdom of the Imam Husayn on the tenth day of the first month, Muharram, of the Islamic calendar. Since the Islamic calendar is a lunar calendar, the date of 'Ashura moves through the Gregorian (Western solar) calendar, going backwards eleven to twelve days each year.

'atabat literally '[sacred] thresholds'. A collective term used to designate the shrines of the Imams in Iraq.

Ayatollah (Ayatullah) literally 'Sign of God'. A designation which was initially that of the highest ranking Shi'i clerics but now given to any *mujtahid*. The highest ranking clerics are called Ayatullah al-'Uzma (Most Mighty Sign of God, usually translated as Grand Ayatollah).

chador a large piece of cloth draped over the head, extending to the ground and usually also pulled across the lower face. Women wear the *chador* over other clothes, especially when going out of the house. It fulfils the Islamic requirement of *hijab* (veiling).

fatwa (*Persian* fatva) judgement made by a *mujtahid* on a point of religious law, usually given in written form.

fiqh, faqih jurisprudence, the process of deriving the *shariʿah* from its sources (the Qurʾan, the Traditions, and, for Usulis, the consensus of the clerical class and reasoning). The person who carries out *fiqh* is a *faqih* (plural *fuqaha*), who in the Usuli School is identical to a *mujtahid*.

ghaybah literally 'disappearance' or 'concealment'. A term applied in Twelver Shiʿism to the occultation or concealment of the Twelfth Imam (see p. 185).

ghuluww, ghulat a pejorative term commonly used in Islamic literature to denote certain Shiʿi sects that believe in doctrines that are now considered to be outside orthodox Islamic belief. The words translate as 'extremism' and 'extremists' and is not, of course, how these sects see themselves. Therefore, in this book the alternative terms Gnostic Shiʿism and Gnostic Shiʿis have been used.

hadith reports of the Prophet Muhammad's words and actions, which were initially transmitted orally before being set down in books. In Shiʿism this is extended to the words and actions of the Imams, although these are also sometimes designated as *akhbar*. In this book these words are translated as 'Traditions' with a capital T.

hawzah (*Persian* howzeh) a seat of learning or centre for Shiʿi scholarship and education, usually consisting of a number of *madrasahs*.

ijazah literally 'permission' or 'authorization'. An *ijazah* of *ijtihad* certifies that a *mujtahid* is satisfied that a student has completed the studies and has the qualifications to become a *mujtahid*.

ijtihad literally 'exertion' or 'striving'. It is used to denote the process of arriving at judgements about the appropriate application of the *shariʿah* in particular circumstances through the application of certain principles of jurisprudential reasoning (*usul al-fiqh*), applying rationality and certain practical principles (*usul al-ʿamaliyyah*) to produce a valid conjecture (*zann*) about the correct answer to a question.

Imam literally 'the one who stands in front'; the leader. For Twelver Shiʿis, the principal meaning refers to the twelve designated successors of the Prophet Muhammad. The Imam of the present age is the Twelfth of these figures, who is in occultation. Other Shiʿi groupings identify other Imams. In this book, this meaning is indicated by capitalizing the word. Imam is sometimes also used by Arab Shiʿis to designate the leader of their community and it is in this sense that the title was given to Khomeini, the first time it was used in that way in Persian. *Imam-jumʿah* designates a leader of the Friday prayers, who usually also gives a sermon (*khutbah*).

imamzadeh shrine of a descendant of the Imams.

khums a religious tax established in the Qurʾan (see pp. 189–90 for more details).

madrasah religious college for training clerics (see pp. 125–7 for more details).

marjaʿ al-taqlid (*Persian* marjaʿ-e taqlid) literally 'a focal point for emulation'. Refers to the fact that in Usuli Shiʿi theory every person who is not a *mujtahid* must choose one to turn to for guidance on all matters of religious observances and social transactions; this *mujtahid* is then that person's *marjaʿ al-taqlid*.

mujtahid a cleric who has been trained and gained certification in *ijtihad* and is thus competent to issues *fatwas*.

mutʿah (*Persian* sigheh) temporary marriage contracted for a fixed time, for a fixed dowry and sometimes with other conditions. In Persian, the word *sigheh* is also used of a woman who marries in this way.

mulla used in Persian to describe a person who has received religious training (sometimes used pejoratively); the more formal designation of such a person would be *ʿalim* (plural *ʿulama*). These words have been translated in this book as 'cleric(s)'.

rawdah (*Persian* rowzeh), rawdah-khan a *rawdah* is a ritualized recital of the story of the martyrdom of Imam Husayn, and sometimes of the other Imams. The *rawdah-khan* is the person reciting this, who is often a professional.

ruhani, rawhani literally 'spiritual'. A term increasingly used to designate a *mulla*.

sayyid in Persian this word denotes a male patrilineal descendant of the Prophet Muhammad. In Arabic its meaning is more ambiguous since the word is also used as a prefix equivalent to the English 'Mr'.

shari'ah the codification of the norms of Islamic conduct derived through *fiqh*. It extends from religious observances, family matters (such as marriage, divorce, etc.), social transactions (such as business dealings) and, under the Usuli School, to virtually all areas of human life.

sigheh see *mut'ah*.

taqiyyah religious dissimulation (also called *kitman*). In Shi'i Islam, permission is given to conceal one's religious identity and even deny one's faith in circumstances where there is persecution or a threat to life or property.

taqlid imitation or emulation of others. In the Qur'an, this is prohibited but this prohibition is interpreted by the clerical class as applying only to the principles of religion (*usul al-din*, i.e. matters of doctrine), whereas the Usuli School considers *taqlid* of a *mujtahid* to be obligatory in matters of the *shari'ah*.

Tashayyu' Shi 'ism.

ta'ziyah in Iran, this refers to the theatrical performance of the martyrdom of Imam Husayn and associated stories. In other countries, it may have different meanings (see p. 158).

Traditions see *hadith*.

'ulama a generic word for religious scholars (singular *'alim*). In this book, 'clerics' or 'clerical class' has been used to translate this term. Although theoretically and historically, a person learned in any of the religious and natural sciences could be designated by this word; with the victory of the Usuli School, it became confined to those learned in religious law and jurisprudence.

usul principle; can refer to either the principal elements or doctrines of the religion (*usul al-din*) or the principles of jurisprudential reasoning (*usul al-fiqh*, the methodology of *ijtihad*).

velayat-e faqih (*Arabic* walayat al-faqih)   the concept that governance belongs by right to those who are experts in religious law (the *faqih*).

walayah (wilayah)   a term which can indicate authority (either temporal or spiritual) as well as guardianship, love, spiritual guidance and sanctity (see pp. 180–1).

waqf (*Persian* vaqf; *plural* awqaf)   religious endowment, the profits of which can be directed to any religious or charitable purpose by the donor. The *waqf* is usually administered by a cleric who can draw a salary for the work involved.

ziyarah (*Persian* ziyarat)   visiting the shrine of an *Imam* or *Imamzadeh* (a particularly holy descendant of an *Imam*). Such visits often have a ritual associated with them including the recitation of a Prayer of Visitation (*ziyarat-nameh*).

Bibliography

The literature in the field of Shi'i studies has become vast and the following represents only a small proportion of the English-language works that I have found particularly useful for writing this book. Exclusion from the list below does not mean that I consider a work to be flawed or without interest.

General works

The following are general introductions to Shi'i Islam:

Heinz Halm, *Shi'ism* (New York: Columbia University Press, 2004).
Moojan Momen, *An Introduction to Shi'i Islam: The History and Doctrines of Twelver Shi'ism* (New Haven: Yale University Press, 1985).
Yann Richard, *Shi'ite Islam* (Oxford: Blackwell, 1995).

The following encyclopaedias have good articles on Shi'i subjects:

Encyclopædia Iranica (vol. I– London, 1982– ed. E. Yarshater); online edition: http://www.iranicaonline.org, New York, 1996–. (Accessed 19 August 2015).
Encyclopaedia of Islam. 1st edn. (eds M Th Houtsma, *et al.*), 4 vols. and Suppl., Leiden: E. J. Brill, 1913–38; 2nd ed. (eds H. A. R. Gibb, *et al.*), 12 vols, Leiden: E. J. Brill, 1960–2005.

The following books cover subjects that range across more than one chapter of this book:

Linda Clarke (ed.), *Shi'ite Heritage: Essays on Classical and Modern Traditions* (Binghampton: Global Publications, 2001).

Seyyed Hossein Nasr, Hamid Dabashi and Seyyed Vali Reza Nasr (eds), *Expectation of the Millennium: Shi'ism in History* (Albany, NY: State University of New York Press, 1989).

Le Shi'isme Imamate (Paris: Presses Universitaires, 1970).

1. The succession to Muhammad

On the life of the Prophet Muhammad from a Shi'i viewpoint, see the following translation of a work by an important Shi'i scholar: 'Allamah Muhammad Baqir al-Majlisi, *Hayat al-Qulub: The Life and Religion of Muhammad*, Vol. 2 (translated by James L. Merrick, San Antonio, TX: Zahra Trust, 1982); a more recent translation by Syed Athar Husain S. H. Rizvi is available on the Internet: http://www.al-islam.org/hayat-al-qulub-vol-2-allamah-muhammad-baqir-al-majlisi. (Accessed 19 August 2015).

For a traditional account of the succession, see Husain Jafri, *Origins and Early Development of Shi'a Islam* (London: Longman, 1979). For an academic account, see Wilferd Madelung, *The Succession to Muhammad: A Study of the Early Caliphate* (Cambridge: Cambridge University Press, 1998).

2. The life and times of the Twelve Imams

For a traditional account of the Shi'i Imams, see the following translation of a key early work: al-Shaykh al-Mufid, *Kitab al-Irshad: the book of guidance into the lives of the Twelve Imams* (trans. I.K.A. Howard, Horsham: Balagha, 1981). See also: Jafri, *Origins* (see above) for the earlier Imams; and Hussain, *The Occultation* (see below) for the later Imams and the Occultation.

For an in-depth study of one Imam, see Arzina Lalani, *Early Shi'i Thought: The Teachings of Imam Muhammad al-Baqir* (London: I. B. Tauris, 2000).

Regarding the Shi'i community during the lifetime of the Imams: on the emergence of a distinct proto-Twelver Shi'i identity and the return of many Zaydis to the proto-Sunni majority in the mid-eighth century, see Najam Haider, *The Origins of the Shia: Identity, Ritual, and Sacred Space in Eighth-Century Kufa* (New York· Cambridge

University Press, 2011); on the period of the later Imams and the Occultation, see Said Amir Arjomand, 'The Crisis of the Imamate and the Institution of Occultation in Twelver Shi'ism: a Sociohistorical Perspective', *International Journal of Middle Eastern Studies* 28 (1996) 491–515; Etan Kohlberg, 'From Imamiyya to Ithna-'Ashariyya', *Bulletin of the School of Oriental and African Studies* 39 (1976) 521–34 and Hossein Modarresi, *Crisis and Consolidation in Formative Period of Shi'ite Islam: Abu Ja'far ibn Qiba al-Razi and his Contribution to Imamite Shi'ite Thought* (Princeton: Darwin Press, 1993); on the separation of the Twelver Shi'is from Gnostic Shi'ism, see Marshall G. S. Hodgson, 'How Did the Early Shi'a become Sectarian?' *Journal of the American Oriental Society*, Vol. 75, No. 1 (Jan.–Mar., 1955), pp. 1–13; on the 'Abbasid Revolution and its Shi'i overtones, see Moshe Sharon, *Black Banners from the East*, 2 vols. (Jerusalem: Magnes Press; Leiden: Brill, 1983, 1990).

3. The political leadership of the Shi'ah

For the specific periods dealt with in this chapter see the relevant volumes of the *Cambridge History of Iran* (vols. 4–7, Cambridge: Cambridge University Press, 1968–91).

On the Safavid period, see Andrew J. Newman, *Safavid Iran: Rebirth of a Persian Empire* (London: I. B. Tauris, 2008).

On the Qajar period, see Hamid Algar, *Religion and State in Iran 1785–1906* (Berkeley: University of California Press, 1969).

For Shi'ism in Lebanon, see Stefan Winter, *The Shiites of Lebanon under Ottoman Rule, 1516–1788* (New York: Cambridge University Press, 2010); for India, see J. R. I. Cole, *Roots of North Indian Shi'ism in Iran and Iraq: Religion and State in Awadh, 1722–1859* (Berkeley: University of California Press, 1988).

4. The intellectual and spiritual history of Shi'i Islam

On the Traditionists of Qom and the rationalists of Baghdad, see Andrew Newman, *The formative period of Twelver Shi'ism: Hadith as discourse between Qum and Baghdad* (Richmond, Surrey: Curzon Press,

2000) and Meir Bar-Asher, *Scripture and Exegesis in Early Imami-Shiism* (Leiden: Brill, 1999).

For the Safavid period: on the interplay between the Gnostic Shi'ism and orthodox Twelver Shi'ism, see Kathryn Babayan, *Mystics, Monarchs, and Messiahs: Cultural Landscapes of Early Modern Iran* (Cambridge: Harvard University Press, 2002); on the conversion of Iran to Twelver Shi'ism, see Rula J. Abisaab, *Converting Persia: Religion and Power in the Safavid Empire* (New York: I. B. Tauris, 2004); on the late Safavids and Muhammad Baqir Majlisi, see Rudi Matthee, *Persia in Crisis: Safavid Decline and the Fall of Isfahan* (London: I. B. Tauris, 2012); Colin Turner, *Islam Without Allah?: The Rise of Religious Externalism in Safavid Iran* (London: Routledge, 2013).

For an example of a work within the School of Isfahan, see James W. Morris, *The Wisdom of the Throne: An Introduction to the Philosophy of Mulla Sadra* (Princeton: Princeton University Press, 1981).

On the Usuli-Akhbari dispute, see Robert Gleave, *Scripturalist Islam: The History and Doctrines of the Akhbari Shi'i School*. Leiden: Brill, 2007.

On Vahid Bihbihani, see Zachary Heern, *The Emergence of Modern Shi'ism: Islamic Reform in Iraq and Iran* (London: Oneworld, 2015).

On the relationship between the Bab and Shi'ism, see Todd Lawson, *Gnostic Apocalypse and Islam: Qur'an, Exegesis, Messianism and the Literary Origins of the Babi Religion* (London: Routledge, 2012).

On the Shi'i theory of political rule, see Abdulaziz A Sachedina, *The Just Ruler (al-Sultan al-'Adil) in Shi'ite Islam: The Comprehensive Authority of the Jurist in Imamite Jurisprudence* (Oxford University Press, 1988) and Said Amir Arjomand (ed.), *Authority and Political Culture in Shi'ism* (Albany, NY: SUNY Press, 1988).

On clerical institutions, see Linda Walbridge (ed.), *The Most Learned of the Shi'a: The Institution of the Marja' Taqlid* (New York: Oxford University Press, 2001).

5. Shi'i Islam as a lived religion

Information on Shi'i popular religion in various parts of the Shi'i world can be found in Alessandro Monsutti, Silvia Naef and Farian Sabahi, *The Other Shiites: From the Mediterranean to Central Asia* (Bern: Peter Lang, 2007).

On the Karbala commemorations, see Kamran Scot Aghaie, *The Martyrs of Karbala: Shi'i Symbols and Rituals in Modern Iran* (Seattle, WA: University of Washington Press, 2004).

For India, especially ritual storytelling, see Toby Howarth, *The Twelver Shi'a as a Muslim Minority in India: Pulpit of Tears* (London: Routledge, 2005) and Syed Akbar Hyder, *Reliving Karbala: Martyrdom in South Asian Memory* (Oxford: Oxford University Press, 2006); and for Hyderabad, David Pinault, *The Shiites: Ritual and popular piety in a Muslim community* (London: Palgrave Macmillan, 1992).

On the Ta'ziyah in various parts of the world, see Peter J. Chelkowski (ed.), *Eternal Performance: Ta'ziyeh and Other Shiite Rituals* (London: Seagull Books, 2010); Peter Chelkowski (ed.), *Ta'ziyeh, Ritual and Drama in Iran* (New York: New York University Press, 1979).

6. The role and position of women

Lois Beck and Guity Nashat (eds), *Women in Iran from 1800 to the Islamic Republic* (Champaign, IL: University of Illinois Press, 2004).

On the role of women in the Karbala commemorations, see Kamran Scot Aghaie (ed.), *The Women of Karbala: Ritual Performance and Symbolic Discourses in Modern Shi'i Islam*. (Austin: University of Texas Press, 2009).

On temporary marriage, see Shahla Haeri, *Law of Desire: Temporary Marriage in Iran* (Syracuse, NY: Syracuse University Press, 1989).

On Shi'i women in India, see Karen G. Ruffle, *Gender, Sainthood, and Everyday Practice in South Asian Shi'ism* (Chapel Hill, NC: University of North Carolina Press, 2011).

On Isma'ili women, see Delia Cortese and Simonetta Calderini, *Women and the Fatimids in the World of Islam* (Edinburgh: Edinburgh University Press, 2006).

7. Shi'i doctrines and practices

On Shi'i doctrines and practices in general, see Mohammad Ali Amir-Moezzi, *The Spirituality of Shi'i Islam: Belief and Practices* (London: I. B. Tauris, 2011).

On the Imamate, see Mohammad Ali Amir-Moezzi, *The Divine Guide in Early Shi'ism: The Sources of Esotericism in Islam* (Albany, NY: SUNY Press, 1994).

On the concept of *walayah* and its history, see Maria Massi Dakake, *The Charismatic Community: Shi'ite Identity in Early Islam* (Albany, NY: SUNY Press, 2007).

On the Akhbari approach to Qur'an commentary, see Todd Lawson, 'Akhbari Shi'i Approaches to Tafsir', in G. R. Hawting and A. A. Shareef (eds), *Approaches to the Qur'an* (New York: Routledge, 1993), pp. 173–210.

On the Occultation of the Hidden Imam, see Jassim Hussain, *The Occultation of the Twelfth Imam: A Historical Background* (London: Muhammadi Trust, 1982).

On messianic expectation of the Hidden Twelfth Imam, see Abdulaziz A. Sachedina, *Islamic Messianism: The Idea of the Mahdi in Twelver Shi'ism* (Albany, NY: SUNY Press, 1981).

8. Alternative Shi'i communities

On the Zaydis and Houthis in Yemen, see Barak A Salmoni, *et al.*, *Regime and Periphery in Northern Yemen: The Huthi Phenomenon* (Santa Monica, CA: RAND, 2010).

On the Isma'ilis, see Farhad Daftary, *The Isma'ilis: Their History and Doctrines* (Cambridge: Cambridge University Press, 1990).

On the Druze, see Robert Brenton Betts, *The Druze* (2nd ed., New Haven: Yale University Press, 1990); and Nissim Dana, *The Druze in the Middle East: Their Faith, Leadership, Identity and Status* (Brighton: Sussex Academic Press, 2003).

For a general account that focuses on the early stages of Gnostic Shi'ism, see Matti Moosa, *Extremist Shiites: The Ghulat Sects* (Syracuse: Syracuse University Press, 1987).

On the 'Alawis, see Meir Bar-Asher, *The Nusayri-'Alawi Religion: An Enquiry into Its Theology and Liturgy* (Leiden: Brill, 2002); Yaron Friedman, *The Nuṣayrī-'Alawīs: An Introduction to the Religion, History, and Identity of the Leading Minority in Syria* (Leiden: Brill, 2010)

9. Shi'i Islam in the contemporary world

More general books on the subject of this chapter include:

Rainer Brunner and Werner Ende (eds.), *The Twelver Shia in Modern Times. Religious Culture and Political History* (Leiden: Brill, 2001)

Graham Fuller and Rend Rahim Franke, *The Arab Shia: The Forgotten Muslims* (New York: Palgrave, 1999)

On contemporary Iranian Shi'ism, see Roy Mottahedeh, *The Mantle of the Prophet: Religion and Politics in Iran* (London: Chatto and Windus, 1985) and Abbas Amanat, *Apocalyptic Islam and Iranian Shi'ism* (New York: I. B. Taurus, 2009).

On Shi'ism in Iraq, see: Yitzhak Nakash, *The Shi'is of Iraq* (Princeton: Princeton University Press, 2003); Faleh A. Jabar, *The Shi'ite Movement in Iraq* (London: Saqi, 2003).

On Shi'ism in the Lebanon, see Rodger Shanahan, *The Shi'a of Lebanon: Clans, Parties and Clerics* (London: Taurus Academic Studies, 2005).

On Shi'ism in Saudi Arabia, see: Guido Steinberg, 'The Shiites in the Eastern Province of Saudi Arabia (al-Ahsā'), 1913–1953', in Brunner and Ende (eds), *The Twelver Shia in Modern Times* (see above), pp. 236–54; Yousif al-Khoei, 'The Marja' and the Survival of a Community: the Shi'a of Medina', in L. Walbridge (ed.), *The Most Learned of the Shi'a* (see above), pp. 247–50; Human Rights Watch, *Denied Dignity: Systematic Discrimination and Hostility toward Saudi Shia Citizens* (New York, 2009); Human Rights Watch, *The Ismailis of Najran: Second-class Saudi Citizens* (New York: 2008).

On Shi'ism in India and Pakistan, see Khaled Ahmed, *Sectarian War: Pakistan's Sunni-Shia Violence and Its Links to the Middle East* (London: Oxford University Press, 2011); Ian Talbot, 'Understanding Religious Violence in Contemporary Pakistan: Themes and Theories' in Ravinder Kaur (ed.), *Religion, Violence and Political Mobilisation in South Asia* (New Delhi: Sage Publications, 2005), pp. 145–64; Justin Jones and Ali Usman Qasmi (eds), *The Shi'a in Modern South Asia: Religion, History and Politics* (Delhi: Cambridge University Press, 2015).

On Afghanistan, see Amin Saikal, 'Afghanistan: The Status of the Shi'ite Hazara Minority', *Journal of Muslim Minority Affairs*, 32:1 (2012), 80–7.

On North America, see Yvonne Haddad and Jane Smith (ed.), *Muslim Communities in North America* (Albany, NY: State University of New York, 1994); Liyakat Takim, *Shi'ism in America* (New York: New York University Press, 2009).

The table at the end of the chapter is based on the table in Momen, *Introduction to Shi'i Islam*, p. 282. The total country population figures have been updated in accordance with United Nations population estimations for 2014: http://esa.un.org/unpd/wpp/Excel-Data/population.htm. (Accessed 17 December 2013). 'File POP/1-1: Total population (both sexes combined) by major area, region and country, annually for 1950–2100 (thousands)' using the tab 'No Change'. Adjustments to the figures for Shi'is have been made in view of information found in the sources on specific countries (see the listings above) and a number of general sources; for example the 2009 Pew Research Center report, *Mapping the Global Muslim Population* at http://www.pewforum.org/2009/10/07/mapping-the-global-muslim-population/. (Accessed 17 December 2013); and http://www.adherents.com. (Accessed 17 December 2013). All statistics have to be assessed carefully since, for example, in some countries such as Turkey, Syria and Yemen, orthodox Twelver Shi'is form only a small proportion of total Shi'is, while figures for the Gulf states have to be read carefully to see whether they refer to the total population or only nationals/citizens.

Index

This index is done on a word-by-word basis and ignores the Arabic definite article "al-". Look up under the element of a person's name by which they are best known; this is usually their title or the last element of their name indicating their pace of origin. Very early names usually do not have these elements and are indexed by given name.